DEPECHE  E

A BIOGRAPHY

Steve Malins

Cooper Square Press

For Zak Malins

First Cooper Square Press edition 2001

Typeset by Derek Doyle & Associates

Published by Cooper Square Press
An Imprint of the Rowman & Littlefield Publishing Group
150 Fifth Avenue, Suite 911
New York, New York 10011

Distributed by National Book Network

Library of Congress Cataloging-in-Publication Data

Malins, Steve
    Depeche Mode : a biography / Steve Malins.—1st Cooper Square Press ed.
        p.   cm.
    Originally published: London : André Deutsch, c1999.
    Includes bibliographical references.
    ISBN 0-8154-1142-1 (pbk. alk. paper)
        1. Depeche Mode (Musical Group) 2. Rock musicians—England—Bibliography. I. Title

ML421.D46 M35 2001
782.42166'092'2—dc21
[B]   2001017081

Contents

Acknowledgements

Most of the material for this book comes from interviews with Daniel Miller, Alan Wilder, Mark 'Flood' Ellis, Chris Carr, Steve Lyon, Anton Corbijn, Daryl Balmonte, Perry Balmonte, John Foxx, Wayne Hussey, Juan Atkins, Brian Griffin, Tim Simenon, Gareth Jones, Dave Bascombe, Gary Numan, Anne Berning, Russell and Ron Mael (Sparks) Andy McCluskey (OMD) and Stevo.

Also thanks for dinners, wine, faxes and assistance to Andrew Fletcher, Martin Gore, Dave Gahan, JD Fanger, Jonathan Kessler, Alan & Hep, Douglas McCarthy, Sarah Lowe, Geraldine Oakley at Sire, Pandora Powell, Karen Stringer and Bong.

Special thanks to Patricia Bush, Zak Malins, Mary Malins, Bernard MacMahon, Gary, Gemma & Saffron and all the gang, Richard & Tina, Ian & Virginia, Steve Hillier, Lee, Steve Webbon, Jimbo, Mal & Hannah, Kevin and John, Danny, Andy, David, Mark, Claire, Sarah, Keith, Isabel & Paul at Q.

Introduction

'We kind of subtly corrupt the world,' chuckled Depeche Mode's songwriter Martin Gore, shortly after the release of their 1986 single, 'Stripped'. He added with a grin: 'If you call yourself a pop band you can get away with a lot more.'

Depeche Mode have 'got away' with an alarming amount since they first appeared as a fledgling synthesizer pop act in 'plus-fours, soccer socks and carpet slippers'. This is a story of a group of individuals who share a chemistry if not a friendship, which has survived drug overdoses, mental breakdowns, panic attacks, heart flutters, alcoholic binges, the loss of the band's first songwriter, worldwide success, cross-dressing, bad haircuts, money, divorce and fashion. In the process Depeche Mode have sold over 35 million albums worldwide, while in the UK every new studio LP they've released in the last 18 years has reached the Top 10.

The dynamic between the band members is central to Depeche Mode's success. It's a bizarre democracy which includes one band member who hasn't contributed to the band on a musical level for years – Andrew Fletcher. It's also the main thrust of this book and I've tried to uncover the personal and musical relationships between Martin Gore, Dave Gahan, Andrew Fletcher, Alan Wilder, Vince Clarke and honorary member Daniel Miller, who has made a massive contribution to the band's success over the years. This twisted, intimate dynamic flows from the songwriter Martin Gore to singer Dave Gahan, whose interpretation of the material is part of the alchemy that creates a Depeche Mode song. Yet Fletcher's supportive, non-musical role is also crucial as he acts as a foil for the non-confrontational Gore, who would not be able to function creatively on a one-to-one basis with Gahan or Alan Wilder, member for 13 years. Alan and

Daniel were both vital in providing insights into Depeche Mode's inner workings but I'd also like to thank 'Fletch' for a couple of evenings when he filled in gaps in my knowledge and Martin for answering faxes full of questions. Both were extremely helpful with fact checking and the occasional 'off-the-record' revelation.

I was amazed when I discovered they'd never been approached about contributing to a biography before but then Depeche Mode are still a blind-spot to many people in Britain. They are one of the biggest bands we've ever produced in this country and yet they remain slightly obscured by memories of their early '80s synthesizer pop past.

Not everyone I spoke to in the course of writing this book wanted their quotes to be attributed but I have tried to generate as much fresh material on the band as possible. Even so, I do owe a debt to all the other writers and journalists who have interviewed the band over the years, in addition to various books and articles on related subjects.

Most of all, thanks to Depeche Mode whose style changes from DIY electronica to blues, gospel and rock have provided a constant source of inspiration over the last 18 years. They're a rarity in being able to touch people who identify with the frailties of the band members, while also being a fine stadium band who can create a massive communal feeling in audiences of up to 70,000.

Steve Malins, London, 1999.

People Are People, 1961–80

Martin Gore was a docile, thoughtful and naturally happy child, born into a working-class family in Dagenham, Essex on 23 July 1961. At that time his stepfather and grandfather both worked at Dagenham Ford Car Plant but the former gave this up to become a driver and relocated the self-confessed 'passive and harmless' toddler and his two sisters to Basildon. Gore's mother found a job at an old people's home, where she still works to this day.

'As a kid I used to be the shy type,' says the daydreaming, acquiescent songwriter. 'I always had none, or few, friends and I spent most of the time alone in my room reading fairytales. I lost myself in fairytale books and lived in another world. In school as well, I had a big shortage of self-confidence. The teachers only seldom heard my voice.'

The main interests of this cautious, reserved child were languages, which he naturally excelled in, and music: 'When I was ten or so, I discovered my mother's old rock 'n' roll singles in the cupboard, stuff like Elvis, Chuck Berry, Del Shannon, and I played these records over and over again, and I realized then that this was the only thing I was really interested in, and it went on from there.'

At 13 the newly converted glam-rock fan (he was particularly keen on Gary Glitter and oddball American duo, Sparks) was given an acoustic guitar and he proved to be a quick learner, spending most nights learning chords on the instrument. He was still at school when he wrote 'See You' and 'A Photograph Of You', later recorded by Depeche Mode. Perry Balmonte, who in years to come would become a musician and join The Cure, was a schoolmate of Gore's at St Nicholas comprehensive in Basildon. 'He was very introverted,' says Balmonte. 'Very quiet and a good student.'

Gore claims he didn't go out much or drink until he was 18 – a barren social patch which he was to make up for later. He did have a girlfriend at school, Anne Swindell, who had already gone out with another schoolmate, a skinny, ginger-haired boy called Andrew Fletcher.

Gore admits, 'I was probably a weird child. Because I quite liked school and stuff. I felt secure at school and didn't want to leave. I played cricket for the school team and got two 'A' Levels in French and German. I failed Maths though.'

After leaving St Nicholas in 1979, Gore took a job in NatWest's Clearing Bank in Fenchurch Street, City of London, a stone's throw from where his girlfriend's ex-boyfriend, 'Fletch', was working at Sun Life Insurance. Martin Gore claims his colleagues treated him in a 'stepmotherly' fashion because he was young and shy. By now he was performing in an acoustic duo, Norman and The Worms, with school friend Philip Burdett, who went on to become a folk singer on the London gig circuit. Reportedly the two old classmates performed a folkish version of the theme from '60s TV series, *Skippy the Bush Kangaroo*, as part of their set.

However, their musical direction changed dramatically one night when Gore turned up at a gig with a Moog Prodigy synthesizer. The set was keenly observed by another local musician, Vince Clarke: 'Martin came along with a synth, which I thought was brilliant. Here was an instrument that didn't need its own amp – you could just plug it into the PA.'

Clarke (born in Woodford in 1960) was a member of the church choir at the time and through the local branch of the church-affiliated Boys Brigade he met another St Nicholas pupil, the aforementioned Andrew 'Fletch' Fletcher. Fletch (also born in 1960) was still a child when his engineer father, housewife mother, brother and two sisters moved to Basildon. He joined the Boys Brigade when he was eight and claims he went to church seven nights a week – 'So did Vince,' Fletcher revealed a few years later. 'He was a real bible basher!'

Clarke was a bit of a loner and an introspective character, while his nervy friend enjoyed winding people up and playing football, becoming a massive Chelsea fan at the end of the '60s when they were London's most glamorous club. Although Perry Balmonte's memory of Fletcher is of a fairly happy child, the young churchgoer has commented, 'I was an incorrigible pessimist, who never saw the bright side of life. I was always reading books about history. I was convinced I was going to become a teacher.'

Balmonte doesn't remember Fletcher ever showing much interest in music at school: 'I suppose he must have been but it didn't show.' However, Clarke, who had taken up the oboe at the comprehensive, was 14 years old when he discovered pop music, although it was hardly cutting-edge, radical stuff: 'It was Simon and Garfunkel who first made me listen to music, I suppose. They really made an impression on me. I thought they were fantastic! So I started learning to play the acoustic guitar. Me and a few of my mates then got together this gospel-folk thing, and we entered a talent competition. At that age you really believe you're the bee's knees, and with the guitar you can make a nice sound almost as soon as you pick it up, so we thought we were brilliant. You sit there planning all the things you're going to buy as soon as you're famous ... all from a local talent show. And, of course, we were awful. Didn't come anywhere at all in the end.'

When punk hit Basildon, Clarke and Fletcher beat a retreat to their collection of Beatles and Eagles albums and in 1977 the duo formed a band together, No Romance In China. The 'band' consisted of Clarke on guitar and vocals, Fletcher on bass and, according to the former, 'One of those Selmer Auto-rhythm drum boxes with the little pitter-patter beats that you put on top of your home organ.' To begin with they played along to their favourite records, such as 'I Like It' by Gerry and The Pacemakers, the Everly Brothers' 'The Price Of Love' and the Phil Spector track, 'Then She Kissed Me'.

A year or so later, their tastes had darkened and Clarke had, funnily enough, become a big fan of the post-punk band, The Cure. Perry Balmonte saw the band's first 'gig' at a jam in a Basildon pub called the Double Six. They played three songs, one of them being The Cure's 'Three Imaginary Boys'. Shortly after the 17-year-old Fletcher left the Boys Brigade, a friend remembers seeing them making another rare appearance at the Woodlands Youth Club, in front of a bunch of 14-year-old kids.

After a couple of years No Romance In China dissolved and Fletcher spent most evenings out with his new girlfriend, Grainne. Clarke briefly formed another group, The Plan, with the ever-enthusiastic Perry Balmonte who has been in-and-out of bands all his life. However, Clarke wasn't happy being just a guy in the background, preferring to be the one in control of the situation, and so he decided to leave the group.

He went back to Fletcher and they started another outfit, Composition of Sound, with Martin Gore. In their first incarnation, Fletcher was press-ganged into playing the bass and had to get a £90 loan from his bank manager for the instrument, while the others both initially played guitar. However, as Clarke wrote new songs, he and Gore switched to primitive Moog and Yamaha keyboards. When Fletcher was also forced to buy a synth several months later, Composition became a fully-fledged electronic band.

'After punk, we all got into Kraftwerk and A Certain Ratio,' remembers Perry's younger brother, Daryl, who is three years younger than Fletch, Clarke and Gore. 'I always found the electronic/futurism scene to be quite dirty and underground, like the early Human League,' enthuses Daryl, who started humping around the band's equipment in return for them giving him a lift in their van when he was doing his Basildon paper round. 'Their single "Being Boiled" was a bit avante garde and hard sounding. I liked the Some Bizzare stuff and Gary Numan, which was a darker type of music than your usual chart music.'

In 1979 Gary Numan had emerged as the enigmatic peroxided leader of Tubeway Army, scoring a No.1 hit with the sparse, otherworldly 'Are "Friends" Electric?' In the '70s there were a few one-off hits for electronic acts, most famously Kraftwerk's 'Autobahn' single which reached No.11 in 1975. But Numan sealed his place as the first major star of synthesizer pop when the follow-up single 'Cars', released under his own name, also went to No.1 in the UK. Over the next three years he had five Top 3 albums and even broke into the American Top 10. Numan's fleeting but significant importance to Clarke, Gore and Fletcher was that he'd shown it was possible to get to the top of the charts as a 21-year-old ex-punk and non-musician playing synthesizer music.

'My only talent musically is an arranger of noises,' confessed the Tubeway Army frontman. 'I was no good on guitar anyway and the synth was dead easy to play.' Gore was also thinking along the same lines: 'To us the synthesizer was a punk instrument, an instant do-it-yourself kind of tool. I think without knowing it we started doing something completely different. We had taken these instruments because they were convenient. You could pick up a synthesizer, put it under your arm and go to a gig. You didn't need to go through an amp so we didn't need to have our own van. After a while we started going to gigs on trains.' Over the next few months, Composition chased after a pack of more worldly, arty electronic pop acts, such as Soft Cell and The Human League, who would break open the charts in the wake of Tubeway Army's gaunt futurism.

Meanwhile Gore had also joined another local band, The French Look. The group's leader was a guy called Rob Marlow who was a very well known character on the local Basildon scene (he's one of Clarke's best friends and was later on a label run by the Depeche Mode man). Friends remember him as being a 'bit like Gary Numan in that he was always the frontman, wanted to play keyboards, guitar and everything else at once'. In The French Look, Gore played keyboards at the back and they had a big bloke called Paul Redman who got into the band because he owned a couple of synthesizers and was strong enough to carry them around.

Everyone knew each other but a less familiar face was the guy mixing The French Look's sound during a rehearsal at Woodlands School – a skinny ex-punk, Dave Gahan. He caught Vince Clarke's attention when The French Look were rehearsing one day and Gahan started singing along to a cover of David Bowie's 'Heroes'. It was just a jam but Clarke, who hated being the frontman, thought, 'He's all right, maybe we should get him into the band.' Gahan never actually auditioned for Composition of Sound, he was in if he wanted to have a go. Clarke invited him to come and see the band at a gig in Scamps, Southend, headlined by one of Perry Balmonte's outfits, the School Bullies.

Composition's performance didn't start too well when Fletcher, who has a reputation for clumsiness, tripped over and kicked the plugs out of all the amps except his own, leaving the bassist to play a solo set for the first couple of numbers. Perry's younger brother, Daryl, remembers the gig: 'This was about April or May 1980, just as I was leaving school, and Perry gave Depeche Mode the support slot when they were known as Composition of Sound. At this point they hadn't become a full synth band yet. There was Fletch on bass,

Martin on keyboards and Vince on guitar and vocals. Dave Gahan was actually at that gig, watching them, and that's when I first got to know him. They did a lot of songs that they ended up recording as Depeche Mode – "Photographic", "Ice Machine" and a few instrumentals as well.'

At one point Composition of Sound supported The French Look at St Nicholas Comprehensive. Gore would change his shirt and then play with the other band. This was also the first gig featuring Composition's new singer, Dave Gahan, who was so white faced and nervous he had to drain a few lagers before he had the courage to walk on stage. His only previous experience of singing in public was the Salvation Army Choir when he was eight. Then French Look went on and during the first song Rob Marlow had an argument with Paul Redman and the gig collapsed because the latter refused to play his keyboards. Not surprisingly they broke up after that.

Daryl Balmonte describes the gig as a '... good night. I was still at the school and we were amazed because Dave instantly brought all his crowd from Southend. All of a sudden, there in a school hall, were about thirty or forty New Romantic weirdos along with all the young local kids. That's when Vince realized that he'd made a good choice.'

Dave Gahan was born in Epping on 9 May 1962 and, like the others, had a religious upbringing thanks to his mother's side of the family, who were involved in the Salvation Army. Unlike his new band-mates Gahan had rejected the church completely and after setting off for Sunday school with his older sister, he would kill the time by riding his bike around. His father left home when Gahan was still a toddler and his mother then uprooted the family – Dave, his sister Sue and brothers Peter and Philip – to Basildon: 'She remarried and I always assumed my stepfather was my real dad. He died when I was seven.'

When Gahan was ten he came home from school to discover, '... this stranger in my mum's house. My mother introduced him to me as my real dad. I remember I said, crying, that was impossible because my father was dead. I was very upset and we all had a huge argument because I thought I should have been told. Later I realized what a hard time mum had bringing us up. I didn't help by getting into lots of trouble.'

Gahan had started bunking off school and ended up in juvenile court three times for spraying graffiti on walls, vandalism and stealing cars, later found burnt out and abandoned. 'I was pretty wild. I loved the excitement of nicking a motor, screeching off and being chased by the police. Hiding behind a wall with your heart beating gives you a real kick – will they get you? My mother often cried bitter tears for me.'

As an early sign of exaggerated rebelliousness, he also got his first tattoo when he was 14, on Southend sea-front, from 'an old sort of sailor guy named Clive' who had a dotted line tattooed around his neck with the words 'cut here'. In stark contrast to the rather timid, church-going faction of Composition of Sound, he also started experimenting with drugs before he left school. 'I had a lot of mates, a lot of people I could go to hang out with that I could pick for different sorts of moods. Violent ones, druggy ones, just girls. A gang of us would go out together and buy a big bag of amphetamines. We'd go to London all night, end up at some party then catch the milk train from Liverpool Street to Billericay. It was a bloody long walk home.'

Gahan claims he learnt about sex 'pretty fast' with female friends of his older sister, and that by the time he was 13 he'd been a soulboy, 'hanging around with the crew from Global Village', the gay club beneath Charing Cross station. He left school in July 1978, after playing truant for most of the last year. For the next few months the cocksure 'geezer' went through numerous dead-end jobs (he says 'about twenty'), including stacking shelves in a supermarket, labouring on a construction site and packing work at Yardley's perfume factory: 'I was bringing home good money, giving mum some, going down the pub, pulling, being a general wide-boy.

'Finally I realized I had no career so I went for a job as apprentice fitter with North Thames Gas. My probation officer told me to be honest at the interview, say I had a criminal record but I was a reformed character, blah-blah. Of course, I didn't get the job because of that. I went back and trashed the probation office.'

In his last year at comprehensive school, Gahan had discovered punk, and followed tours by The Damned and The Clash. 'I wasn't really into what The Clash were singing about because I didn't really understand their first album. But I used to go and see them because I liked their attitude and the energy.' He was able to mix his main interests, punk and art, by enrolling in Southend Art College where

Gahan was 'going off to see Generation-X and The Damned. I had original Sex shop gear. We used to stick labels on the outside and come down to the gritty London clubs like Studio 21.'

Although Gahan wasn't the only 'alternative' person in Basildon, it was impossible to get a flourishing scene going there, so people like him went to London or Southend where the locals were more tolerant. 'John Lydon and George O'Dowd [Boy George] used to come to Southend,' he recalled. 'George came to model and nick stuff. He got into trouble for that. They were flamboyant people, like Steven Linnard (now a successful fashion designer), a big change after my rough and ready Basildon mates. Rowdy but artistic.

'I got bored with that but for a while it was exciting. I had a double life, mixing with the art-school mob, then going home to Basildon. I'd go to the pub wearing make-up, but 'cos I knew the local beer-boys, the Spanners, I was OK.'

According to early-80s schoolboy and gear-humper Daryl Balmonte, 'Dave was always a bit of fish out of water in Basildon. In the '70s it was a very violent place. He used to get the train up to all the clubs in London, and the pub opposite the station was the hub of the violence. So he would be standing outside, a 15-year-old boy in full make-up and he'd get a lot of stick. So that's his memory of Essex Man, which is probably why he ended up living in America. Whereas Fletch and Martin were more low-key. They used to go to the Towngate Theatre, where the bar in there was a bit more Bohemian, sort of hippie-like. People in patchwork jeans would get up and play acoustic guitars. So their view of the town was very different to Dave's encounters with the real thugs.'

In 1979 Gahan met his girlfriend Joanne at a Damned gig. 'She was one of the Billericay punks,' he remembers. Bizarrely, one of her favourite bands was the original punk incarnation of Tubeway Army, so she used to go and see Gary Numan play at various gigs around London. By the time Numan had switched to electronic music, Gahan was also a fan and so the couple drove around the country watching various gigs on his major tour in late 1979.

Shortly after Dave Gahan joined Composition of Sound, the fashion-conscious singer suggested a phrase he'd spotted on the front of a French magazine, Depeche Mode – which translates as 'Rapid Fashion' – as a new band name. Clarke admits, 'We just liked the sound of the words.' To make themselves appear even more artily exotic, the band initially insisted on pronouncing the name 'Depeshay'. According to friends of the band, this name change was settled on after Gahan played six or seven dates with Composition of Sound but no one can agree on the exact time when they made the switch. Calling themselves Depeche Mode was a strange affectation for a bunch of working-class lads from Basildon but Gahan had developed a taste for flashy, pretentious posturing through his visits to London clubs in 1980.

'Depeche Mode were very naive, as all lads of 18 are really,' grins Daryl Balmonte. 'They really were quite a bizarre mix. Dave came more out of the punk scene, Fletch used to always be on about Graham Parker. Martin was into Kraftwerk, Jonathan Richman, lots of different things. Dave saw The Clash when he was 14, got straight into Billy's, Studio 21, all that stuff. I think Vince spotted something in Dave. He attracted a lot of attention.'

The underground club world enjoyed by Gahan gave him an edge on most of his Basildon peers, although the suburbs would eventually catch up when the Cult With No Name metamorphosed into the ludicrous overground cult, the New Romantics. This scene was spawned by London club-life in spring 1978 when Billy's opened, just off Dean Street in the West End. At first it was only open on Fridays, attracting an arty, gay crowd but then two of the regulars, Rusty Egan and Steve Strange, took over on Tuesdays to establish 'Club For Heroes'. Flyers were handed out to promote it as a Bowie night (the flyers read, 'Fame, Fame, Fame, What's Your Name? A Club For Heroes').

Although they played Bowie records, it was his approach to image which was just as important. Self-styled fashion guru Peter York summed it up in the '80s when he wrote, 'Bowie's music came with the look. Troubled boys and girls waited for his next incarnation the way the good folk of Fashionland wait for Paris. The look was a way of life.' Billy's also established a way of life through a very exclusive door policy. The club effectively remoulded the '60s Mod ethic into a new form of dandified flamboyance which was ruthlessly patrolled by the self-appointed fashion policeman-cum-doorman, Steve Strange (real name Steve Harrington, a former punk singer in the Moors Murderers). Bowie actually dropped in one night to check out the club and later patronized the scene by filming his transvestite promo video for 1979's 'Boys Keep Swinging' single in Billy's. A year later Bowie's Pierrot Clown outfit in his 'Ashes to Ashes' promo was clearly influenced by the curious sights in Billy's but he maintained his air of superiority by using Steve Strange as an extra in the video.

Meanwhile Strange had evolved into the 'Face' of the Cult With No Name, inspiring Molly Parkin to write in the *Sunday Times*: 'His larger than life attitude has been the secret of the Strange success. At a time when the British economy is suffocating, Steve Strange is firing on all creative cylinders, an example of superb self-promotion.' *NME*'s punk writer Julie Burchill was less enthusiastic: 'This new rave, Steve Strange etc., is nothing more or less than glam rock that's opened the dictionary by chance at "romantic" rather than "bisexual".'

After Billy's, Strange moved on to Blitz, which created a new tribe, the Blitz Kids. Boy George was right at the centre of this surface-only lifestyle where clothes and Mod-like élitism offered an escape from dole-life. 'Punk was safe – we were spinning forward in a whirl of eyeliner and ruffles,' says the garnished pop star. 'Getting a reaction was the ultimate goal ... As long as I was being photographed and noticed, I had a purpose, a reason to get up and dress up. Foundation and powder first, then a cup of tea while it settled. Eye-shadow was applied with fingers. I couldn't afford brushes, it was all instinctive. Last was always the hairpiece, hat and earrings. Then I twirled in front of the mirror for an age.'

In stark contrast, George's lover and band-mate in Culture Club, drummer Jon Moss, was appalled at the gossipy spite and sense of emptiness behind the fluttering eyelashes of the club-goers. 'Nice exterior, very dressy – but underneath, dirty. There was no spirit, no faith, no religion. Ungodly. The Blitz thing was like walking into hell, it was like Berlin in the '30s.' John Foxx, a chisel-cheeked ex-art-school student and founder of British synthesizer pioneers Ultravox, was also unimpressed: 'There's a very music-hall element to rock 'n' roll music. At its best it's Ray Davies; at it's worst its the comedy clown stuff – the New Romantics. I went down to Blitz once to see for myself. It was kind of interesting but that was as far as my involvement went, even though inevitably I was implicated as being part of that scene.'

Tony Hadley from Spandau Ballet, who were Blitz's resident band
for a while, has a different perspective: 'The Blitz scene wasn't a load
of pretty, effeminate things posing and talking about art and literature. Bollocks to that! Blitz was lads getting completely out of their
heads and trying to pull girls. We just happened to dress differently
from the people down the normal pop disco.'

Bitchy, streetwise, bisexual, extravagant and escapist, for a short
while this unnamed club scene was a creative jump forward from the
rotting, stagnant punk scene. By the time the media dubbed its
protagonists as 'New Romantics', its only appeal was to offer a romp
in the Boots make-up counter for anyone who wanted to affect being
a bit 'strange' and 'different'. Fletcher, Gore and Clarke would
become associated with this pulped, popularized dressing-up binge
but for now they were sufficiently seduced by the cold, exclusive
glamour of the original London scene to allow Gahan to christen
them with a faux-exotic name.

Meanwhile Composition of Sound rehearsed almost every night in
Vince's garage, prompting his mother to complain about the 'bloody
clacking' of fingers on keyboards as they practised with headphones
to conceal the noise. Gahan used to come down to rehearse and
mess about with the band's COS skateboard between bursts of
earnest showmanship in front of his new mates. Later they took over
a storage room at the local church for rehearsals. Fletcher: 'The vicar
used to just let us have the place. You just had to be nice and polite,
and you weren't allowed to play loud.'

The band's follow-up gig to Gahan's nervous debut in St Nicholas,
was at a biker's club in the Alexandra Pub, Southend. They were a
bizarre sight as they arrived with synthesizers and their new Futurist
mates but went down a storm – even the bikers loved it.
Composition's early sets included a lot of songs which they never
went on to record, such as 'Reason Man', the Everly Brothers' 'Price
Of Love', 'Tomorrow's Dance', 'Television Set', 'I Like It' and 'Ghost
Of Modern Time'. One of the highlights was 'Photographic', a jerk-
ily atmospheric song, performed by Gahan in a vaguely robotic
monotone which betrayed his early enthusiasm for Tubeway Army.
The track was a favourite of their young fan Daryl Balmonte, who
started getting paid for carrying their gear after a sell-out show in The
Venue, London: 'When you listen to "Photographic", it was quite

dark. There were some songs like "Television Set", "Reason Man" and a song called "Addiction" which were hard electro.'

Basildon's young hopefuls were still only three months old when they made their first recording, which consisted of three Vince Clarke songs, including 'Photographic'. They decided to use them for their debut demo-tape and after sending it out they were contacted by booking agents at two tiny but important venues. One was an old Oi and punk hang-out, the Canning Town Bridgehouse. 'The first few nights at the Bridgehouse, it was very empty,' says Daryl Balmonte. 'They gave them a Wednesday night residency and the band literally used to pull half-a-dozen people.'

The other offer was Crocs in Rayleigh, where on 16 August 1980, they started a residency at Saturday night's 'synth disco', The Glamour Club. To the young schoolboy Daryl Balmonte, ' ... it seemed quite an old, early-twenties crowd. You might get the Kemp brothers from Spandau Ballet coming down. It was quite underground, fashiony sort of people.' Culture Club's Mikey Craig, a regular face in the ruck of carefully applied Max Factor and posturing drinkers, remembers a 'bunch of rockabillies, skinheads, New Romantics and Kid Creole look-alikes'.

In fact, through Craig, Culture Club played their first live show at Crocs on 24 October 1981, attended by various members of Depeche Mode. Boy George writes in his autobiography *Take it Like a Man*, 'Crocs was Southend's premier freak club, made famous by local chart stars Depeche Mode. It drew a mixed crowd, office boys and secretaries, white-faced Futurists in rubber and dog-collars, trendier types in Westwood pirate hats, rockabillies with high tops and flat tops. We were relieved to have done our first gig, and in front of a celebrity audience – Dave Gahan from Depeche Mode was there.'

A young DJ, Stevo, who by 1980 had already made his name in the electronic scene as an off-kilter, unpredictable but influential enthusiast, remembers seeing Depeche Mode at Crocs in Rayleigh. 'It was a big open space with no decor at all except you could fit a lot of people in there and it had a bar. At the time it was a very fashion-oriented crowd. People were dressing up but unfortunately fashion was starting to take a priority over music. People like Spandau Ballet and Duran Duran irritated me because they had success by jumping on an industry-built scene. They had no part of an electronic scene, as far as I was concerned. Human League, Depeche, Soft Cell were synth acts but the others were rock 'n' roll bands with frilly shirts.'

Despite leaving school illiterate Stevo, real name Steve Pearce, had earned enough money through labouring on a work experience scheme during his final year at school, so that in 1979 the 16 year old bought a mobile disco on hire purchase. He started playing an 'electronic music/disco' residency on Monday nights at the Chelsea Drugstore in London's Kings Road, followed by a regular night at the Clarendon in Hammersmith. 'I was terrorizing the dancefloor in Chelsea,' laughs Stevo, 'by playing some very left-field music, things like Chrome and Throbbing Gristle, alongside Kraftwerk and Yellow Magic Orchestra. Then you'd go to the Ritz and they'd be playing Roxy Music and Bowie and it was very gay and there was lots of make-up. That was the scene which engendered the New Romantics. At the time I was an anarchist on a musical level and I felt it was immensely important to break down all the boundaries musically and open it all up. So to suddenly have it undermined by the national newspapers running pictures of people with silly haircuts was hugely frustrating.'

After his dancefloor selections attracted interest Stevo was invited to compile an 'electronic music chart' in the music magazine, *Record Mirror*, followed by a regular Futurist Chart in *Sounds*. 'I didn't like the term Futurist,' says Stevo. 'It came from a *Sounds* editorial. Then it became linked with Visage and all that, which made it a bit of a joke. The heavy, aggressive music didn't break through.' (The name was appropriated from the Futurist art movement, founded at the turn of the century. In 1909 Italy's Filippo Tommaso Marinetti published the first 'Futurist Manifesto', demanding the destruction of art's old guard and calling for a younger generation to create a modern movement.) Although Stevo was suspicious of the Futurist tag, he tried to define it on his own terms by filling his new chart with demos sent to him by up-and-coming bands. 'I was getting a lot of good material so I started to think about putting together a compilation album and I wanted Depeche Mode on it,' recalls Stevo.

Although intrigued by Stevo's suggestion of a Futurist compilation LP, the band were cautious and indecisive about the project. They'd decided to take their demo-tape around various record companies, only to be rejected by everyone. 'When we first took our tape around we didn't get anything from any of the record companies,' revealed Fletcher in 1981. 'Stiff Records sent us this real sarcastic letter – something like, "Hi, budding superstars ...".'

Gahan: 'Yeah, me and Vince went everywhere, visited about twelve companies in a day. The indie label Rough Trade were our last hope. We thought, they've got some pretty bad bands, but even they turned us down! They were all tapping their feet and that and we thought, this is the one – then they went, "Hey, that's pretty good, it's just not Rough Trade".'

In the office that day was a 29-year-old independent record boss who'd already been at the forefront of electronic music as a musician and entrepreneur. Daniel Miller had started listening to synthesizer music at Guildford Art School, where he attended a film and TV course from 1968–71. 'I was always a massive music fan and I grew up during a great period for rock and pop music in the 1960s ... There had been such an explosion of styles between 1964–8 but by the end of the '60s when I started at college, I'd just got fed up and frustrated with rock music. There didn't seem to be any experimentation any more, so free jazz and electronic music were the two things I became interested in. I began to discover German bands such as Can, Faust, Amon Düül, and, a bit later on, Neu! and Kraftwerk. I thought what they were doing was incredibly original and exciting. They were creating new sounds, things that I wanted to hear really. I was a bit sniffy about Brian Eno, Roxy Music and David Bowie at the time because I was really into Neu! and Kraftwerk, and I felt the British acts had used a lot of those ideas and put them into pop. Of course in retrospect I realized that was very clever. I hated all the British progressive rock bands like ELP, I was just into German electronic music.'

After working as a disco DJ in Switzerland – 'I was a ski-bum, basically' – he returned to the UK at the height of punk. 'I got into punk because of the energy and excitement of the period. For a long time kids had been really distanced from musicians, whereas when I was growing up they were the same thing. I never thought that music was about being able to play incredible solos and having vast amounts of equipment, so with punk I liked the do-it-yourself attitude.'

This DIY attitude spilled over into the new electronic scene. 'Synthesizers had become cheap and affordable,' explains Miller, 'and there'd been this creative explosion through punk so that you now had English bands like Cabaret Voltaire and Throbbing Gristle who were doing really interesting electronic music. All these factors inspired me to do something for myself – just for a laugh. Before I went to Switzerland I was film editing, so when I came back I did some film stuff again to earn some money. I was working ridiculous hours but it meant I could buy a very cheap synthesizer and a four-track tape recorder.'

Miller formed his own one-man band, The Normal, and recorded two songs, 'Warm Leatherette' (inspired by J.G. Ballard's novel *Crash* and later covered by Grace Jones) and 'T.V.O.D.'. 'I think I called it The Normal because I wanted to demistify it and make it very bland,' says the rarely interviewed Miller, who completed the enigmatic package by setting up his own label for the release, Mute.

The low-key musician had no interest in approaching an established record label with his material. 'There were lots of articles in the music newspapers about how to make your own single,' he recalls. 'It was very simple and not too expensive to get some test pressings, so that's what I did.' The self-appointed label boss didn't know anything about retail or distribution and ended up going to the Rough Trade shop on London's Portobello Road. The store was originally an essential outlet for punk and independent releases and from 1978 onwards the Rough Trade business had expanded into a label and distribution network, helping the careers of such diverse artists as Cabaret Voltaire, The Fall and reggae artist Augustus Pablo.

Daniel Miller walked into the shop and told them he'd got a test pressing of his single and would they be interested in buying a box of them if he got some more made? 'I met Rough Trade's boss Geoff Travis and I went to the back of the shop. They played "Warm Leatherette" and I was going "Oh, my God", because I wasn't used to someone hearing something I'd done. Anyway they loved it and said if I let them distribute it they'd help me press up 2,000. So that's what we did. The single came out in May 1978, picked up some good reviews and sold out very quickly.'

The inhibited, guarded Miller was 'taken aback' at the critical acclaim for his indie-distributed project and decided to explore further: 'I'd started to get to know the people at Rough Trade really well. I hung out there and helped them out a bit. Then an offer came in to play live and I thought, I can't really do it on my own. I'd recently met another guy, called Robert Rental, who also made synth music in his bedroom. We got to know each other and decided to form a little group to do this one gig which neither of us wanted to play on our own. That was actually put on by the DJ Colin Favor, who's now a techno DJ, as a celebration of this new kind of electronic music. There was Throbbing Gristle, Cabaret Voltaire and us.

'That continued into doing a Rough Trade tour, supporting Stiff Little Fingers. It was a bit painful but good fun. We went down extremely badly. Stiff Little Fingers were a conventional punk band and here we were, these two guys on stage with synthesizers and a backing tape, just making noise because we weren't really playing songs.' When Miller got back from the short tour he found a pile of tapes had arrived on his doorstep from artists who'd liked The Normal record and wanted to do a similar small-scale deal with Mute: 'I received one that I really liked, which was a band/singer called Fad Gadget. Deciding to work with him was the turning point, I guess.'

Fad Gadget was the self-mutilating creation of Leeds art student Frank Tovey, who mixed dark electronics with bleakly humorous observations on urban life. His 1979 single 'Back To Nature' was Mute's follow-up to The Normal, with Miller running the tiny label from his north-west London flat. Over the course of his next few singles, including 'Ricky's Hand' and 'Fireside Favourites', the innovative Fad Gadget developed a hard, rhythmic synth style and an extreme, self-destructive persona which was a long way ahead of its time. Nine Inch Nails' Trent Reznor surely owes Tovey a creative debt, although sadly Fad Gadget is a long since defunct and largely forgotten alter ego.

Over the course of the following year Mute started releasing experimental records by Non, a front for San Francisco artist Boyd Rice, who made uncompromisingly left-field electronic music. These included singles with four holes in the middle drilled by Rice himself for 'multi-axial rotation', which could be played at any speed. Mute's first-ever album was *Die Kleinen Und Die Bosen* by DAF (Deutsche Amerikanische Freundschaft), an LP of minimalist electronic dance music which would prove influential on later 'Industrial' and techno scenes.

Daniel Miller also dreamt up the Silicon Teens, an imaginary, adolescent synthesizer band who were allegedly redefining pop culture by recording an album of classic rock 'n' roll songs, such as Chuck Berry's 'Memphis Tennessee' and Heinz's 'Just Like Eddie'. The Silicon Teens' *Music For Parties* became a cult favourite (some major labels even approached Mute with offers for the band, not realizing they didn't actually exist) and signalled Miller's conviction that a new form of all-synthesizer, teenage pop group would emerge in the early '80s.

Although Miller acknowledges that Gary Numan was the first solo star of synth-pop music, he points out that there are guitars and/or drums and strings on the artist's albums: 'Numan was good and he made a lot of inroads into electronic pop culture. I liked the Tubeway Army *Blue* album (so-called because it was originally released on blue vinyl), that was a really good record but at one level it wasn't pure enough for me because he still used drums and guitar.' He continues, 'Synth-pop music was an historical inevitability. There had been nothing like that before, and then there was this rash of singles which all seemed to come out at around the same time. They all came from a love of electronic music, cheap synths, and the inspiration of punk.'

Miller's passion for innovative synthesizer artists made him an obvious A&R contact when Depeche Mode walked into Rough Trade in late 1980. 'They said, "How about this man", pointing at Daniel, who'd just walked into the room,' recalled Gahan. 'He took one look at us, went "Yeech!", walked out and slammed the door!' Clarke: 'People kept saying, "No, it's not our cup of tea, but play it to Daniel. He's starting his own label." But Daniel was in a really bad mood the day we saw him, said he didn't like it and stormed off.' Clarke and Gahan came back from Rough Trade to report that Daniel Miller, who was a bit of a hero to Fad Gadget fan, Martin Gore, was a 'right grumpy old bastard'.

Twenty years later Miller is keen to relate his side of the story: 'I guess it was autumn 1980, and I was very involved with Rough

Trade. There had been some kind of fuck up at the manufacturers about a sleeve for one of the early Fad Gadget singles and I was really in a bad mood. I remember going upstairs and Scott Piering, one of the top promotions people in the country who worked out of there, said, "Here's a tape, I don't know if you're interested in it." I saw these scruffy looking New Romantic types hanging out there, and I was running out and that was it. I didn't even listen to it. I just said, "I can't, I've got to rush." '

Miller had missed his first opportunity, leaving the door open to Stevo, who had now announced he was going to launch his own record company, Some Bizzare, to release his long-planned compilation of Futurist demos. 'Depeche Mode were at the Bridgehouse during one of my evenings out in Canning Town and I had a chat with them about my label and the Some Bizzare album,' recalls the entrepreneurial Stevo. Vince Clarke laughs at the memory: 'We were young and impressionable, and Stevo was saying things like, "Oh, I can get you a support tour with Ultravox!," which was a dream come true to us.' Although the band were excited by Stevo's enthusiasm, the ever-cautious unit still weren't ready to commit to anything just yet.

'Within a month of that first meeting I saw them play,' says Daniel Miller, who was about to have his second bite at the cherry. 'I didn't even associate them with the band who were in the Rough Trade office. They were supporting Fad Gadget at the Bridgehouse in Canning Town and I thought they were brilliant. I don't even know why I bothered to watch them but I remember the evening quite well. Fad Gadget had just finished a sound check and normally I would have gone off with them but for some reason I stayed behind and watched this group who looked like a dodgy New Romantic band. I hated the New Romantics but what came out of the speakers was incredible. I thought, "Well, everybody plays a good song first," but it just got better and better. Most of the songs they played that night actually ended up on the first album. They were incredibly unpretentious and you have to remember that at the time most electronic music was by people like me who had a slightly arty background – The Human League or Cabaret Voltaire. We were all slightly older, so we had that big Krautrock influence.

'In my head I'd had this vision of a much younger band who were going to come out of the electronic scene, which was basically the concept behind my own imaginary group Silicon Teens. They were a fake group but we billed them as the world's first all-electronic teenage pop group. You didn't have to be that smart to figure out there were going to be people whose first instruments were synthesizers rather than guitars. That was how I perceived Depeche Mode although later on, I realized that wasn't strictly true and they could play guitar. But this was the idea I had in my mind as I watched them at that gig.'

Miller met them backstage afterwards and said, ' "I'd really like to do something with you, a single or something." I saw them again the next week, just to make sure. I was working with Boyd Rice from Non, and he came down to that second show and he was blown away as well. I had another chat with them and pretty much that was it.' According to Gahan, 'Daniel came along again and said he could put out a record. If after that we didn't want to stay, we didn't have to. It was the most honest thing we'd heard.' Vince Clarke: 'Daniel offered us a deal, just for one single. We couldn't decide which offer to take up because Stevo was still interested. I can't remember why we went with Daniel but that's how it all started off.'

The two parties shook hands and didn't bother to seal their agreement with a written contract. Miller was passionate about establishing a rebellious, independent spirit at the label, both through its artists and business practices. In any case Mute was still a very small operation when Depeche Mode joined Fad Gadget and Non on the roster. 'At that time, I had one employee,' says Miller from Mute's bustling, well-staffed modern offices in London's Harrow Road. Back in late 1980 he worked from his home in north London, near Golders Green.

Although Miller and Depeche Mode had entered into an informal, verbal agreement, Stevo was still very much around, sniffing out possibilities. The music industry maverick claims, 'Depeche Mode were very confused about whether to go with Mute or Some Bizzare because we were in a very strong position in terms of media exposure. So I walked backstage at one of those early gigs and said to Daniel, "I just told Depeche Mode that you're a lovely guy and they should go with you." I told them that Daniel was very honest and trustworthy. By that time I had The The and Soft Cell, while Daniel had Fad Gadget on his label, so artistically his heart was in the right place. We've kept a very close relationship since. If I've been in trouble Daniel's helped me out.'

Miller confirms this eccentric, spirited and instinctive pioneer of alternative music (in the '90s Stevo's Mayfair offices would include a private chapel and a confession box for would-be-signings to go through a solemn hand-over ritual when they arrived with demo tapes) has been an ally, not a rival: 'I'd actually been working with Stevo for ages. First of all, when he was a DJ I used to send him all our Mute releases. Then he started to promote concerts at the Clarendon under the banner, Stevo's Electronic Parties. All our bands did them – DAF, Fad Gadget, Boyd Rice. I was good friends with Stevo and he spoke to me about the Some Bizzare album. He wanted to get Throbbing Gristle, Cabaret Voltaire and me for the project. There were a lot of tapes that came in and he decided to put all these young bands, who nobody had heard of, on to the record. I don't think there was any real rivalry between us. I'd heard Soft Cell ages before Stevo, because Frank Tovey [Fad Gadget] was at college with Marc Almond. And they'd sent him a tape to play to me before I'd heard Depeche Mode, which I quite liked but I wasn't completely blown away with it. Stevo had seen Depeche Mode a few days before me and he was really into Soft Cell and I was into Depeche. He said, "Well, if you have Depeche Mode, I'll have Soft Cell." I think Depeche Mode wanted to work with me anyway but in the end I did end up producing the Soft Cell single "Memorabilia". And we agreed that Depeche Mode should do a song for Stevo's Some Bizzare album.'

Stevo: 'I remember very clearly Daniel and Soft Cell recording "Memorabilia". I walked into this little East End studio at 10.30 a.m. I was drunk. It was Daniel Miller's birthday and he'd been up all night, so I said, "Happy birthday, Daniel" and he spewed all over the floor. It stank. I still reckon that's what gave the record its raw edge. Have you ever tried mixing a record in those conditions? You just wanted to get out of there.'

At the end of 1980 Depeche Mode went into an east London studio to record 'Photographic' for the Some Bizzare album. 'I wanted to put a really good song on Stevo's album, but not absolutely the best one,' says Miller, who acted as an informal producer on the session. The band rigged up their equipment and their new mentor asked them to play 'Dreaming Of Me', 'Ice Machine' and 'Photographic' live in the studio. Their set-up at the time was a Moog Prodigy synth, a Yamaha CS5, a little Kowai synth and a Dr Rhythm – a very basic, programmable drum machine. Miller had some synthesizer equipment which was slightly more sophisticated, but not much. He had a couple of synths and an ARP 2600 modular synth with its optional analogue sequencer. 'I remember Vince going "wow" when he saw that,' laughs Miller. 'He was really into the sequencer because he was into a very precise sound, so we used that on "Photographic". We did that track very quickly, it was played and mixed in a day.'

Daniel Miller was excited at discovering a teenage pop band who were also a very simple, pure electronic act. 'The special thing about Depeche Mode was that they were very minimalist, there was no sound or part that didn't need to be there. It was very functional. It was the only way they could do it because they had very basic equipment. There was only monophonic, not polyphonic, synths so they could only play one note at a time – there were no chords. They used their limitations very well. I'd been sent a lot of tapes at the time that were very self-indulgent, rambling pieces of music that weren't very good. This was so un-self-indulgent and that was what appealed to me.'

Miller's zealous, purist attitude towards electronic music was partly inspired by Kraftwerk's minimalist approach to their massively influential '70s albums, *Man Machine* and *Trans-Europe Express*. In an extremely rare interview, the band's Ralf Hutter revealed, 'We can convey an idea with one or two notes, it is better to do this than to play a hundred or so notes. With our musical machines, there is no question of playing with a kind of virtuosity, there is all the virtuosity we need in the machines, so we concentrated our work towards a very direct minimalism.'

At the end of 1980, Depeche Mode enjoyed their first ever press when the Basildon *Evening Echo* ran a story on the local band. The writer concluded, 'They ... could go a long way if someone just pointed them in the direction of a decent tailor.' Fletcher subsequently confirmed their sartorial nightmares: 'I used to wear plusfours, soccer socks and carpet slippers. Martin would paint his face half white and Vince looked like a Vietnamese refugee. He'd tan his face, dye his hair black and put on a headband.' Boyd Rice remembers the first time he met Vince Clarke at London's Bridgehouse: 'He looked like Lucille Ball!'

Dreaming Of Me, 1981

In February 1981 Stevo released his long-awaited dream project, the Some Bizzare album. Opening with the very pretty, plucked minimalism of Blancmange's 'Sad Day' (a very different recording to their later hits 'Living On The Ceiling', 'Blind Vision' and 'Waves'), it was an imaginative, eclectic record which went beyond the monochromatic, robotic imagery associated with pop Futurism. Alongside Depeche Mode, Soft Cell also debuted on the record with their psychopathic mutant song, 'The Girl With The Patent Leather Face', as did Matt Johnson's The The, whose nameless track featured blank vocals and paranoid, urban atmospherics. Bill Nelson, ex-Be Bop Deluxe, appeared as Eric Random on the Jell song 'I Dare Say It Will Hurt A Little' but many of the other acts were obscure and remained so – the derivative Neu Electrikk and Naked Lunch, for instance.

The *NME*'s Chris Bohn focused on Depeche's 'Photographic', describing it as 'very assured, neatly structured with entwined synth melodies which are partially marred by the '30s Futurist lyrics, but saved by the persistant quiver of a melody line.'

The Some Bizzare album was dominated by some of the era's Futurist musical 'conventions': most of the electronics were stark, minimal and symmetrical; primitive drum machines propelled the songs with an awkward cybernetic jerkiness; and the DIY productions encouraged detatched monotones from the assorted vocalists. Nevertheless, this 'Futuristic' pop was certainly very different to the gaudily ornate but musically more conventional New Romantics. 'We were Futurists,' said Dave Gahan a few years down the road, 'because we were involved with people who wanted to be individual. The New Romantic thing meant people all looking the same,

23

however flamboyantly. Futurists were an extension from punk. That was our following at the time.'

Nearly 20 years later Stevo is impassioned about the link between Some Bizzare and a pulped version of an art movement dating from the birth of the century: 'Nobody really wanted to be called a Futurist. It suggested you didn't have a sense of humour and were some kind of a science fiction nerd.' By early 1981 Gary Numan had spent two years sharing bleak, totalitarian sci-fi with his audience, creating his own Futurist legacy. 'Because we play synthesizers,' said Gahan in '81, 'we're supposed to look strangely at people and not smile.' Fletcher agreed:'We get people who think "synthesizers ... they must be moody". A lot of Numanoids come to our gigs.' Depeche Mode didn't really fit these expectations. They weren't remotely sci-fi and although Gahan was a fairly static performer, sometimes rendered almost immobile by nerves and a lack of experience, he never appeared aloof, distant or otherworldly.

Despite the LP's flawed associations, Depeche Mode's contribution to the Some Bizzare album inspired the British music media to scrutinize them for the first time. *Sounds'* Betty Page wrote the first major feature on the band, redefining the term 'Futurist' by wrestling it away from an image of fey, artistically elitist fops. In early 1981 Page wrote, ' ... dispel from your minds the untenable notion that Futurists are either bored mummy's boys tinkering with expensive gadgets or desperately earnest avant-garde merchants trying to preach the gospel according to Kafka: the current emergence of elec-tronic-based bands is at a truly grass-roots level – an increasing number of fresh-faced young men (and women) are taking to synthe-sizers and drum machines for their amusement rather than cheap guitars, to create cut-price, instant tunes.'

By the time Page interviewed the band, they'd caught the atten-tion of major record labels who were looking to poach new talent from the indie sector. Miller recalls, 'Very soon after we decided to do a single together and before it actually came out, the band started getting quite a high profile in the press and several labels came after them, offering a lot of money. The line these people gave was, "Oh, yes, of course, Mute is a lovely label but you'll never have a hit. And they've got no international set-up." '

Depeche Mode turned these offers down, placing their trust in Miller who was proving to be a very discerning career and musical guide. Vince Clarke told *Sounds* magazine: 'We've got a better chance on Mute. Daniel's been good to us and we like the way he operates. We listened to a few other companies but we decided to stick with him. He had a big success with the Silicon Teens, and we've got the same sort of lightweight feeling to us. Daniel's got a good nose for things like that. He's an underestimated man.' In return, the relatively worldly Miller felt a keen responsibility to make sure he did ' ... the best job possible for Depeche Mode. It was also very important to Mute Records and the whole alternative side of the industry for us not be ghetto-ized into being a very small sideline. Otherwise we would just end up being a free A&R source for the majors. We wanted to develop a label and work with an artist over a long period of time.'

Clarke's apparently vehement resolve that Daniel Miller's label was right for Depeche Mode sealed their immediate future together. As the band's only full-time member (the others were still working or at college) his ambitious drive kept them moving forward when the others were non-committal or at least, not very communicative. The compliant Martin Gore was happy to go along with Miller and Clarke, although if there hadn't been a shy but determined character pushing the band in that direction, who knows if they would have stayed with Mute Records? In 1988 Gore commented, 'Why didn't we sign to a major? It was quite tempting. Looking back, I can't imagine why we didn't go with them, it was just a stroke of luck we didn't. I mean, can you imagine four 18-year-old boys with no cash being offered sums of money like £200,000? But it was the best decision we ever made.'

Daniel Miller was very aware of Gore's docile nature – in fact it had actually turned into a band joke: 'Martin's a non-confrontational person, so he tends to let things go unless he feels really strongly about it. We used to call it the Arsenal syndrome, because he told this story once. When we started working together we had that usual conversation about which football team do you support and he said, "I suppose I support Arsenal." I said, "What do you mean?" He told me he used to go with his friend's dad but added, "I must admit I haven't really enjoyed it for the last five years but I really didn't want to say anything, so I've kept going." That sums up Martin completely. He doesn't deal with things. He'd prefer to be bored every Saturday afternoon rather than upset somebody by saying he didn't want to go. It's quite a sweet kind of thing really.'

Even the more demonstrative, eager Gahan confesses, 'The real reason we didn't sign to a major label is probably that we were so indecisive it passed us by. Daniel Miller was advising us too, although he never pushed us to stay with him. He did say that whatever they offered, he would do his best to match, and if we wanted singles in the charts, he'd do his best to get that for us too.'

Miller is quick to point out that Depeche Mode were very enthusiastic about the alternative, indie set-up at Mute, which appealed to all the band members. 'I think being with a label where the people who ran it were very close to the group was important to them and that is what being an independent label is about. They wanted to be in the indie charts and, in any case, they didn't like the people they'd met from the major labels.'

The speed of the band's progress had taken them by surprise, leaving them unprepared. Miller sensed the most bewildered were Gore and Fletcher. 'Dave and Vince were ambitious but the other two were not sure. The feeling I got from them was that they were like an amateur band just doing it because they enjoyed it. They had only just started to realize they were really good.' Fletcher has confirmed this: 'Vince was on the dole, always pushing and pushing. He was very ambitious. Martin and I are not ambitious people. We're lazy people.'

By now Gore and Fletcher were operating as almost an individual unit within Depeche Mode. 'In the early days Fletch used to be the outspoken half of Martin,' reveals Miller. 'Fletch and Martin are in some ways two halves of one person – they complement each other perfectly. Andy is completely pragmatic, very honest, doesn't mind a confrontation and in fact, quite likes it; Martin's dreamy, artistic, and will avoid confrontation at all costs.'

In early 1981 the pair were still working in the city and had no intentions of chucking in their jobs, particularly Fletcher who knew he was not a natural musician. The fervid Gahan was the most impressionable member of the group, but the others were naturally cautious and suspicious about change. This circumspect streak in the band allowed Fletcher and Gore to wait and see how successful Depeche Mode became before they considered quitting the security of their jobs. They trusted Daniel Miller's advice, enjoyed the atmosphere of an independent label and, importantly, the operation was informal enough for them to shake hands and jump ship at an early stage. Miller still didn't ask for a written contract with the band. 'We had a non-contractual 50/50 split within the UK and 70/30 split income for the rest of the world in their favour, which is a very good deal for a new band,' says the Mute boss nearly 20 years later. 'They are potentially on the same deal now but the deals we have abroad means a great deal more per record sold comes in for them. It is the same 50/50 split between us and them, but, obviously, the amount we split is a lot more than it used to be!'

Fletcher: 'We went for points, percentage of the profits. There's no way a major would have given us the points deal we've got with Mute. We had to go for the first two years without much money, though, because we didn't get a huge advance.'

Whatever the band's initial reasons were for staying on Mute, their friend Daryl Balmonte was convinced they'd made the right decision. 'Daniel was turning into their mentor,' he says. 'They were very lucky to find him. I think if a textbook manager had come along there would have been a lot of pressure to get as big as possible as quickly as possible, like Duran Duran and Culture Club, and they would have experienced the pyramid effect, straight up and straight down. But Daniel allowed them to make their own decisions and sometimes their own mistakes, so they built up naturally. Depeche Mode were the Silicon Teens in reality. He'd found a band that he'd made up in his head, and I don't think he intended to see that only last a year. He was thinking more long term.'

Their immediate future resolved, the all-electronic four-piece went into Blackwing Studios, located in the deconsecrated Church of Hallows in south-east London, to record Vince Clarke's 'Dreaming Of Me' as their first single for Mute. Miller had discovered Blackwing when he was recording the Silicon Teens project, requiring a studio with a big control room where he could set up all his synthesizers. 'Most people who worked in studios took the attitude "If you don't have a drummer and a guitarist then this isn't proper music, and what are those black boxes and you don't even know how to play,"' remembers Miller. 'However, Eric Radcliffe, the engineer at Blackwing, was immediately excited by the idea of working with a synth act. He didn't have an electronic music background but he was a very creative musician and had a science background. I think he was doing a PhD in laser technology. We used to have a lot of problems with the synthesizers because they weren't really designed to do the things we wanted from them, so Eric was a big help.' In fact, for several years all of Mute's artists recorded at Blackwing, and in the early '80s the synth-pop outfit Yazoo even gave a nod to Radcliffe by naming their debut LP, *Upstairs at Eric's*.

Meanwhile, Daniel Miller and Depeche Mode had selected 'Dreaming Of Me' as their debut single because they agreed it represented a mid-way point between their poppiest material and some of the darker, less melodic tracks they'd been playing live. According to Gahan, 'This was an obvious first single. We had about twenty songs but Daniel Miller, as an outsider at the time, helped us choose one. I think it's a classic pop song.'

'It was very exciting,' says Miller, grinning, 20 years later. 'I remember my thirtieth birthday very clearly because I'd just seen the sleeves for "Dreaming Of Me", and the band were playing a gig at the Rainbow which the DJs/promoters Steve Strange and Rusty Egan were calling the People's Palace. This was the first big public New Romantic gig and the pair had put on all these synthesizer bands, Ultravox, Metro, the robotic dance troop Shock. Then they invited these second-raters Depeche Mode to open. It was the first time the band had played in front of a big audience and a lot of the long-term fans say that's when they first saw them, so they obviously made a good impression.'

Depeche Mode then played at Cabaret Futura, a 'Berlin-esque' Futurist club on 16 February 1981 and Mute's 13th single, 'Dreaming Of Me', arrived in the shops four days later, backed by the mechanical 'Ice Machine'. *NME*'s Chris Bohn reviewed the single: 'Despite the narcissistic title, "Dreaming Of Me" is as sweetly unassuming a slice of electronic whimsy as anything by Orchestral Manoeuvres In The Dark. Deadpan vocals, programmed rhythm rejoinders and a candy-floss melody make for a pleasant three minutes.' *Sounds*' Betty Page described the song as 'sweet, simple, precise and lightweight synthetic pop', but was curious about whether the band were ready to develop their sound by incorporating a live drummer. Dave Gahan dismissed this, not with the purist horror of a true Kraftwerk devotee, but for more pragmatic reasons: 'I don't think it'll happen now. The tapes we've got now sound like real drums anyway. I know Orchestral Manoeuvres In The Dark were put down for using a drum machine on stage but the worst thing they ever did was to get a drummer. It was really bad after that. We don't need one anyway – it's just another person to pay.'

Depeche Mode enjoyed hearing their record being played by Radio 1 DJs Peter Powell and Richard Skinner, although it didn't breach the Top 75 until a month after release, eventually peaking at a very promising No.57. Fletcher later confessed, 'The biggest thrill I'll ever feel was when we went into the charts at fifty-odd for the first time.' 'It really was a major event in those days if you went into the Top 75,' recalls Miller. 'Woolworths would buy it and you'd get telegrams from all around the world saying, "Can we license this record?"'

Mute and Depeche Mode had not only proved that their alliance could break into the charts, they were also attracting the well-informed attention of American record company boss Seymour Stein, who'd signed Madonna to Sire/Warner Records in the early '80s. Miller and Stein had already worked together in licensing The Normal's 'T.V.O.D.' single and Fad Gadget for release in America. The record-hungry U.S. executive had developed the habit of flying into England and heading straight for the Rough Trade shop in Notting Hill where he would ask, 'What have you got that's interesting?' 'That's where I met him,' notes Miller. 'I told him I'd got this new band and asked him if he wanted to come and look at them. So he went along and loved them as well.'

As usual Daryl Balmonte was helping out with the gear at that gig: 'He came to Sweeney's disco in Basildon in late April '81. This New York guy who'd discovered Madonna – he came to Basildon! Sweeney's wasn't a very leftfield kind of place. It was a full-on Basildon disco but the manager of the place realized Depeche Mode were happening. The band love characters and Seymour Stein was a riot. I remember he took us out for a Chinese dinner and held court with all these fantastic stories about the music business. He became very fond of the group and felt very involved in them, although once they became big the Warner Brothers machine started to take over.'

Fletcher subsequently related the tale with a tone of skin-pinching bemusement: 'Here was this big U.S. record company president who'd signed Talking Heads and The Pretenders, coming to this small club which held about 150 people. We didn't even have a dressing room. We had to meet him on the stairway. He signed us from our first single. He's quite an incredible character really.'

In addition to thrashing out a deal with Sire, Miller was working hard on establishing licensing deals in Europe. He started to make new business contacts with people who could offer advice and experience as he expanded the label, hooking up with a guy called Rob Buckle, who ran Sweden's biggest indie label, Sonet. 'Through Rob I started to learn a bit about international,' says Miller, 'and the pair of us travelled around Europe setting up licensing deals for the band's next single, "New Life".'

Depeche Mode continued playing gigs throughout the spring and summer of 1981, ranging from Southend's Technical College and a Thames Boat Trip, to supporting Fad Gadget at the Lyceum in London, where journalist Paul Du Noyer enthused: ' ... stealers of the show were probably Depeche Mode, the group from Basildon. Depeche Mode are three synths and a singer, visually in the Spandau Ballet mould, but musically a very interesting proposition in their own right.'

Depeche Mode also ventured outside southern England for the first time, playing dates in Leeds, Birmingham and Cardiff. They used the rest of their spare time – with the notable exception of the unemployed Clarke who filled his days booking dates and organizing the band – in Blackwing, recording new songs. 'The way the sessions were structured was quite odd,' remembers Daniel Miller. 'Martin and Fletch both had day jobs in banking and insurance. Dave was in college at Southend Technical College, and Vince was on the dole. Vince was very much the driving force behind the band. He was the person who organized the gigs, who wrote most of the songs, did the musical arrangements and figured out how they would play them. He was also the driving force in the studio. He had a very clear idea of how he wanted the songs to sound and was self-assured and confident about it. Vince's ability with the equipment was starting to improve as well.

'I would be at Blackwing in the day to give Vince a bit of advice on how to get sounds, help him with the technology and some arrangement things. Then Fletch and Mart arrived after work in their dodgy suits and would be far more interested in eating their takeaways and playing the games machine. Not much has changed I suppose! Then we'd say to Martin, "We need an extra melody on this, can you come down?" He'd usually complain, "Oh, do I have to, I'm just having my Chinese?" He'd come down with this Chinese meal in one hand and play an amazing melody with the other.' When Dave Gahan was at the studio he would fret about how the music was sounding and constantly question whether things were right or not. This unique in-studio behavioural pattern of a spirited but agonized Gahan buzzing around as boffins twiddled their synthesizers to the vague disinterest of the self-enclosed unit of Fletcher and Gore has lasted throughout their career.

By the time of the 'New Life' release in June 1981, Depeche Mode had performed almost 50 gigs and scored a chart hit but Gahan admits, 'We didn't feel secure when "New Life" first came out.' The song was a joyously upbeat, dancey pop track with nonsensical, rather puerile lyrics. 'Vince's songs are odd because they don't mean anything,' said Gore at the time. 'He looks for a melody, then finds words that rhyme.'

'Dreaming Of Me' had already alerted the attention of the industry and some music fans but in the summer of 1981 Depeche Mode became fully-fledged pop stars. In the same week that the supportive Richard Skinner aired a Depeche Mode Radio 1 session (featuring Vince Clarke's 'Boys Say Go!' and 'Photographic', and Gore's two songs 'Big Muff' and 'Tora! Tora! Tora!'), 'New Life' entered the British charts. Over the next month it climbed to No.11, giving the band their first *Top Of The Pops* appearance along the way. 'It was all right,' says Fletcher of this TV breakthrough. 'At first I felt a bit of a prune. Like pressing a keyboard and pretending you're really doing it and singing into a microphone with a lead going nowhere. Halfway through you think, "God, what am I doing here, looking a prat in front of millions of people? We've got used to it now, it's just funny now."

By the time 'New Life' had finished its 15-week chart run and stalled at 500,000 sales, Gahan had quit his art course. It's been claimed that the necessary ego-boost for the singer to make this decision came after his tutor at Southend Art College sent him to do work experience in central London. The frontman found himself the centre of attention as a crowd of girls gathered while he dressed the window of a department store. In any case, half a million sales were enough to persuade the ultra-cautious Fletcher and Gore to leave banking and concentrate on the band full-time.

In 1981 Depeche Mode looked and behaved like boys next door who dabbled in eyeliner, rather than presenting an image of self-conscious fashion dandies. According to one newly converted fan, *Melody Maker*'s Steve Sutherland, the four boys appeared to be, '... all malleable puppy fat, equally at home over tea with your gran, or snogging down the disco.'

'Depeche Mode were not in the slightest bit elitist,' says Miller, who was turned away from Blitz by Steve Strange due to his lack of sartorial flair. 'I understand that elitism was important to a certain type of club culture but I didn't like it. Depeche were a pop band. A lot of the New Romantic music was crap because it was fake Bowie – more rock than pop. I was interested in electronics and not making any compromises in the use of rock dynamics.'

Depeche Mode's Basildon roots also separated them from the more self-aware scenes in London, Birmingham and even Leeds and Sheffield, where an aura of arty underground cool clung to The Human League, Cabaret Voltaire and Soft Cell. 'I guess a lot of the other synthesizer bands were from towns with vibrant club scenes,' considers Daryl Balmonte, 'whereas Basildon has always been mistakenly seen by the media as a joke town.'

'In Britain people are obsessed with where you're from,' comments Miller. 'It has a lot to do with class. You're from Manchester, you're from Birmingham ... it's much cooler to come from Manchester rather than Birmingham. Fuck knows why. I think Basildon has a certain image which isn't really correct. I thought of Basildon as a nice little country town but it's actually a pretty heavy place.'

In contrast to their alienated or knowingly ironic synthesizer rivals, Depeche Mode came across as a charmingly naïve pop band, with Gahan explaining to one writer, 'We're P.U. You know, pop and up.' Vince Clarke corrected him, 'The phrase is U.P. and it stands for Ultrapop!' Critics responded to them in precisely the fashion that Daniel Miller had first envisaged – as a Silicon Teens-made flesh, a teenage pop group working with new technology and celebrating it without indulging in heavy sci-fi atmospherics or art-school pomp. Steve Sutherland enthused, 'Damn near the most perfect pop group these two lucky lug'oles have sampled all season. They have a set of knowing but naive, intense yet idiotically simple two-minute gems that stand quiff and earrings above the ever-growing pile of synth-pop fad followers. Suss enough to play by the rules, but brilliant enough to break them.'

From late 1980 through to 1983 British music went through an inventive period when vaudeville, irony, humour, ambition, innovation, technology and fashion combined in some fantastic pop stars and songs – all with the required feeling of built-in obsolescence. One of this era's typically bizarre, extreme transformations was Adam and The Ants' revamp from a struggling punk act into dandified American Indians for their first hit, 1980's 'Dog Eat Dog', complete with white, stripey make-up, two drummers and the song's dumb, glammy hook. A year later Adam Ant knowingly summed up his creative affectations with the line 'Ridicule is nothing to be scared of' from his 1981 chart-topper, 'Prince Charming'.

Just as surprisingly, in May '81 the undergound electronic group The Human League reinvented themselves as a witty 'electronic Abba', with singer Phil Oakey openly admitting his mercenary ambitions: 'I wear make-up because people will listen to our records more if I wear make-up, or if I've got a silly long haircut on one side. It's a gimmick, and if that's necessary to make people listen, then that's what you've got to do. The more people you can actually get to, the better. Mind you, the pierced nipples are a problem, actually. I get little girls ringing me up and asking me how to do them.'

Of all the post-punk bands who aspired to chart success after years of credibility and poverty, The Human League made the most daring transition. Almost overnight the media deemed it was 'all right' to be selling records like there was no tomorrow, especially as these new acts made an issue out of their punky, DIY credentials and seemed aware of their own disposability (this idea was later crushed by their regular comebacks in the '90s). The Human League's producer Martin Rushent, who played an essential role in shaping their classic 1981 album *Dare*, expressed an Everyman attitude towards the new technology: 'All this equipment is the great equalizer, doing away with all that virtuoso crap.'

In 1981 Soft Cell broke through with their cover of an old
Northern Soul anthem, 'Tainted Love', described by the *NME* as
'perfect – the functionary textures of electro-pop shaken and shaped
to invoke the remorse of a forgotten jukebox ...' 'Tainted Love'
reached No.1, launching Marc Almond as a misfit pop star: 'I wasn't
particularly tough at school, how I survived was making people
laugh,' he claimed, plugging his outsider status to the hilt. 'I'm interested in the loser, the person who has to struggle to survive ... I feel
really at home with people who are outsiders.' Music writer Mary
Harron was sensitive to Soft Cell's willingness to expose their frailties, accurately summarizing: 'After the New Romantic's blasé, don't-
muss-my-image notions of cool, Almond was an inspiration because
he never quite brought off his image – usually failed horribly – and
didn't care. And because he was a real pop star, he gave a kind of
glamour to failure. The video for their single "Bedsitter" combined
images of rumpled clothes on the floor, bowls of cornflakes and dirty
teacups with the romantic image of going out to dance and forget it:
the reality of lonely, grubby adolescence and the myth of Clubland,
fused into what looked like a perfectly attainable dream.'

Soft Cell's cute, youthful perversity; The Human League's sussed
employment of two down-to-earth Sheffield girls as backing singers,
OMD's jumpers and earnest voices, and Depeche Mode's cherubic
synthesizer pop were all in stark contrast to the hautily aspirational
New Romantics – from Steve Strange's assertion that he always liked
to be 'different and avant garde' to Simon Le Bon's reported
comment that the best thing about being famous is that 'you can eat
smoked salmon 24 hours a day'.

This pop-fuelled atmosphere was ideal for the ordinary teenage
ambitions of Depeche Mode and in June they recorded a new, infec-
tiously catchy track, 'Just Can't Get Enough'. There was a delay
when they didn't tune up their instruments before the session and
realized later that nothing was in tune with anything else. It hardly
mattered as 'New Life's extended four-month chart life meant that
they had to wait until the autumn before they could release the
follow-up.

After completing this new track, the band set off on a short trip
around the country, playing clubs in Brighton, Manchester, Leeds
and Edinburgh, where they were face-to-face with a mixture of New

Romantics and a trickle of pop fans. Daryl Balmonte remembers, 'It wasn't until their first album, *Speak and Spell*, came out that they got a teeny audience. In 1981 they were still very hip with the post-Studio 21 crowd.' Daniel Miller added another job to those of record company boss, A&R man, producer and friend – he also went on the road with them. 'In the very early days I was driver, tour manager and sound man,' he laughs.

In August the *NME* published a Depeche Mode front cover, taken by Anton Corbijn who blurred the frontman Dave Gahan and focused on the men behind him. 'I was really disappointed,' says Gahan. 'I was on the front but ... I wasn't. It was quite cheeky of him. It went completely over my head, the whole photograph. I remember thinking, What a bastard! He's got me completely out of focus.' The interview, conducted by Paul Morley, offered a positive, intellectualized slant on the New Pop phenomenon, although conspicuous by his absence was a 'depressed' Vince Clarke. The band's quiet, slightly strange songwriter was keeping his thoughts to himself but he later revealed how he felt claustrophobic within the routines of a successful pop act. 'It was the way the whole thing was going. I lost my enthusiasm. It was turning into a production line and that was worrying me. The techniques were improving to an extent and the way we were playing but even then I found there were things in the way, preventing us from experimenting. We were so busy, there was something going on every day and no time to play around.'

This was a dangerous place for the young Basildon boys to find themselves in, because all the forces of the music industry were treating them as a fad – their plugger Neil Ferris was doing a fantastic job in securing their singles daytime airplay but had no interest in building their credibility. The music press delighted in their innocence, which of course could only be short-lived, and Daniel Miller was determined to prove Mute could have a hit pop band. 'They maybe did too much press and TV,' concedes the Mute boss, 'but it's difficult. Mute was a young label and the band were still teenagers. Unfortunately they got saddled with this teenypop image which has never gone away in this country.'

On 7 September Depeche Mode released 'Just Can't Get Enough' as their third single, charting at their highest placing so far – No.8.

This ultra-pop song, crafted in bright but deceptively rich analogue sounds by the band and Daniel Miller, has remained a favourite with the fans. However, for every critic who mused over the track's teeny passion, there was another who felt Depeche Mode's singles were becoming a little too perky and childlike. *Record* Mirror's Sunie summed up this alternative opinion when she wrote of 'Just Can't Get Enough', ' ... hugely enjoyable, bouncy and boppy and very close to irritating.'

On 19 September Depeche Mode played a benefit concert for Amnesty International at London's Venue, then they set off for their first-ever gigs in Europe. It was a short trip consisting of four dates in Hamburg, Amsterdam, Brussels and Paris. Inevitably the band's frilly shirts and Max Factor make-up prompted the European press to file away Depeche Mode as a New Romantic band. Gahan remembers: 'We must have done 30 interviews on the Continent, where they asked if we were "Bleetz Keedz", then have them print our denials right next to those awful shots of us wearing frilly shirts and eyeliner.' More importantly during this short trip overseas, Daniel Miller observed, ' ... a rift growing between Vince Clarke and the other members of the band. It got to the point where they weren't talking to each other.'

Clarke's annoyance with the day-to-day routines of promoting Depeche Mode had turned into an entrenched hostilty against the whole process. He felt out of sync with the other band members who, at this stage, were willing to do whatever was required of them, so he withdrew from them as well. It wasn't much of a surprise when Clarke visited each member in turn to tell them he was leaving the band. 'They'd been expecting it,' explains Clarke. 'I'd been going through a gloomy phase, so they knew something was up. But I still had to go round to their houses and tell them.'

Daryl Balmonte remembers the wilful but virtually silent songwriter informing him about his recent decision on the first day of the band's upcoming UK tour. 'I don't think anyone was surprised when Vince left,' says Balmonte. 'Vince started acting a bit quiet for several months before he quit. *Smash Hits* used to do these flexi-discs on the cover and Andy and Mart were on holiday, so he went in and did it on his own with Dave on vocals. I remember Fletch saying, "I don't think Vince needs us." He just seemed to be happy doing things his way. Vince didn't have a band mentality whereas the others saw themselves as being part of a gang. He likes to lock himself away and spend his own time on a project. Vince is a difficult man to get to know. It's weird because all three of the original Composition of Sound members could be mistaken for being hard to approach. I think it's probably more of a church thing than a Basildon thing.'

Fletcher: 'Vince was important to the concept of the band. Without him, we wouldn't have known where we were going. He was the driving force. It's weird, really. I don't think he ever regretted leaving. I think he felt he could do it all by himself, and it's true, he could.'

According to Miller, 'No one thought about the band splitting up. Everybody close to them knew that Martin was a really good song-writer. Even on Vince's tracks his melodic contributions were very good. They'd recently given up their jobs, they'd had a couple of hit singles, so it was obvious that they weren't going to give up. Martin would write the songs and Fletch took over a lot of the other roles Vince had – the organizing side of it. You have to remember that because they were on Mute, we only had three or four bands, so they were all really important to us. And the band are very resilient and articulate about what they want to do.'

On the surface the resolve of Miller and Depeche Mode after losing the musician who'd written all the band's hits is astonishing. This was an extremely competitive period in British pop music when exciting new acts were breaking through almost on a weekly basis, including Teardrop Explodes, ABC, Culture Club, The Associates, Simple Minds, Japan, The Cure, Ultravox, Visage, Wham! and Spandau Ballet. Gore has commented, 'Looking back I think we should have been slightly more worried than we were. When your chief songwriter leaves the band, you should worry a bit. I suppose that's one of the good things about being young. If we had panicked, we probably wouldn't be here today.'

'I think Vince was maybe a bit surprised at how we reacted,' clarifies Fletcher, 'but we were fairly prepared – the general atmosphere had been getting really bad. It was like us three and Vince on his own. He just felt that we were becoming public property, he didn't like what was happening to Depeche Mode, didn't like being famous and didn't like touring.'

All parties agreed to keep quiet about Clarke's decision until after
their UK tour in autumn '81. 'Vince announced to us he was leaving
quite early on,' recalls Miller, 'but we decided to keep it quiet because
we were just about to sign the American deal with Sire Records and
we didn't want to freak them out by telling them that the band's main
songwriter was leaving!'

On 31 October the band set off on their first British tour with
Clarke still in tow, in order to promote their forthcoming debut album
Speak and Spell. The support slot on these completely sold-out
dates were the electro-pop duo Blancmange, who'd also appeared on
Stevo's Some Bizzare album. Despite Clarke's hushed-up decision to
leave, Daryl Balmonte insists, 'They did socialize with Vince on the
first tour. They're very resilient. They just figured, "OK, he's leaving
but that doesn't stop all of us going out together and having a
laugh."'

Balmonte, who roadied on the tour, remembers the audiences as
' ... quite a mix really. There were some young fans but there was
still an element of the old raincoat brigade because it was another
club tour, with the band often going on stage at midnight. A lot of the
venues had a minimum age limit, of 18 or over, places like the Top
Rank in Birmingham.' Fletcher was developing his own theory about
the age difference between the people who bought their records and
those he was playing to at their gigs: 'I don't think tours play a major
part in what we do. I think most of the people who bought our
records have never been to a gig in their lives, and will never go to
one. They'd rather see a picture in a magazine.'

Out front, the charismatic Dave Gahan was exhibiting early signs
of showmanship but it was very inhibited compared to the exaggerated, rock 'n' roll swagger that would emerge in later years. The band
had no strong sense about how they wanted to present themselves.
They were badly dressed, a mish-mash of New Romantic cast-offs
and cheap high street stuff, and to make matters worse the synthesizers' immobile placings on the stage (as opposed to guitars) limited
what they could do as performers. Gary Numan had solved the problem with lavish light-shows and frozen body language; The Human
League had used slide projectors to create distracting images behind
them and Kraftwerk had built their own robots. 'We don't do photo
sessions any more,' explained Kraftwerk's Ralf Hutter in the late

'70s. 'We had physical dummies, replicas of ourselves made. They are plastic and more resistant to photographs.'

Depeche Mode weren't the only electronic band who were finding it hard to match image with music – OMD's Andy McCluskey, who resembled a young geography teacher more than a pop star, admitted: 'Our visual image is a mess. We look like a bunch of idiots who just walked in off the street.'

Backstage, Gahan and Gore spent most of the time with their girlfriends, Joanne and Anne, both of whom helped out – Jo started running the fan club and Anne worked on the merchandise store. Daryl Balmonte, who had just left school, was now effectively their full-time roadie, creating a very friendly, close-knit atmosphere behind the scenes. Everyone on the tour felt a real sense of loss when Vince Clarke played his last gig with the band at the Lyceum, London, on 16 November. Once the show was over the original songwriter walked away, turned and gave them a wave.

In November Mute released the band's debut LP. 'This was another exciting time,' says Miller. 'As the record was coming out we got our first office, and I upped the staff to three or four. That was in Seymour Place in the West End.' *Speak and Spell*, which was credited as co-produced by Daniel Miller with Depeche Mode, peaked at No.10 and stayed on the charts for 32 weeks. It included the two hit singles, 'New Life' and 'Just Can't Get Enough', plus tracks which were mostly favourites in the band's live set. The incongruous cover image of a swan was not entirely successful but it did make the band stand out from their pop contemporaries who preferred to plaster their faces all over their albums.

The sleeve designer/photographer Brian Griffin had done quite a few famous covers in the late '70s and at the start of the new decade, including Elvis Costello's *Armed Forces*, Joe Jackson's *Look Sharp* and Iggy Pop's *Soldier*, along with LP images for Teardrop Explodes, Echo and The Bunnymen and Devo. 'I got myself an agent and he had a lease on a shop in Seymour Place,' remembers Griffin. 'The agent had the first, second and third floors and he came in to see me one day and said that a little record company had moved in downstairs and they needed a sleeve for one of their bands. So all I had to do was go down one flight of stairs and there was Daniel with a couple of other people. It was a very small set-up. I spoke to Daniel,

met Depeche Mode and took the brief. That first meeting was really
funny because they seemed so passive. No real intensity, it all seemed
very throwaway. They became more intense the longer I worked with
them. Anyway, I shot the cover image in my studio in Rotherhithe.
Goodness knows why I put a swan in a plastic bag. I have no idea.
Their reaction was doubtful.'

'It was awful,' said Gahan shortly after the album's release. 'The
guy who did it, Brian Griffin – he also does the Echo and The
Bunnymen sleeves – when he was explaining it, he was going "imagine a swan floating in the air, floating on a sea of glass", and it
sounded really great. It turned out to be a stuffed swan in a plastic
bag! It was meant to be all nice and romantic, but it was just comical.'

Reviews for *Speak and Spell* were mostly up-beat, with *Sounds*
describing it as, 'trendy electro-disco beats go hand in hand with
choirboy melodies and a merry-go-round of neo-folksy synths to
make a perfectly uncontrived pop soufflé.' *Melody Maker*: 'So obviously bright, so clearly sparkling with new life, it's a wonder they
don't burn permanent dancing shadows on to the walls.' *NME*'s Paul
Morley probed a little deeper: 'Depeche Mode take the shiny, skim-
ming, superficial, predictable NICENESS of "teenbop" – the passive
patterns of Slik, the fresh bounce of Bay City Rollers – and enamel
it with intelligence and insolence. Depeche Mode introduce literacy
into bubblegum.' *Record Mirror* gave it a maximum, five out of five,
defining it as 'a charming, cheeky collection of compulsive dance
tunes, bubbly and brief like the best pop should be.' But the journalist highlighted the darker song, 'Photographic', as one of the album's
standout moments, arguing: ' "Photographic" is like Numan at his
best, but better: all the sinister phrases, both lyrical and musical, but
with a rapid danceable beat instead of the solemnity that Gazza's
always laid on with a sequinned trowel.'

Speak and Spell is very 'bubblegummy' and naive sounding but
there are subtle hints of a band willing to explore more atmospheric
musical areas and themes. Vince Clarke contributes the moodily
symmetrical electro-pop of 'Photographic', 'Puppets' and the dream-
like 'Any Second Now' to this darker direction but more importantly
Martin Gore's 'Tora! Tora! Tora!' and the excellent instrumental 'Big
Muff' point the way to Depeche Mode's future. *Speak and Spell* also

retains the pure electronic sound of their live shows, mixing Kraftwerk-like clarity with purposeful, teenage pop tunes. Daniel Miller emphasizes, 'We never used polyphonic synths to play chords so everything had to be built up. We felt that didn't have anything to do with electronic music and I still believe that.' Even so, within a couple of years, Dave Gahan was expressing reservations about the album, no doubt prompted by a listen to the horribly twee 'Boys Say Go' or 'What's Your Name?' 'When I hear tracks from *Speak and Spell* I get embarrassed, although at the time I thought it was great!'

In December 1981 Mute officially announced that Clarke had left. Once the tour was over bad feeling quickly set in between Clarke and the band, fuelled by the aggressive, competitive natures of Gahan and Fletcher. 'It wasn't amiable at all,' says the hyperactive, emotional Gahan. 'There was a lot of bad feeling on both parts. It was about a year before it finally died down, and until then it was pretty vile.'

At the same time the band placed an advert in the back of the *Melody Maker*, reading: 'Name Band, Require Synthesizer Player, Must Be Under 21.' Their first American tour was booked for January 1982 on the back of 'Just Can't Get Enough' which had done well in the U.S. clubs, so they needed someone to play Clarke's melody parts live. They had no intention of getting a permanent replacement for their ex-songwriter. One of the keyboard players who turned up for the audition was a 22-year-old from Hammersmith, west London, Alan Wilder.

Born on 1 June 1959, he was not only older than the members of Depeche Mode, he was from a more liberal, middle-class background. 'The Hammersmith youth isn't so rebellious there, like in Basildon, although my parents weren't rich or poor. In school I mostly stayed in the background. I only found music and language to be absorbing.' By the time Wilder graduated to St Clement Danes Grammar School, aged 11, he was playing piano, flute and he soon became a member of his school orchestra and brass band. 'My parents wanted their kids to have a musical education. One brother is a pianist and accompanies all kinds of singers, the other teaches music in Finland.

'After I left school in 1975 I was unemployed all the time. My parents advised me to apply to recording studios. I think I got rejected about forty times. Eventually I got to be a tea-boy at one studio [DJM studios in London's West End] where I met my idols at the time, the Rubettes. I also played in a little soft-rock band which was called The Dragons. Then I moved to Bristol to get the chance to rehearse more. After that I played in several jazz and blues bands, including a pub act, Real To Real. I also had a short time in a New Wave band, Daphne and The Tenderspots [he called himself Alan Normal] who released one single, "Disco Hell".' After that Wilder joined the Hitmen (whose lead singer Ben Watkins went on to form Juno Reactor), played a few live shows and saw the advert in the *Maker*.

The funny, sharp-witted Wilder reveals, 'To be honest before I joined Depeche Mode, I didn't know the first thing about electronic music. At the audition almost all of the people who showed up were fans and I think my nonchalance was greatly appreciated by Dave, Andrew and Martin. Besides I could play along with them immediately. The thing that I remember about that rehearsal was they were all in their Marks and Spencers woolly jumpers. They were incredibly shy. Martin still is but in those days he was unbearably shy. He would make you feel really uncomfortable simply because he was so uncomfortable.

'The audition was a little tricky. I'm sort of middle-class and they were working-class lads. Musically I thought they were a bit naive sounding but there was something interesting about it, and I was sort of in a desperate situation where I would take just about any gig at the time.'

Wilder also noted Daniel Miller's role as inspiration and protector: 'Daniel was very careful about every decision to do with Depeche Mode in those days. In fact, even before I went to the audition I had a meeting with Daniel first – everyone did. He was vetting people and then I was allowed to go to the audition. Out of the last two contenders whom they invited back, I don't think I was his choice. They initially saw about twenty people, then Daniel asked for two of us to come back, and the other guy had a couple of songs which Daniel quite liked and I think he felt that this other bloke was a bit more like them. Daniel probably saw that I was very different in my background and the fact that I had a musical training. Whereas I don't think the band even considered that – they just thought, he can play the parts and he looks all right, we'll get him in. Anyway, Daniel rang me up and told me I'd got the job although it was made very clear that they only wanted me to play on tour with them.'

Miller: 'It was down to two people and I think I slightly favoured the other guy but they said they wanted to go with Alan, so I said, fine. It was really just to have a live player. We weren't looking for a full-time member of the band. I think Alan was a bit disparaging of them because he could play their songs with one hand but it worked and he didn't really have to be taught anything.'

'When I joined Depeche Mode I didn't really like their music at all,' concedes Wilder. 'Martin, Dave and Andy were really nice fellows, so I decided to stick with them for a few months. I've never had any regrets ...' he deadpans.

At the end of 1981 the three original group members returned to Blackwing to record a new single, 'See You' – without Clarke or Wilder. Miller discloses, 'That was the first track we did without Vince. Martin came up with this song and it was very basic, just a melody on a Casio synth and Martin tapping the beat with his foot. The song was all there but in terms of arrangement and sound there was no indication of which way to go. It was very different to Vince who'd had a much stronger sense of what he wanted but the atmosphere in the studio was very exciting and quite positive. No one had any doubts about carrying on.'

Leave In Silence, 1982

Alan Wilder played his debut gig with Depeche Mode at Crocs in Rayleigh in January 1982, shortly before they headed off for their American shows. 'Daryl Balmonte was there,' recalls the keyboard player. 'He's been there since they played at Crocs in the early days in their plus-fours and talcum powder in their hair. I remember he still only looked about 12 years old. In those early days him and Dave were virtually inseparable.'

Meanwhile Daniel Miller had applied for American visas and discovered a problem – Dave Gahan's juvenile record didn't cause any trouble but Alan Wilder had a shoplifting conviction which he hadn't disclosed at the audition. 'When I was 17 or 18 I went out with my girlfriend and we were completely broke, so we stole some food and we got caught,' he admits 20 years later.

The hitch was sorted out and on 22 and 23 January the band played two shows at The Ritz in New York. Both were well attended thanks to the underground success of 'Just Can't Get Enough' and Seymour Stein's enthusiasm at a time when he was a very big player on the American music scene. *Speak and Spell* made its full American release in spring 1982, creeping into the Billboard Top 200 at 192. However, it received a mixed reception from the U.S. music critics who were still keen on 'rock dynamics'. *Trouser Press* was one of the American magazines that felt uncomfortable with the band's Kraftwerk-like combination of synthetic purity and instant pop melody: 'Depeche Mode utilizes commercial song formulas with almost unerring precision. Three minutes at a time can be enjoyable: more forces you to come to terms with their limitations. A simple, predictable sonic palette (synth only) heightens the difficulty.'

They returned to England in time for the release of their fourth

44

single on 29 January 1982. 'That's a real lovey-dovey one,' says
Gahan. Gore: 'It was the first "real song", the first piece of pure electro.' Although 'See You' isn't one of their best songs it was a vital
success for the band, reaching No.6 – their highest chart placing so
far and achieved without the assistance of Vince Clarke who'd
offered them a new song, 'Only You', after leaving the band.
However, Depeche Mode turned it down because they thought it
sounded like another track and Clarke moped off, later using it with
some success for his new band Yazoo.

While they impressed observers by scoring their biggest hit so far,
Depeche Mode were going through an awkward transitional phase.
'See You's deft, moody keyboard lines hardly balanced with its horribly trite, teenage lyric. The pop newcomers also still had no idea of
how to present themselves or their music. They lurched from suits to
M & S jumpers and leather. One photo session even portrayed them
in cricket whites, holding bats. Spindly, ginger-haired Fletcher recalls,
'After '82 we started to look more casual again. What we have on
stage is more or less what we wear everyday. It's always been one of
our major problems that we have no definite image. We come across
as pretentious when we try to do something that isn't ourselves, but
when we act naturally we come across as being pretty anonymous.
The band with the best image in the world is Pink Floyd, they're a
really faceless group.'

Their other problem was an ideological confusion in the Depeche
Mode camp regarding the exploitation of the disposabilia of teen
magazines and children's TV, and a growing desire to build the
band's career through weekly music magazines such as *NME* and
Melody Maker and more credible music programmes. Daniel Miller
appointed Chris Carr as their press representative, with the young
pop act joining a publicity roster that included Siouxsie and The
Banshees and The Associates. Carr was very aware of the band's
image, lampooned at the time by punk poet Attila the Stockbroker
as bland, haircut music in his poem, 'Nigel Wants to Go and See
Depeche Mode'. 'I despised a lot of their early singles,' says Carr,
establishing a familiar pattern amongst band collaborators. 'They
were really wimpy as a band. Depeche Mode were so unsure about
who they were and what they wanted to be. They were wimpy as a
collective, because to say that Dave was wimpy as an individual would

be very misleading! However, there was a point after Vince had left when suddenly we realized that we've got something here, and that if we didn't control and focus it, it was going to be lost. So we started seeking the *NME* stamp of approval. But on the other hand you still had their plugger Neil Ferris and the Radio 1 camp, who were going, Pop, Pop, Pop.'

As Gore confessed they had very little understanding or control of their image: 'In 1981, when *Speak and Spell* came out, we were 18 years old; we were young, we were naïve, we didn't have a clue! From one day to the next we were being thrust on TV, we were being put into the press, and at that time we thought we should do every interview that came along, and we didn't particularly care about our image; we were just kids, y'know? It took us a long time to get to grips with what was actually happening, how to take control of our image and the things we put out to the world.'

Alan Wilder recalls some of his early TV appearances with unmistakeable horror: 'The worst one was this thing we did at Alton Towers,' he says emphatically. 'We had to mime to one of our songs while we wandered around the gardens with hands in our pockets. All of us had terrible clothes on and I'd say it's Depeche Mode's worst moment.'

Meanwhile, fresh from their recent Top 10 success the band started rehearsing for a second British tour in February. 'On that tour Daniel was very hands on,' asserts Wilder, who was starting to learn more about synthesizers and elecronic music from the Mute Records founder. 'He'd created a lot of the analogue sounds on *Speak and Spell*, then those sounds would be duplicated on tape for the tour. If they were in keyboards, Daniel would programme them. We used to rehearse at Blackwing, where we'd set up the four-track tape machine, two PA speakers facing us, we'd run back the tape music and play three keyboards. Martin was the one who would tell me which parts I should play. It would be, "Oh Vince used to play this part so you'd better do that one". That was really all I did on my first tour.'

Depeche Mode set off on 10 February 1982, playing a Radio 1 'In Concert', before opening the tour proper at the Top Rank, Cardiff. This time the 15-date journey around the UK, which included two sold-out nights at Hammersmith Odeon, heaved with teen hysteria. Gahan, who was the main object of adulation, had received his initiation into the frenzied world of the teenage pop fan when he was left exposed at a personal appearance in London's Camden Palace: 'I was practically pulled apart. It was really scary, when I got inside I was trapped and there were people clawing at me, ripping my clothes, pulling my hair – I was so frightened I ran and hid myself in the loo. I just didn't want to come out. I think that was one of my worst experiences – those kids could kill you.'

Wilder: 'The response from the fans on that tour was amazing. You'd go out and play these really simple pop tunes and the audience would go mental for it, so I knew this was something that wasn't going to end overnight.' Meanwhile, the hired musician had his first opportunity to spend a lot of time with his new colleagues since being frozen out of the 'See You' sessions. 'On that tour all the girlfriends used to come along,' he remembers. 'Dave was putting on a lot of puppy fat because he'd sit on the coach with his girlfriend Joanne and they'd pile through this collection of crisps and Mars Bars. All the band were in their woolly-jumper phase when I first met them. I was meek and mild and nice too, but also a bit more worldly.' Daryl Balmonte recalls with a grin, 'Alan was also a big one for jumpers and he had this ridiculous, long Dr Who scarf which we all hated. So we stole it and threw it away.'

'It wasn't easy fitting in,' says Wilder, *sans* scarf almost two decades later. 'In fact to this day I don't think I ever quite fitted in. They were a very close-knit unit and to some extent still are – well, Martin and Fletch are. With their particular background, being work-ing-class kids who'd all gone to school together, they were very tight but also unworldly.'

Balmonte: 'Alan was this nouveau hippie who'd grown up in Hammersmith. I mean, he was from grammar school, he didn't come from a comprehensive in Basildon! He thought we weren't grown up enough. I can remember doing a gig in the Lyceum, we got there and the gig wasn't ready, so we were playing tag, and the stage crew were like, "Who the fuck are these kids?" And I don't think Alan ever quite understood that side of us. Mind you I don't think it bothered Alan that much, that he didn't fit in with our weird mentality.'

The alert west Londoner also observed the strange dynamic of the band he'd just joined: 'Fletch and Martin have a very strange rela-tionship which I don't know quite how to describe. They're sort of like Laurel and Hardy. I've always felt that Fletch's role is to be Martin's mate, to be his voice on occasion. They're inseparable. I don't think Martin could be in Depeche Mode without Fletch, and that's Fletch's role, to be there for Martin. He's needed because Martin is really difficult to get through to. Don't get me wrong, I like Martin a lot, he's a lovely bloke in many ways but he doesn't show much of himself. He's very shy unless he's completely drunk and then he's completely extrovert. You can't talk to him about his feelings and if he's got a problem with something he won't say what it is, he'll just have a slightly forlorn look on his face. You might find out what's wrong through Fletch so that's a useful role for Andy to be Martin's voice on occasions. Martin finds it difficult to express himself verbally and I've never felt totally comfortable with him. I don't think I've got to know him through all this time. I don't think in all this time that I've ever really had a good conversation with him.'

'I think Mart and Fletch are dependent on each other,' confirms their old schoolfriend, Daryl, 'although for different reasons, and to different degrees. They're very loyal to each other and I think it must be weird for other members of the group at times because it seems like a faction within the band.'

Wilder: 'Daniel Miller is also quite a difficult person to know. Having done the song 'Warm Leatherette' when he was The Normal, people have an idea of what he must look like and of course he's the complete opposite – this oversized bloke shuffles in looking a bit dishevelled and it's Daniel. He's the bloke who sits down on the platform floor of the train station with his cap out. And he was this mentor and father figure to the others. He was very much the guiding light, not manipulating them, but overseeing everything. So all my dealings with them tended to go through Daniel and for a while I didn't have too many direct conversations with the other band members. Obviously I did on tour but in the run-up to the shows, things like what songs were going to be played, what I should wear and so on, that would come mainly from Daniel. It was a very odd thing really, and that feeling of distance didn't go away for a long time. It was Daniel who said, "Well, actually they won't need you in the studio for their next single."

'Dave was the most open of all of them. Dave can tell you about his feelings for hours and he'll burst into tears. He's completely the opposite to Martin. I could communicate and talk with Dave much better than with Martin or Fletch because he's a more affable, outgoing kind of character. Whatever faults he may have, there's a very endearing side to him. And he's also very funny, which is something people don't realize about him. He's a brilliant mimic, really sharp – not verbally, but visually. He used to have us in fits when he was doing his Tony Hadley from Spandau Ballet. He could do our plugger Neil Ferris – it was really hysterical. Neil used to wear the brightest whitest trousers and tight jeans, like the Radio 1 DJ Peter Powell. He used to bounce in, very energetic, and Dave had him down brilliantly. So I guess generally speaking I got on better with Dave, and I think we both had a few problems with Fletch, so from that point of view we felt as one.'

By now Dave Gahan's relationship with the nervy, willowy Fletcher had set into a pattern ranging from friendly banter to genuine irritation. According to Daniel Miller, 'It's true that even now Dave and Fletch don't mind having a good verbal scrap. Usually it will be about absolutely nothing, or it's a misunderstanding. And quite often they'll be agreeing with each other. I've heard some hilarious conversations where they're both arguing because that's the only way they can communicate with each other – through argument. You can have a meeting with the band and within seconds they're at each other. From day one there's always been tension between Dave and Fletch but it can't be that bad otherwise they wouldn't still be working together. If you asked them what their arguments were about, they probably wouldn't remember, or even who won them. As time goes on they're much more careful about avoiding confrontation. We try to avert potentially dangerous situations, so that it doesn't degenerate into an argument, but 18 years on they are still bickering.'

At the end of the tour Depeche Mode played a secret gig at their old haunt, the Bridgehouse, watched by *Melody Maker*'s Paul Colbert, who wrote: 'The venue was packed to the rotary towels in the toilets. Heaving bodies, flashing feet and that was just the bar staff.' The promoter, Terry Murphy, tried to pay the band £1,000 but they insisted the money went to the renovation of the pub.

Their first European tour opened in Rockola, Madrid on 4 March 1982, followed by shows in Stockholm, Hamburg, Hanover, Berlin, Rotterdam, Oberkorn, Paris and Mechelen. They also played two dates on the Channel Islands. Their gig in Paris at Le Palace would be their last in the country for two-and-a-half years. 'They're so unfriendly there. I'm sure it's something to do with our name,' said Dave Gahan. 'Mind you I wouldn't like to see a band called Woman's Own over here that much.'

Anne Berning, who later worked with the band's German label Intercord, remembers the young synth-pop act arriving in her home country for the first time. 'They were broken in the German pop press with songs like "Just Can't Get Enough". Our teenage music magazine *Bravo* picked up on them and ran a lot of features. When I grew up they were always regarded as a teeny-pop band. They were very hip with the mainstream teenagers but that was all.'

Alan Wilder: 'We were constantly being asked to do press for pop mags like *Bravo*. Crappy pictures and all that rubbish. The German record company basically did the same sort of things that Neil Ferris was doing in England, which was to milk it for all it was worth.'

In the month following their European dates Depeche Mode, minus Alan Wilder, went back into the studio. 'I did understand that they didn't want to be seen to be replacing Vince,' says a circumspect Wilder. 'They wanted to show the world that they could do it on their own without him. I understood all that, but nevertheless it was very frustrating for me.'

On 26 April Depeche Mode released the insubstantial 'Meaning Of Love' as their next single, reaching No.12. Although this was a respectable position Vince Clarke's newly formed Yazoo, a duo featuring local Essex girl Alf (Alison Moyet), reached No.2 with 'Only You' – the song Depeche Mode had rejected. Naturally this was gratifying for Clarke and an irritation for his former band, especially as the media encouraged some inter-group rivalry. *The Face* reviewed both singles and concluded, 'Depeche Mode could learn a lesson from this ...' To make matters worse 'Meaning Of Love' sounded like a pallid imitation of a Vince Clarke song, as Gore attempted to ease the transition to his more melancholy style of work. Given Depeche Mode's confusion and insecurity behind their Basildon bluster it wasn't surprising that resentment against their ex-songwriter festered for a while in 1982. 'There was rivalry and I wanted to be fair to everybody,' says a diplomatic Miller. 'Depeche Mode were making great records and so were Yazoo. If you look at that period I didn't sign any artists for a couple of years – from the time I first started working with Depeche to when I signed the Birthday Party in 1983. I couldn't sign any artists because I didn't have the time or the energy – that was all spent on the bands I had. Although there were problems neither side made it an impossible situation. No one said, "Well, if he's going to be on the label, we're going to leave," or anything like that. It was never quite that bitchy.'

Even so, in spring '82 Gahan sniped, 'Vince has done a few adverts, a few jingles ... We were offered a Tizer advert, but we just couldn't do it.' On another occasion he was more conciliatory: 'We all think Yazoo are really good, honest. We went to see them at the Dominion in London and were really impressed, especially with the slideshow. We occasionally bump into Vince in the corridors of Mute but we never see him socially. Then again he never stops working long enough to go out.'

Daryl Balmonte: 'I think there was natural boys' jealousy. Nobody wanted Vince to sink but Depeche wanted to sell more records than him. But then they were competitive with everyone. I can remember we did a gig at the ICA and Daniel came in and told Dave that Soft Cell's "Tainted Love" was No.1. And Dave said, "Yeah, I'm jealous."'

Now settled into a steady, crisp-gobbling domesticity with his girlfriend Joanne, Dave Gahan decided to erase his juvenile offender past by removing a tattoo on his arm. It was a disaster. Chris Carr remembers, 'We used to call Dave "Pizza Man" because the guy from Harley Street that removed the tattoo did it with a laser. It was a complete bodged job and looked like somebody had put a hot iron on him. This was a time when Dave wouldn't smoke a spliff, he wouldn't drink. He was Mr Sensible. Martin and Fletch would be out there drinking and doing what they were doing and he would take me aside sometimes and say, "Wankers. I did that when I was a kid."'

On 7 May 1982 Depeche Mode began a short American and Canadian tour, playing eight club dates in New York, Philadelphia, Toronto, Chicago, Vancouver, San Francisco, Pasadena and The Roxy in Los Angeles. Daryl Balmonte, who roadied on the tour remembers, 'There was still a big buzz about the band. We had a powerful record company behind us and when we got there the band were very optimistic about their chances in the States.' However, Gahan's skin had bubbled up into an infection, so he had to perform the shows with his arm in a sling, restricting the group's effectiveness somewhat as he was the only animated character on stage.

The three original band members spent the rest of the summer in Blackwing studios, recording Depeche Mode's second album with Daniel Miller and studio engineers John Fryer and Eric Radcliffe. This left an increasingly frustrated Alan Wilder still kicking his heels: 'I was unhappy to have been excluded from the making of it, considering I had been touring and performing with the group since the beginning of that year and they expected me to help promote it after its release.'

On 16 August Depeche Mode released their sixth single, 'Leave In Silence', which sent out a warning signal when it peaked at a lowly 18. Its more evocative, introspective style had failed to secure the band's usual airplay but artistically it was a considerable improvement on 'Meaning Of Love'. Martin Gore: 'We all believed in this one – perhaps too much.' Inevitably they were very disappointed with the single's sales. 'It's very rare to capture an atmosphere on a single, but that's one we did it on,' said a gratified Gahan. ' "Leave In Silence" had everything – melody, sound, mood, everything. It's one of my favourites.' He added, 'When we released "Leave In Silence" it was a gamble. It didn't get nearly as much radio play as our past records had got. It didn't go as well but the fact was it wasn't played as much. The radio didn't see it as a single; they saw it more as an album track.' The song did have its critics, notably Paul Weller who complained, 'I've heard more melody coming out of an arsehole.'

The new album, *A Broken Frame*, was released on 27 September and got as high as No.8. The award-winning sleeve, once again designed by Brian Griffin, was a major improvement on *Speak and Spell*. 'There was quite an intense meeting about this one,' says the photographer. 'I had a location finder and she found this cornfield in Hertfordshire, lower-East Midlands really. We decided to go for a bit of Soviet social realism. That cover took on a life of its own. Eventually it ended up on the front cover of *Life* magazine in January 1989 for a feature on the best photographs of the decade.'

Fletcher, the skinny band propagandist claimed *A Broken Frame* ' ... is a lot weightier than the last album, not so lightweight and poppy.' Few people today would describe the LP as 'weighty' but it is a strange, fractured record which ranges from slender pop tracks, such as the dreadful 'A Photograph Of You', to the more enigmatic, oblique 'My Secret Garden'. Part of the problem was that Gore had been thrown into the deep end by Clarke's departure and filled the album with songs he'd written over the last few years – 'See You' and 'A Photograph Of You' dated back to his mid-teens. The band's naturally cautious collective nature also resulted in a subtle change of style after their main songwriter went AWOL, rather than a reinvention. Behind the scenes Daniel Miller realized that the album wasn't different enough from *Speak and Spell* for people to notice the new man at the creative helm: 'Martin would write "Meaning Of Love", which was him trying to be really poppy, whereas "Leave In Silence" was pure Martin Gore. "Photograph of You" is real pop but "Shouldn't Have Done", that was more downbeat and I think it took a while for people to catch on that that was the sort of thing that Martin naturally comes up with.'

Depeche Mode did try out some fresh sounds which took them a small, tentative step away from the clean synthetics of their debut. Andy Fletcher enthused, 'There's a lot of percussion on the new album, you know, just hitting things, plus there's walking and marching and that sort of thing, but nothing you could really call an instrument.' Gahan interjected, 'There is a saxophone, but you wouldn't be able to make it out. It's recorded backwards and it sounds like an elephant.'

Daniel Miller believes: 'There are a lot of myths surrounding Depeche Mode that are really untrue; like they only started using guitars on their last two albums. The first guitar was used on *A Broken Frame*. They have an approach to the music which is still based on setting themselves rules, even if they break them. If you don't have a concept that way then your music becomes very indulgent and like everybody else's. We made all our own sounds, we didn't sample off records.'

Reviews for the album were very up and down. Chris Burkham inadvertently revealed his rootsy, conservative musical tastes in *Sounds*: 'The main problem for Depeche Mode is that the use of synthesized sound, to the exclusion of almost everything else, within a pop song is rather limited. The reason that Yazoo – to pick a slightly obvious comparison – manage to make their songs succeed on more than the perfunctory "nice tune" level is the way the hard synthesized beat is juggled against Alison's vibrant vocal style ... David Gahan's voice serves the instrument – barely intruding, always obeying, never giving any orders – instead of playing off against the flat sheen on the Moog.'

NME were more enthusiastic: 'What can be appreciated is their quickening concision, their increasing artfulness, Martin Gore's impressive songs, songs that connect firmly with the folk-wisdom and folk-metaphysics of the vanished Vince.'

However, *Melody Maker*'s Steve Sutherland, who was a fan of the band's first album and singles, mocked the attempts at development: '*A Broken Frame* sounds like puerile infatuations papering over anonymity ... the lyrics have matured from wide-eyed fun to wild-eyed frustration, but the weary words of "Leave In Silence", just like the glib ones of "Just Can't Get Enough", are words and nothing more.'

A couple of years after the album's release Dave Gahan had achieved enough distance from the project to admit, 'I think we all feel that *A Broken Frame* is, in retrospect, our weakest album. Definitely. It's very, very patchy. Very badly produced.' The album failed to maintain the commercial momentum of *Speak and Spell* either, both in the UK and internationally. 'I'm convinced we wouldn't be here today if we had signed to a major label,' says Gore, recognizing the value of Miller's patient, nurturing approach to the band. 'After the initial success of *Speak and Spell*, *A Broken Frame* was a very quiet period for us. It didn't do nothing but it didn't do anything astounding, and I think we would have fallen into second-album syndrome and would have been dropped by our third album.'

Nevertheless their fan-base turned out in full force for their autumn UK tour, a 20-date marathon which included two more dates at London's Hammersmith Odeon in October. Although the audience was still crammed with delirious teenage girls, the on-stage hand-clapper and air-puncher, Andy Fletcher, also observed a hardcore of very laddish fans. 'The blokes see us like lads, electronic versions of the Angelic Upstarts,' he argued. 'You get those sort of people outside the dressing-room door going, "Oi, Andy". You have to speak to them in your best Cockney accent. You go, "Yer, all right, 'ang on." You get the little girls that you have to be really nice to because they're like your little sister.'

Just before Christmas 1982, a Mute press release announced that Wilder was joining Depeche Mode as a full-time member. 'Daniel phoned me,' grins Wilder. 'I think the band found it difficult to be the bearer of good news, as well as bad.'

The Landscape Is Changing, 1983

'Get The Balance Right', the first song to feature Alan Wilder on keyboards (who also wrote the B-side 'The Great Outdoors') was released on 31 January 1983. Softly sung and melancholic but propelled by a dancey electronic rhythm, the track was interpreted by Gahan as being 'about telling people to go their own way. It also takes a dig at people who like to be different just for the sake of it. You've just got to reach the right balance between normality and insanity.'

The single reached No.13 after climbing from its debut chart position of 32, hardly a significant turning point after the dip in sales with *A Broken Frame*. Its year-opening presence in the charts was a deliberate ploy by Daniel Miller who was keen to turn the corner with the band. However, Martin Gore is an efficient rather than prolific writer so this was the only song available to them. Perhaps because of the absensce of other choices, the group were unsure about the quality of 'Get The Balance Right' and their doubts were aggravated by a sense that they needed to move on and find a new style. The single was yet another track recorded at Blackwing with the same team – Miller, Radcliffe and Fryer – albeit with new digital equipment. Martin Gore admitted a few years later: 'That's actually our least favourite single. It was hell to record. I hate it and I wrote it.' Andy Fletcher: 'We had a lot of problems, it was a kind of an interim period between equipment and it just didn't happen.'

However, the 12" version was seized on by black American DJs who spun it in eclectic, electronic club nights in New York, Chicago and Detroit. The band's uncomfortable relationship with the British press was irritated again by some damning reviews, in particular *Time Out*'s John Gill: 'I have often wondered why God bothered with Depeche Mode.' However *Sounds* were closer to the truth when they declared 'the muted brass and percolating synth bubbles provide the perfect foil for a brilliant pop song'.

To promote *A Broken Frame* the band went on yet another America/Canada tour, but despite the support of K-ROQ and the clubs, Depeche Mode were stuck on a plateau as the original media buzz faded away. This jaunt was followed by dates in the Far East which made a big impression on the band. They were mobbed by 500 fans when they arrived in Hong Kong's Tai Kak Airport, leaving them a bit shaken. Over the next few days they came face-to-face with a very different way of life. Gahan was shocked by the sight of young boys and girls offering themselves for money in Bangkok: 'From the age of about ten, I can remember things quite vividly that just didn't seem right. Then you see things that are poorer than you've ever seen – people begging and little kids coming up to us with disgusting, dirty clothes hanging off them, showing themselves or holding their hands out for food. When you experience that, you begin to understand what a lucky position all of us here are in.'

As soon as they were home Gore started writing new songs with the experiences of the Far East still fresh in his mind. 'He wrote pretty much all the next album in a couple of weeks straight after those trips,' recalls Wilder. 'They seemed to come together pretty quickly and it was obvious that all these bizarre places such as Bangkok had opened up a few eyes in the band.'

Andy Fletcher was also maturing in his role as the one who 'joined up a lot of the dots' in Depeche Mode's day-to-day working life. The group didn't have a manager or a written contract but were set up in such a way that it was possible for them to function without requiring either. Daniel Miller was a trusted friend, adviser, producer and record company boss; they had a regular and increasingly slick touring crew who wanted to continue working with them for as long as possible, and even the head of their American record label, Seymour Stein, was involved from the start. Fletcher wasn't a manager or business boffin (which was alleged by the press in the next few years) but he did take an interest in everyday details: meetings with their plugger Neil Ferris or the accountants, hotel arrangements, and he even studied maps to work out quicker routes on tour. Effectively he did whatever was needed in order to maintain Depeche Mode as an aggressively independent force, although his direct input as a musician lessened. He continued to suggest ideas but stopped playing on the album recordings, quite simply because Alan Wilder could play the synthesizers better than anyone else in the band.

When Depeche Mode returned to Britain to start work on their next album they were determined to alter their style through changing technology, different studio personnel and a new recording environment. After scouting around, Miller and the band decided to record the LP, which would be entitled *Construction Time Again*, at John Foxx's Garden Studios in Shoreditch. 'Daniel rang me up because they wanted to use the Garden for Depeche Mode,' says Foxx. 'I suggested the studio's engineer Gareth Jones to them as he was used to electronic music. In the early '80s most studio technicians were baffled by little black boxes and didn't know how to deal with synthesizer music.'

The nervy, hyperactive Gareth Jones, who'd first been turned on to electronic music by Walter Carlos' 'Switched On Bach', recalls, 'I'd worked with John Foxx on his *Metamatic* album and he'd decided to invest in a tape recorder and mixing board and basically set up a studio in a warehouse in Shoreditch. I didn't invest in it but I did help him set it up. I was his engineer really over that period. Somehow Mute heard about it. Until then they were a very small label, working mainly out of Blackwing in south London. Depeche Mode were obviously looking for somewhere different to perhaps help them make a new kind of record and they came round to check the studio out. They needed an engineer of course and in those days it wasn't common for people to turn up at a studio with their own engineer. When John introduced me to Depeche Mode, I didn't get it really. They were some commercial band who'd had hits on the radio that I wasn't really into.'

The Garden's location, near Spitalfields market in east London, placed Depeche Mode in a derelict, industrial area of the city which was also a source of inspiration to one of the godfathers of industrial music – the Some Bizzare act, Throbbing Gristle. Led by charismatic, alternative sex guru, Genesis P. Orridge, Throbbing Gristle created a mixture of chaotic metal noise and pure, spookily clean electronics in the basement of a factory warehouse at the edge of Hackney Fields. The site, a plague pit in medieval times, was filled with metal debris from the old factories which the group used in their music. Down the road in Shoreditch, Depeche Mode also set out with a tape recorder, scanning the local area for pipes and scrap metal in search of interesting beats and textures for their new album.

Kraftwerk popularized the incorporation of everyday sounds into music with their early-70s hit 'Autobahn'. However, the Dusseldorf act took a very different approach to Throbbing Gristle because they created an 'idealized' version of the world around them. They waved a tape-recorder microphone out of Ralf Hutter's Volkswagen when driving down the German autobahn, then returned to their Kling Klang studio to replicate it on synthesizers. Hutter: 'You can listen to "Autobahn" and then go and drive on the motorway. Then you will discover that your car is a musical instrument. In these sorts of ideas, there are plenty of things that can be funny; it's a whole philosophy of life which comes from electronics.'

On their 1977 album *Trans-Europe Express* Kraftwerk continued to explore man's relationship with modern machines through mechanized travel – in this case by rail. Hutter: 'The movement [of trains] fascinates us, instead of a static or motionless situation. All the dynamism of industrial life, of modern life. We really speak about our experiences, of life as it appears to us. Even the artistic world does not exist outside of daily life, it is not another planet, it is here on Earth that things are happening.'

It was Throbbing Gristle, however, who started using the term 'industrial music' after recognizing that their immediate environment had completely shaped their sound. Orridge: 'When we finished our first record, we went outside and we suddenly heard trains going past and little workshops under the railway arches and the lathes going and electric saws and we suddenly thought, we haven't actually created anything at all, we've just taken it in subconsciously and recreated it.'

There were other layers to Orridge's use of the word 'industrial' which would find echoes in Martin Gore's decision to name Depeche Mode's 1987 album *Music For the Masses*. 'There's an irony in the word "industrial",' said Orridge in 1983, 'because there's the music industry. And then there's the joke we often used to make in interviews about churning out records like motor cars – that sense of industrial. Up until then pop music had been based on the blues and slavery, and we thought it was time to update it to at least Victorian times – the Industrial Revolution.'

Like Kraftwerk, Throbbing Gristle also enjoyed seeing themselves as laboratory technicians or scientists rather than musicians: 'We've been very lucky because Chris Carter is totally into electronics,' said Orridge, who would later become friends with Martin Gore, 'and buys all the specialist magazines, and as soon as anyone even does research on something, we know about it. We know as quick as a "scientist" what's going on, and what's possible ... He gets circuits and builds them, tests them, and then finds whether they're of any use, and sometimes he alters them so that he's inventing new things for us to use immediately. So we're like a workshop as well ...'

Daniel Miller was of similar importance to Depeche Mode, fulfilling a role which allowed them to keep up with the 'industrialization' of music through new technology. But where Depeche Mode and Throbbing Gristle veered off in wildly different directions was their approach to songwriting. While the Basildon pop group concentrated on pop melody, the Hackney metal-thwackers were resolutely avant garde, aiming to re-educate the listener to a fresh way of listening to music. 'People at first expect us to play music with melody lines and riffs and so on,' noted Orridge, 'and they're a bit confused when we start and they realize that it's not built that way – you're dealing with sound as sound, you're actually building sound like somebody builds a car – then they're all right again because they start listening to it. They're disciplining their brain to listen to it as a sound, blocks of sound, units.'

Throbbing Gristle were more melodic than their Austrian counterparts SPK. They took their name from a group of West German psychiatric patients who, inspired by the Baader Meinhoff Group, attempted to form their own terrorist group and died while making their first bombs in their hospital room. SPK used flamethrowers and, allegedly, ate sheeps' brains on stage! Meanwhile in Germany Einsturzende Neubauten assaulted stages with drills and anvils and created rhythms with metal sheets. In early 1983 Martin Gore went to see them stage their Metal Concerto at London's Institute of Contemporary Arts.

Even in the early '80s industrial music's heavy, mechanized attitude seemed to attract extreme left-wing and right-wing groups, with the latter adding a fascistic element to the genre. 'I think we've given birth to a monster, uncontrollable, thrashing, spewing forth mentions of Auschwitz for no reason,' complained Orridge in 1983.

Meanwhile Depeche Mode's move towards an industrial-influenced sound on their next album was also prompted by other influences which were very close to home. In 1982 Daniel Miller himself had contributed to a project, *Easy Listening for the Hard of Hearing*, with Mute's Boyd Rice and Fad Gadget, where the trio built up 'found' sounds from non-musical instruments. Although this was a pure experiment in sound and texture, by now a piece of new technology had been invented (and quickly discovered by Daniel Miller) which would allow Depeche Mode to use and even manipulate industrial noise in a way that would make it possible to work in a pop context.

The early digital samplers, in particular the £40,000 Fairlight, were ludicrously expensive but they offered the chance to stretch sounds in time, adjust the pitch and fuse different noises together. The Fairlight was swiftly followed by the pricey Synclavier which Depeche Mode started using, although when the cheapest new sampler, the Emulator 1, arrived on the market at a more reasonable £5,000 that became a key band gadget. Depeche Mode were initially alerted to the new technology by Yazoo, who'd seamlessly moved into sampling a little earlier. 'Vince had got one of the first Fairlights in the country,' notes Daniel Miller, 'and that was really my first experience of sampling. The Fairlight was a great instrument, quite limited but very important. Vince used it quite a lot on that first Yazoo album. He and Depeche Mode were always trying to push the technology. Unlike other acts such as Ultravox and Duran Duran who had become rock bands, we were always looking for ways of discovering new sounds, things that had never been heard before, let alone in a pop context.'

The sampler offered fantastic creative possibilities which were explored by American hip-hop acts in the '80s and in the '90s became an essential musical tool for the likes of modern 'electronic' acts, Massive Attack and Tricky. Sampling culture also offered a new radicalism in pop music, as acts began to steal bits of music from each other, and then build songs as collages – partly their own creative ideas, the rest from a series of different sources. Zoo Records boss Bill Drummond and ex-Zodiac Mindwarp guitarist Jimmy Cauty, calling themselves Kopyright Liberation Front, tested Britain's copyright laws when Abba sued the band over their 1987 Justified Ancient's album, *What the Fuck's Going On*. It was later reissued as *The JAMS 45 Edits EP* with the samples removed.

Depeche Mode avoided sampling beats or sounds, as they were paranoid about getting sued. Gareth Jones recalls: 'I remember a couple of occasions when we did sample drums. There was a Led Zeppelin track which we used but none of that stuff made it to the final releases. They just didn't want to steal bits from other people's records. There was also this slight worry in the background about copyright which no one wanted to fuck with and still don't to this day. I remember on Depeche Mode's 1997 album, *Ultra*, I did a bit of vocal recording and mixing and there was one demo with a beat off another record. I was going "this sounds wicked," and they were saying, "No, no, it's off this record and we can't do that." '

Unfortunately the sampler also encouraged some of the worst music of the 1980s as the thrill of being able to recreate orchestras and brass sections within a machine blinded a lot of artists. According to John Foxx, 'Gareth was the "Klangmaster" – a genius with sound – and he encouraged Depeche Mode to seize on sampling as a way of doing that heavy, industrial type of music, whereas so many people were thrilled because they could make what I call "posh" music with samplers. They tried to replicate the sound of an orchestra or real guitars. Synthesizers should sound like themselves but so many people were trying to make them imitate natural instruments. It was horrible. I think every piece of new technology goes through the formica stage, where people tried to imitate wood. In the '70s Rick Wakeman attempted use synthesizers as if they were a classical instrument and came up with ludicrous pompous material, totally failing to use the real possibilities of the instrument. The same happened with sampling, where everyone rushed around making their music "posh". Now, of course, it sounds horribly dated. Then others like Depeche Mode saw it as a form of creative thievery and were at the forefront of that.'

Gareth Jones, who has a 'scientific education', remembers being apalled by this unimaginative use of the new technology: 'Depeche

Mode never used samplers in that fake way. For a lot of people it was a great thing because suddenly they could have a digital recording of a cello or a trumpet, and you could then play your own melody on it. A boring use of it perhaps, but obviously it's used a lot in film soundtracks and advertising. You had to face a quality loss in the sound but at least you didn't have to hire an orchestra or a trumpet player. All you're doing is emulating another instrument. We never used them to emulate something, the whole point was you could put your own sounds in it.'

Like Foxx and Depeche Mode, the increasingly marginalized but keen electronic exponent Gary Numan, who started sampling sounds for his proto-industrial 1984 album *Berserker*, also remembers this as an exciting new phase in technology-led music. 'I went out and about dragging drains and manhole covers across the ground, hitting anything I could find in search of the perfect sound. At one point we even tried to sample the carburettor on my Ferrari,' he says, recalling one of sampling's more flamboyant real-world effects. 'You could hear it sucking in air, which I thought was a fantastic effect.'

However, Depeche Mode went a lot deeper into 'found sound' than many of their enthusiastic contemporaries. 'I think Gareth was very important in helping Depeche Mode move effortlessly from analogue synthesizers to the world of sampling and digital technology,' says Foxx. 'So many of the original pioneers floundered or alienated their fan-base because they weren't using so many Moogs, or whatever.'

Gareth Jones's enthusiasm for this new approach was certainly infectious. 'They wanted to change their sound and they had an idea about what they wanted to do. I wanted to make it harder, raucous, because that's was where I was coming from. I was into more underground music. I was living in a squat in Brixton and I had the attitude that if something was commercial then it couldn't be any good. I just had a bolshy perspective.'

Depeche Mode's new adventure in metallic noise began with the installation of Daniel Miller's Synclavier at The Garden. Gareth Jones, who'd become a fan of The Normal after John Foxx played him the 'Warm Leatherette' single, discloses, 'The Synclavier sounded high quality although I think it was mono at first and we gradually updated it so in the end it was doing lots of voices.

'One of the main things we did in addition to the sampling was we got into acoustic basses. We'd made a big control room at The Garden, which was fairly unusual in those days, and great for them because they could put all their synths up. They had quite a big collection of synths, even then. John Foxx and I had made a little tiled corridor that went under the street and we also had a couple of live rooms. So for the album recording I put amps all over the place, miked up all these different rooms and fed out the synths through all these amps. The idea was to create more texture and atmosphere.'

Outside of the studio, the band roamed around east London looking for good sounds. Alan Wilder: 'We wanted sounds that you couldn't get out of synths, so we went to a scrapyard up the road near Brick Lane. I remember we'd do things like go out and hit the ground with a hammer, just so we could capture the sound of concrete.'

The album's most experimental song is 'Pipeline', a track almost completely constructed out of these found sounds. 'That song is all sampled metal,' beams Jones, who is still extremely proud of the recording. 'We went to disused railway yards and I bought a high-quality tape recorder, beautiful technology with reel-to-reel tape. One of the band had been out and found this yard with loads of pipes, corrugated iron and old cars, and we took some drumsticks and hammers out with us. We were really into ambient space as well, so when we were sampling we'd have one sound close to the hammer and another right back down, as long as the wire would go, so we had this acoustic perspective. On "Pipeline" it's possible there might be some bass synth but all the melodies are created out of sounds we'd discovered in these scrapyards which was pretty radical at the time. We recorded one melody after another to tape, and when we mixed it we didn't use any artifical reverberation or any EQ. All the reverbs on the instrumental parts are from the railway yards where we sampled the original noises, so it's a bit special really. We were sampling the acoustic sound of the world.'

Daniel Miller, who still had a very active role in the recording process, reminisces, 'We would bang, crash, scrape, pluck, blow anything in order to make an interesting noise. The classic sampling track is "Pipeline" where all the sounds were recorded on location. Even the vocals were recorded on location. We took the backing track out by the railway line in Shoreditch and Martin sang on location in an arch. You can hear the trains in the background and all sorts of stuff.'

Ironically the new equipment also opened up the opportunity for the band to use guitars. 'Using sampling justified us using guitars,' notes Miller. 'It's not splitting hairs, there really is a big difference.'

The possibilities of found sound meant that all the band members contributed musically to *Construction Time Again*. The non-musicians Gahan and Fletcher enthusiastically listened out for exciting, textured noises in the area, armed with Jones's tape recorder. However, they were still a slightly unusual bunch consisting of three distinct units – Fletcher and Gore, Gahan and Wilder – with Miller as a sort of patriarch. And now Jones was thrown into the mix.

'I really liked Gareth,' grins Wilder warmly. 'He was so enthusiastic, when we first met him he just wouldn't stop talking. He's very hyperactive. I think he enjoyed the direction we were taking but there were times when he found it very difficult to be in the studio with us. We were these different characters and we'd all be doing different things. Half of us were mucking about in the studio, someone else might be on the piss in a pub nearby, one of us might actually being doing something useful. So there was Daniel and Gareth amongst these kids at play.'

Wilder recalls how Andy Fletcher would usually be the target of jokes when Martin Gore started getting bored in the studio. 'Martin and Fletch's bizarre relationship used to spill into the studio. It was almost as if they hadn't really fully lived out their childhood and they'd do really strange things. They used to play this game where Mart would hide his mate's glasses case and Fletch would go into a panic about it. This would happen on a daily basis and it would become really frustrating to anyone such as Daniel, Gareth or myself who were trying to get a synth sound, or something to do with making a record. We'd be fiddling about and you'd hear, "Mart, Mart, where's me glasses case? Come on, what ya' done with it? I know you've hidden it." And then Dave would join in and start taking the piss out of Fletch. So for half an hour there would be mayhem while Fletch looked for his glasses case and eventually it would have to resort to him threatening violence before Mart would give it back. This was a routine which started from when I first worked with them and there were one or two similar things which they did over and over again.'

In fact Fletcher was usually the butt of everyone's jokes because his edgy, nervy nature meant he was easiest to wind up. 'There was a lot of piss-taking at Fletch's expense,' explains Wilder. 'In the early days he was so very highly strung and incredibly thin because of all the nervous energy he used to burn. He would often be very panicky and you know how when people are nervous they cover it up by going into silly voices and doing silly things – he used to do a lot of that kind of thing. I think this was all part of a lack of self-confidence and even-tually it manifested itself in serious depression. By that time glasses cases weren't being hidden.'

However Wilder emphasizes that ' ... not all of the piss-taking was in Fletch's direction. Daniel was quite moody in the studio, taking things very seriously. He'd spend hours and hours, days and days on a synth sound, and get very uptight about it. I didn't mind that because I knew he cared and wanted to do something special. Anyway, he's a big fat bloke and he always used to have his trousers hanging down so you could see his arse crack. He'd be standing there on the synth being quite intense and we'd toss peanuts at him, trying to get them down the back of his trousers. He could get a bit stroppy when that happened.'

After recording was completed at The Garden, the band decided to look around at other studios to mix it, as Foxx's studio only offered a 24-track. While this was going on Gareth Jones went to Germany to check out a local Berlin band who wanted him to produce them. 'The group's manager said he wanted me to do the recording in Berlin but I wasn't keen. So he said to me, "Well, at least let me show you the studio," and he took me to this big penthouse Solid State studio in Hansa with 56 channels [the only one like it in the world at the time]. It was a five-studio complex, very hi-tech, so I was really excited. Daniel Miller was actually over in Berlin at the same time because Nick Cave [who was on Mute] was recording in Hansa Studio 2 which is the big hall. It's a massive ballroom, great acoustics, a wicked vibe. Anyway Daniel and I hooked up and I said, "Look man, maybe we should mix Construction here?" Daniel was getting the Berlin vibe, so he was into the idea.'

The other major benefit of finishing the recordings in Germany was that it actually worked out cheaper than in London. Jones: 'The pound was strong, which helped make it very economical. The band could come over and stay in a top hotel, ship the gear over and it would still be cheaper than a mixing facility in London.' 'It was cheap,' agrees Miller, although in retrospect he points out other important advantages. While Britain had a flourishing alternative market in 1983 (many of the acts were being nurtured or unleashed by Stevo at Some Bizzare), the initial thrill of synthesizer pop had long gone. An increasingly conventional rock-and-pop approach to technology was creeping into the charts which would soon lead to one of British music's most stagnant, uninspired periods in the mid-'80s. By being out of the country a lot of the time, Depeche Mode were not exposed to this sterile but popular conservatism. Miller recalls, 'There was nothing happening in Britain – the '80s were as boring as fuck in the UK – so it was good to get out of the country. That was probably important looking back because it meant they weren't force-fed the crap pop frenzy that was going on in England. Being in their own environment gave them confidence to be different. It kept them on a creative path.'

The group members were instantly excited at the prospect of a new city and a swanky place to stay. Hansa also had an appealing musical history with David Bowie famously recording his Berlin trilogy – *Low*, *Heroes* and *Lodger* – there in the late '70s. The Englishman and his friend Iggy Pop both lived in Berlin for several years, with Pop's Bowie-produced albums *The Idiot* and *Lust For Life* also recorded at Hansa. The claustrophobic atmospherics of these recordings were partly influenced by the studio's location, overlooking the Berlin Wall.

'I had a great time there,' enthuses Daniel Miller. 'We were literally working next to the Wall. You could see into East Germany. Berlin was this little island in the middle of East Germany and that has an uneasy, edgy effect on you – you can't get away from it.' 'As soon as we arrived, everyone got the Berlin vibe and started wearing black leather, me included!' grins Jones. Berlin in 1983 hadn't changed much in the years since Bowie and Iggy Pop had left the city. According to Pop, 'Berlin was like being in a ghost town but with all the advantages. The police in Berlin have a totally laissez-faire attitude toward, shall we say, "cult behaviour". And it's such an alcoholic city – someone is always swaying down the street.' Bowie: 'Berlin is a city made up of bars for sad, disillusioned people to get drunk in.'

'It opened their eyes to a completely different way of life,' says Miller. 'You could finish work in the studio at two o'clock in the morning and go out and have a drink. There was also a special atmosphere in the city which has to do with its history. The West German government wanted it to be the jewel in their crown, so it was a propaganda tool. Unless you were born and brought up in Berlin there was no reason for people to go there really, or for companies and enterprises to start there. So the West German government changed the laws for people in Berlin. There was no conscription for young people in Berlin and if you wanted to start a business you got a lot of tax breaks. Because of that a lot of the people who did move there were young, artistic and creative. So it was a place full of studios, artists and people interested in alternative lifestyles and it's a 24-hour city. It was a very sexual place. It had a sense of eroticism, adventure and excitement and obviously that led a lot of people down dangerous paths. People had excessive lifestyles there, staying up for four or five days, taking a lot of drugs and doing radical things in art.'

For Depeche Mode this was a real opportunity to lose their inhibitions in a foreign town with a reputation for debauchery, art and extremism. 'I don't think any building has that much influence on a band's development,' argues Wilder. 'Hansa was a great place and we could do some interesting things there but I don't think that was a major contributor to anything. I think it was just the fact that we were away from home and we'd been let out to play – going to clubs all night, sampling the night-life. Martin in particular liked going abroad for these reasons because he could let himself go a bit more.'

Gahan, however, wasn't so unreserved. Along with the slightly older Wilder, he was the most worldly member of the band and he was in a long-term relationship. He told journalists, 'Martin's just being the way he always wanted to be. He missed out on his teens, missed out on just going out, seeing different girls every night and getting drunk all the time. He's living that now. It's not a bad thing – everybody should go through that phase.'

Wilder: 'It was definitely an important phase when some of the band became more worldly. There was a lot of change in them as people, less so in Dave I suppose. It wasn't dramatic with him but I noticed he sort of thinned out a bit and got more wiry and was more aggressive in his manner. Perhaps he was starting to feel some sort of pressure in his personal life with Jo.'

Martin Gore had split up with his girlfriend of three years, Anne Swindell, to whom he'd actually been engaged at one stage. As a slightly odd twist in the band's incestuous history, Anne started seeing Vince Clarke two or three years later. During the mixing of *Construction*, Gore started a new relationship with a Berlin local called Christina. After returning to Basildon for a short time to live with his mother and sister, over the next few months he found a flat in Berlin and began a new life in the city. The band's publicist Chris Carr remembers, 'We all used to go this club where it was steel-cladding on the floor, on the walls and the ceiling. If there had been a fire in there we would have been human burgers. We'd drink a few tequilas then go off somewhere else. Martin had a few different places that we'd visit at different hours. There were a lot of girls around but the groupies used to freak him out. Some of them were a bit too aggressive and fantasized that they knew him and he found that hard to deal with. He hates confrontation and was very awkward about situations like that. Women always go to Martin and he had a big group of girlfriends. I wouldn't call it a decadent group of people but let's just say they expressed a lot of affection for each other! Martin's girlfriend Christina had a good friend called Nanni who was this very statuesque, model-like girl. She used to be an unofficial guide to the city. Christina, Nanni and their friends would also come over to London from time to time. They were nice people and Martin likes a crowd. I think alcohol helped him get over his shyness with women. There's a very feminine side to Martin but he's always been one of the boys. This might surprise some people but he definitely doesn't get on better with women than with men.'

This period highlights the contrasting personalities of Gahan and Gore as the former remained extremely watchful about himself, while the young songwriter blended naturally into an increasingly hedonistic, playfully erotic lifestyle in Berlin. Chris Carr noted the ease with which Gore absorbed new experiences at a time when Gahan was fighting his indulgent nature: 'Osmosis is what Martin's name should be. He distils stuff and takes what he wants out of it. I think Dave's found an equal, and Dave does think in those terms, whether he's conscious of it or not. He tries to suss people out – how strong are these people? Are they with me, or I am on a different level to them? In the same way, Dave needs to prove things to himself, "I'm going to do this, I'm going to do that, I'm going to quit this, I'm going to quit that." Whereas the appearance is that things come easy to Martin. In Martin's company you're influenced by his generosity of spirit and just general vibes. It's easy to be embarrassed in his company.'

Coincidentally Gareth Jones fell in love with a singer in a German band and also moved into Berlin. The highly-strung producer recalls, 'I'm a bit older than Depeche Mode but we all grew up together during this period, especially Martin who decided to live in the city. That was obviously quite different to working there when all our time would be divided between the studio and bars. We didn't go to the theatre, or the opera, or anything like that.

'There's something weird living in a walled-in city seemingly surrounded by a hostile enviornment, because Berlin was this jewel of capitalism, an amazingly functional city. Loads of people seem to like Berlin but I don't know why really. It just seemed very different to London. Berlin felt streamlined and almost futuristic and it had all these dark bars that you could go to any time of day or night. All these freaks would be in there, dressed in black, in cellars, factory warehouses and dark bars. That clearly influenced Martin's dress-sense after he'd been there for a while. There was also certain permissiveness in the pornography and licensing laws.'

While most of these life-changes would feed into future projects, the first excerpt from the new album *Construction Time Again* was released on 11 July. 'Everything Counts' combined new technology with a great pop song, shooting Depeche Mode back into the Top 10 when it reached No.6. In addition to the metallic percussion, one of the song's most memorable hooks is a sampled shawm (a Chinese oboe). If that wasn't startling enough, the song's lyrics now sounded positively world-weary. 'It's about things getting out of hand,' said Gore, 'business getting to the point where individuals don't count and you'll tread on anybody.'

Gahan: 'This was a real turning point, probably one of our favourites, and very powerful lyrically. Gary Bushell didn't like it, but he's a 40-year-old skinhead – what can you say? We find him quite amusing.'

On 22 August Mute released *Construction Time Again,* which also reached No.6 on the back of their recent chart hit. The band had recaptured their momentum, rewarding Miller's faith in them, although many of the critics who'd embraced the band as a perfect pop group – i.e., a short-lived act with a couple of memorable singles – were still digging in their heels, refusing to take their attempts at maturity as worthwhile or serious. But amongst the reviewers were some writers who were enthusiastic about Depeche Mode's change in direction. *NME*'s Mat Snow: 'You'll find no "Meaning Of Love", "See You" or even "Leave In Silence" here. *Construction Time Again* avoids the personal. It's on its soapbox, thinking aloud about the world and its woes with a voice in equal measure acute, uncertain, naïve and gauche. But there's an honesty, almost a shyness, that convinces you that Depeche Mode aren't just another bunch of two-bit pop stars sounding off the party-line to garner some intellectual credibility. They have made a bold and lovely pop record. Simple as that.' However, as Fletch conceded with a self-awareness rare to most successful pop bands: 'We've still got a long way to go before people will be proud to have Depeche Mode albums in their collection.'

Alan Wilder contributed two songs, 'Two Minute Warning' and 'The Landscape Is Changing', on his first album as a full-time member. 'I was never encouraged to write songs, it was my idea to try and contribute,' he explains. 'I actually proposed quite a lot of songs at the time and we chose a couple to record. I did another one on the next album but I realized I actually wasn't very good at writing pop songs so I stopped doing it. I'm sure the only reason the band recorded some of my songs was they thought, Oh, Al's putting all these songs in, we should try a few. At one point I did try to persuade Martin to co-write because I thought as a team we might be able to write some good songs together but he completely blanked that idea. He wasn't into it at all. That was fine. He just said he couldn't write that way. I can understand it, especially now, because he never has written a song with anyone else. I think the whole song comes in one go for him and then it's done.'

In restrospect, *Construction Time Again* is shot-through with a renewed enthusiasm and the industrial texturing alloys it with a maturity lacking in their first two albums. In addition to 'Everything

Counts', there are a couple of fantastic pop songs – the wistfully sung 'The Landscape Is Changing' and closing track, 'And Then ...'. The experimental 'Pipeline' still retains a magical atmosphere and 'More Than A Party' possesses a dynamic urgency absent from either *Speak and Spell* or *A Broken Frame*. Sixteen years later it's inevitable that elements of the album's very rigid musical style have dated, reflected in Gahan's comment, 'Maybe we were trying too hard ... sampling too much. Musically, some of it was very forced.'

The album's cover artwork instantly drew attention to the songs' non-personal themes, briefly reinventing Depeche Mode as a politicized band. According to Brian Griffin there was a loose concept agreed on – that it should be a landscape photograph but contain an image of an industrial worker: 'I'd been doing sleeves for Echo and The Bunnymen which were all shot on beaches and glaciers, so I think that fed into my idea for the sleeve. My assistant's brother used to be in the Royal Marines, so we thought we'd get him to do the modelling for the image. We went to Mont Blanc in the Swiss Alps, taking a real sledgehammer with us. That caused us a few problems because it was the first thing to come off the aeroplane. It was wrapped in a black plastic bin liner and I could hear it clunking down on that steel-sheeted conveyor system, so of course the customs people immediately pounced on it. Anyway, after we sorted that out, the benefits of having an ex-Royal Marine became very clear because we took a cable-car up the mountain and then had to do some climbing with heavy photographic equipment until we found the right spot.'

The worker image paralleled Wilder and Martin Gore's depersonalized lyrics which proclaim common-sense ideas about the industrial world in a disarming, very simplistic pop language. 'The Landscape Is Changing'' expressed Wilder's concern about the environment ('Thousands of acres of forest are dying/I don't care if you're going nowhere/Just take good care of the world'). According to Gore, 'When Daniel first read the lyrics of the album, he said, "Oh yeah, this'll go down all right with the Green Party." ' 'Shame' invited people to forget their social differences ('Do you ever get the feeling/That something can be done/To eradicate these problems/And make the people one?'), while 'And Then ... ' incites a 'Universal revolution ... Let all the boys and girls/Shape it in their hands'. As

Wilder observes, 'It's hardly deep.' At the time Gore described the new songs as, ' ... dealing with the problems of the world and things like that. That's what you get from listening to The Clash, I suppose.'

Gore's melancholy songwriting also mirrored a growing, half-articulated sense of disappointment with the world around him, which he hinted at in 1983: 'It's difficult to pinpoint what it is?' said the bemused musician, whose distress at the loss of his innocent perspective struck a powerful chord with the band's fans. 'You get older and you see more of the same. Whether it's just seeing more or seeing it through different eyes, I tend personally to get disillusioned by a lot of things. Things that used to seem great don't seem so great any more. Perhaps I'm just a very pessimistic person.'

Gore established himself as a great pop songwriter on *Construction Time Again* but not as an insightful social observer. And yet X-Moore, an *NME* writer and member of the political band The Redskins, treated Depeche Mode as 'comrades' when he interviewed them. Not long after this Fletcher did his best to debunk X-Moore's left-wing interpretation of *Construction Time Again*: 'X-Moore claims the album was virtually a rewrite of the *Communist Manifesto*. I mean, that's just silly,' he said. Wilder told the writer, 'When we decided on the theme for the album, the first word that came up was "caring" and that's the main idea behind it.' He was then very surprised when he saw the article: 'We couldn't understand what he was getting so excited about.'

In reality Margaret Thatcher's rise to power had polarized political opinion in the 1980s, stigmatizing pop groups who revelled in glamour, fame and money as 'right-wing reactionaries', and making pseudo-communists of anyone who expressed a 'caring' social perspective. Depeche Mode's naivety opened themselves up to patronage by the *NME* (aided by a little sleight-of-hand by Chris Carr, whose main objective was to overcome their 'pop' image) but Gore hadn't intended his songs to be interpreted in such a radicalized political way.

On 7 September the four-piece opened their 23-date UK and Ireland tour at the Regal, Hitchin. The stage featured the band on risers, surrounded by three wooden towers with light playing through Venetian-style slats. Mat Snow from the *NME* wrote, 'Their show is a careful mixture of spectacle and intimacy. Alan Wilder and Martin

Gore appear first on stage, being gradually enveloped in smoke as they brew up a swirling instrumental overture. Then Andy Fletcher walks on, as amiable and unstuffy as they come. Belying his back-stage nerves, he casually switches on the backing-tape machine sitting centre-stage as he strolls over to his synthesizers. Just by that casual press of a button, he sums up Depeche Mode's appeal; the technology of their music-making is instantly demythologized. You don't have to be a genius or rich or good-looking to stand a chance. Just like that other quartet of boys next-door 20 years ago, Depeche Mode bridge the gap between performer and the audience by show-ing the potential for magic in the most familiar, accessible things.'

The tour, which ended with three sold-out nights at London's Hammersmith Odeon, was a boisterous, self-indulgent affair. 'I think the band's full-on hedonism started in 1983,' says a sightly grizzled Daryl Balmonte. 'They were always up for it. All of them. They never missed any gigs in 20 years – well, we cancelled one in South Africa for Alan Wilder's kidney stone, and there was one when Dave lost his voice in Australia, but that's it. They're almost superhuman and if you can be efficient when you're partying hard, you tend to keep going.'

By the close of the tour, *Construction*'s opening track 'Love, In Itself' was in the charts, but it stalled one outside the Top 20. From the start the band were not sure they were making the right choice. Gahan: 'This is the s-s-s-s-s track. It had a very soft vocal, with a lot of s-s-s-s-s. It sounded awful. I was a bit disappointed with this, it could have been brilliant. There was a lot of fighting within the band over choosing this.' Fletcher: 'There weren't a lot of obvious singles on *Construction Time Again* and some of us wanted to use "And Then ...".' He added, 'We had a lot of problems with the equipment with this one, just trying to get that softness of sound we wanted with-out it all blurring was a real nightmare. It's one that's always good live, though.'

Wilder confessed in late 1983 that the 'band are successful but we can't afford to take a year off' and by 1 December they were back on the road for another long tour – 18 dates in Europe, although effec-tively it was just Holland, Belgium, Scandinavia and 13 nights in German, including three shows at Hamburg's Musikhalle and one at Berlin's Deutschland Halle in front of 10,000 people. In Gore's recently adopted country, the band had scored a Top 10 hit with 'Get

The Balance Right' and *Construction Time Again* had recently reached No.7. *Speak and Spell* was also a gold-selling album in Germany although *A Broken Frame* didn't make much of an impression. Fletcher was happy but a little puzzled by the band's growing stature in Germany because, just as they were celebrating a commercial breakthrough, the new single 'Love, In Itself' reached just No.28: 'It's pleasing that we've finally had a hit somewhere apart from England. But it's hard to understand why. After the album had done really well over there we put out "Love, In Itself" as a single and it bombed. We can't work that out. It may be that the success is just a freak ...'

The impassioned Gahan was thrilled at Depeche Mode's commercial progress in Germany: 'It's an exciting market as well. We enjoy it over there, actually doing gigs over there. You can see something's happening, that we're building. We can see ourselves getting bigger every time we go over there and play.'

You've Got Your Leather
Boots On, 1984

For the first few months of 1984 Depeche Mode's world was centred in Germany where, apart from a London session in Islington's Music Works studio, the next album was written, recorded and mixed. Martin Gore's new demo-ed songs established *Some Great Reward*'s tone of innocence corrupted by experience, set to a militaristic beat. While Berlin's darkly lit hedonism drew Gore like a moth to the flame, life in the grey-skied city could also be isolating, empty and boring. The writer's solitary moments in his rented flat in Charlottenburg, central Berlin, also inform the album. By now the most potent influence on his writing was his relationship with Christina, expressed while still in its first blush. Fletcher told the *Melody Maker* in early 1984: 'Martin's in love again, see? The point is to see something important and to write about it honestly, even if it is only important to yourself. Some people tend to think that love songs shouldn't be treated seriously, that it's only if you're writing about social problems that a song becomes serious.'

In these new songs Gore writes with simplicity about the power games, cruelty, vulnerability, complicity, selfishness, selflessness, insecurity, innocence and experience at the core of a new relationship. They're very sexual songs, offering some intriguing images: 'I'd put your leather boots on/I'd put your pretty dress on' ('Something To Do'); 'You treat me like a dog/Get me down on my knees' ('Master And Servant'). After the admirable but not entirely success-ful social observation of *Construction*, Gore's writing for *Some Great Reward* sounds like a man who is finding his voice – ambigu-ous, erotic, teasing, provocative, funny, shot-through with male ego, fragile but not willing to submit: 'I wouldn't sacrifice anything at all to love', he declares on 'Stories Of Old'. 'Lie To Me' explores how lovers offer each other part-truths which are paradoxically necessary for a relationship to blossom – 'So lie to me/But do it with sincerity'. 'It Doesn't Matter' is a fragile love song, twisted by the conviction that the relationship won't last, while 'Somebody' is a tender ballad sung by Gore to Wilder's piano accompaniment, about mutual support, trust and sexual freedom.

Meanwhile, the cost effectiveness of working in Berlin was proving to be irresistible to Daniel Miller whose small roster of Mute acts all recorded there. Fad Gadget even started drawing fresh creative inspiration from the place, writing the song 'Collapsing New People' about the nihilistic youth of the city. In 1983 Mute's new signings The Birthday Party, who lived in Berlin, recorded their *Mutiny* EP in Hansa. The band split up not long after but singer Nick Cave continued to live in the metropolis as a musician and junkie, drafting Blixa Bargeld from Einsturzende Neubauten into his Bad Seeds line-up. In Ian Johnston's biography of Nick Cave, *Bad Seed*, Bargeld recalls a small bar, the Risiko, through which most of The Birthday Party's social life would pass in 1983: 'The Risiko was basically run by an alcoholic who put all his money into buying a bar. He opened it and renovated it. It was nothing more than a place to get drunk in. In the beginning it looked fantastic but then the walls were covered in blood, everything was broken and all the money had been spent on other things rather than buying more alcohol.'

Chris Carr, who was working with Nick Cave at the time, intervened after observing that Mute were inadvertently financing the singer's heroin habit: 'I had to go in with Mick Harvey to see Daniel, and say, "Stop advancing money aganst royalties to Nick Cave and Roland Howard because they are junkies." People used to nick stuff from Mute and sell their own records to pay for their addictions.'

According to Carr, Dave Gahan not only used to do a fantastic impression of a wasted junkie but had a wicked 'Nick Cave' in his repertoire. 'Initially Depeche Mode used to laugh at Nick,' says Carr. 'Dave's a great mimic and he did Nick Cave to perfection. He used to laugh at Cave, and say, "What's Daniel doing with that bloke and pouring good money after bad?"'

Gore, while indulging in the city's nightlife, recognized that in this company he was not exactly a reptilian debauchee, so he chose to debunk the Berlin lifestyle in a characteristically vague 1985 inter-

view: 'I lived there for two years, went out to some clubs and knew a
few people, but I didn't take it very seriously at all, though it might
have had some subconscious influence. The Berlin scene is a bit of a
myth – the idea that it's full of weirdos and junkies, though there are
quite a lot. The clubs are quite good but not as shocking and different as people imagine.'

During the making of *Some Great Reward*, one of Depeche
Mode's favourite hang-outs was The Jungle, which they used to
arrive at around midnight. It was a trendy sort of place, a mixture of
cafe and club, regularly frequented by Bowie during his time in the
city. The Jungle was quite brightly lit and when you entered the first
thing you'd see would be people sat at tables, looking at each other
and posing. There was a dancefloor at the back but no one ever went
in that part. By the early hours of the morning the band would end
up in small clubs, big enough only for a handful of people, or late-
night cafés and bars.

Initially Depeche Mode were regarded as a teenage pop band by
local Berlin musicians and Alan Wilder recalls, 'Every now and then
a member of Neubauten would turn up in the studio to see Daniel.
They'd ignore us because we were so uncool. They'd sort of mutter
in German and then leave again. So we kind of met them that way,
except for Blixa whom we met a few times.'

Blixa Bargeld had a more open mind about the electro-pop band,
which he expressed to Daniel Miller. 'There was mutual respect,' says
the Mute founder. 'Blixa and Martin always got on very well and I
think Blixa felt that Depeche Mode were pushing the boundaries in
the pop area. One of the enjoyable things about Berlin was that you
could go out clubbing and there would be a lot of other musicians
around who came from completely different areas of music.'

For Miller, Mute's freshly nurtured Berlin roots made a lot of sense
because '70s German acts Neu!, Can and Kraftwerk had all been a
massive influence on him, although he recollects with a stab of disappointment, 'I used to meet German kids and I'd say to them, 'do you
like Neu! and Kraftwerk' and they'd go, "Oh, no, we like Bob Dylan
and Jimi Hendrix."' Despite a lack of enthusiasm amongst the local
population for their own musical heritage, Miller and Martin Gore
shared a keen interest in various small German labels, especially
Berlin's Atatac.

Meanwhile, the first fruits of these new Hansa sessions was 'People Are People', released as their tenth single on 12 March, two days after they completed a five-day tour of Italy and Spain where Gore noted: 'In Spain we get a stamp put on all our records with '"Dance Music"on it!' 'People Are People' became their biggest hit so far, charting at No.4 in the UK, and spending three weeks at the top of the German charts. 'I don't think that in Britain they ever experienced the hysteria that surrounded them in Germany,' argues Balmonte. 'I even remember one of the big German TV shows using the song for their coverage of the Olympics in 1984. All of a sudden they couldn't walk down the street in Berlin without being mobbed.'

On release in America, 'People Are People' gave the band their first hit as it crept into the Top 40 and finally peaked at No.13. 'We wanted a harder edge on "People Are People",' commented Gahan, who was starting to fend off some of the industrial comparisons. 'Daniel was going to sign Test Department at one stage but we hadn't sat down and listened to them – in any case, Test Department and Neubauten are more into Art and we're more into songs.'

'People Are People' is a very immediate, catchy song, separated from the likes of 'Just Can't Get Enough' by the toughened-up sound of the production and rhythm. 'We were aware that the single was quite close to being a disco single,' mutters Wilder, 'and we didn't want it to be like all the millions of others that were out.'

However, Gore's lyric (completely untypical for the *Some Great Reward* album) about 'all sorts of differences between people, not just racism', borders on irritating, especially the frighteningly memorable, 'People are people, so why should it be/You and I should get along so awfully'. The songwriter also flutters introspectively as he sings, 'Help me understand what makes a man hate another man', which was too much for some people; a fragile, vulnerable hook to others. Wilder defends Gore's words, pointing out that 'People Are People' does have a 'soulful' feel to it. 'Sometimes I find Mart's lyrics over-simplistic but they're so deeply felt, you know. He's writing about things he cares about. It's a very difficult art and he's very good at it.'

None of Depeche Mode defend the promo-video which was one in a growing line of cringe-inducing clips as the band roamed around the World War II battleship HMS Belfast, pretending to play it as a musical instrument and making an obvious anti-war statement. While Gore had conceived metal-bashing as a 'very visual' new aspect to the band, it didn't look very impressive in this clip. Nevertheless the song is strong enough to overcome the visuals and by way of credible compensation, the single boasted a mix by the ultra-hip On-U-Sound producer Adrian Sherwood.

The success of 'People Are People' placed the band at an all-time high, and they vibed off each other in Berlin where Daniel Miller shot some of their off-guard moments on Super-8. No deep, severe tensions between the contrasting band personalities were evident at this high point in their career. Wilder acknowledges, 'I think we all look upon that period in Berlin as one of the most exciting. The feeling in the studio was very dynamic and we had a lot of fun in Germany because there was all this success and there were a lot of fans around. People were always wanting to take us to their clubs. We were on TV all the time and we kept running into all these other English bands, such as Frankie Goes To Hollywood and Spandau Ballet. We'd end up having drinking competitions with them and they were all a good laugh. So there were a lot of good times then and we all went out together a lot.' In fact during an interview in 1984 – starkly contrasting with his views now – Wilder presented himself as the band's ' … confidential agent and if any of them has a problem they come to me. This, however, doesn't mean I'm the boss of the group. I'm just a little too sensitive for that. Martin Gore is the one in charge.'

Friends of the band argue there were periods in Depeche Mode's career when Gore and Fletcher would open themselves up to Wilder and talk about all their personal feelings. There were also many times when the Basildon pair felt the sharp but surly Wilder was impossible to read, frustratingly secretive and very clever at hiding all his real emotions from the rest of the band. 'In many ways Alan is a natural loner,' commented one onlooker. 'If anything, he was the quiet one who would listen to what the others had to get off their chests but he would always keep his own thoughts to himself. No one knew what was going on in his head.'

Martin Gore recently described Wilder as a 'misanthropist', to which Wilder replies. 'I don't have a huge army of so-called "friends" because I don't suffer fools gladly and I'm also not so insecure that I need an entourage of sycophants singing my praises all the time. I'm very selective about the people I socialize with. I suspect Martin meant that I was cynical and sarcastic which is pretty much right.' One thing is for sure, Depeche Mode have always been a very English, insecure, shy, dysfunctional collection of individuals whose hang-ups and lack of communication form part of the creative tension in the band.

By 1984 Miller was signing new acts and expanding Mute as a label, aware that despite the odd misunderstanding, Depeche Mode were able to run themselves with greater independence from about 1983 onwards. Wilder argues that, 'In the very early days a lot of Depeche Mode's decisions would be made by Daniel. You know he'd have a quiet word and say, "I think you should do this" and they'd say, "Oh all right then." But of course as everyone became more experienced we realized we could have more control ourselves.

'This meant we had to have meetings but it was difficult to get people together. The attitude was always, Oh do we have to? If anyone made a decision on behalf of the band without discussing it with the others then that would piss people off. Everything had to be run by all the members of the group. This often made it very difficult to get even a simple decision made but you couldn't run it any other way because there is no leader or dictator in the band. If we really needed an independent arbitrator we'd draft in Daniel.'

Fletcher bustled about in his role as the 'communicator' who tried to make sure people got together to discuss things – sometimes to the irritation of the band members, who would exert their revenge when an opportunity arose. Fletcher's legendary clumsiness left him vulnerable, often creating moments of pure slapstick. 'There was a classic scenario on stage once when Fletch ran up to the podium,' recalls Chris Carr, 'hit it really hard and sprawled right across the stage. Your heart goes out to him because all he had to do was get up on his podium and he couldn't even do that. Dave took the utmost delight in that and it was the band joke for the next few days.'

The sessions for *Some Great Reward* were co-produced by Gareth Jones, Daniel Miller and the band. Jones remembers, 'I engineered the first one and then for the second album I kind of plucked up my courage and asked them if I could be on the production team.

They said, Yes, because they were fair-minded people and they got the vibe. Daniel was still very important in the studio. He worked extremely hard at taking Martin's demos and orchestrating them, building up the sounds. He's analogue synth master. When he was co-producing, almost every synth line went through his ears as well.'

Now living in Berlin, Jones was introduced to Einsturzende Neubauten by Miller and started working on their *Halber Mensch* album, which came out in 1985. 'I was doing all this heavy metal noise with Neubauten – *Halber Mensch* was really an attempt to move great big slabs of sound around using primitive sampling – and it was jumping across into the Depeche sessions. I'm not saying that I was the driving force but there was this incredible synergy so that everyone wanted to go in the same direction.'

The sampling technology meant that Gahan and Fletcher were once again contributing some interesting musical ideas. 'I remember we were working in Hansa,' says Jones, 'and Fletch noticed there was an automatic aerosol on the toilet door and it made this great sound. He came in, full of enthusiasm, and said, "Gareth, we've got to use this." There was a very good atmosphere in the band.'

According to Wilder, to fill up the spare time in the studio, 'Fletch and Mart did a jokey album, which I helped out on. We'd go to the other room in Hansa, I'd play piano and Mart would be on guitar. We called the album *Toast Hawaii* because that was his favourite dish in the restaurant below Hansa.' Fletcher would eat Toast Hawaii, which was toasted ham, cheese and pineapple, almost every day during the making of *Some Great Reward*. 'We made a cassette of the album,' continues Wilder with a grin, 'and I took the LP cover which is a picture of Fletch as Plug from the Bash Street Kids. Daniel didn't want to release it. I really can't imagine why.' After pausing for a moment, Wilder adds, 'We wouldn't have done that sort of thing after about 1984 or '85.'

In addition to experimenting with Hansa's acoustics, Martin Gore decided to create a natural environment for himself when he sang the love song 'Somebody' naked in the Hansa studio cellar. 'Martin would take off his clothes at the first opportunity,' laughs Wilder. 'He's fascinated with his own body. Usually it would only take a few drinks and he'd be stripping off!'

Wilder's last song for Depeche Mode was recorded for the album, the moody 'If You Want'. 'I probably liked it at the time,' he says with a grimace. The track's couplet, 'Exercise your basic right/We can build a building site', still prompts a pained expression and a shake of the head from the musician. More importantly he and Daniel Miller forged a very creative 'production' partnership in the studio during the making of *Some Great Reward*. Unfortunately, at times the pair's love of fine detail proved counter-productive. Wilder: 'I remember we spent seven days mixing the track 'Master and Servant', and then we accidentally left the snare drum off at the end. That shows you how far up our own arses we were. We just couldn't hear the track at all. Daniel is a bit of a perfectionist and I don't think there is too much wrong with that, but there's no doubt Martin would get very bored in that kind of situation. It was a nightmare for him to sit in the back of a room listening to someone twiddling a sound for hours and hours.'

In June, Depeche Mode agreed to a work-related distraction from their studio sessions when they played a one-off festival date with Elton John at Suedwest Stadium, Ludwigshafen. John spent 45 minutes sat on some steps chatting with Gore and complimenting him on his songwriting. Then, on 20 August 1984 the band released the anthemic 'Master and Servant' as the new single, backed by '(Set Me Free) Remotivate Me'. Opening with the sound of Daniel Miller hissing and spitting, the song's manic, nerve-jangling rush took it to No.6 in Britain and four places higher in Germany. Gore's use of S&M imagery as a metaphor for life (notably, servitude at work, impotence under governments or authority, the power struggles of families and so on) is immediately established with the song's shrieking intro, 'It's a lot like life'. However, many people still interpreted it as a pure S&M song and their theories seemed to ring true as Gore metamorphosed into a fetish club clone over the next year.

The band's increasing fondness for black leather stamped their heavier identity in the promotional work for the single. Gahan felt a lot more comfortable with this band image, despite the fact the singer's own peroxided flat-top was never a great success: 'When we first started, we were wearing leather, basically the gay leather look. That was from most of our friends. It was our best look. Gradually we just came back into it. It's a good strong image, a powerful one. It's not really an image as such but it looks good and it's the sort of stuff we'd wear anyway.'

Wilder was also looking the part, with an amused John Foxx noting the young man's transformation into an iconic rock 'n' roller. 'I was very interested in the way Depeche Mode reinvented themselves,' says the former Ultravox frontman. 'The way Alan Wilder changed into this young Bob Dylan with a biker jacket. They became serious young men and avoided their fate as an electronic Bros.' Gahan even started calling the bequiffed Wilder, 'Slick'.

Gore went the furthest in experimenting with clothes, make-up and jewellery. He perfected a style which mixed together his innocent features and thin-boned body with fetishistic leather straps, dresses, lipstick, a necklace and black, chipped nail varnish. Part cherub, part Goth; simultaneously sexual, feminine and ludicrous, Gore won a lot of new fans by allowing his audience to project their own sexual fantasies on to him but he had no obvious agenda. During live shows he remained inconspicuous at the back for most of the performance, only emerging into the light for his solo spot, 'Somebody'.

Gore acknowledged the influence of S&M clubs, both in London and Berlin, on his new 'look'. 'I found the atmosphere in those clubs was very friendly. I'm sure I did get some ideas from going to those kinds of places. Maybe it's to do with my dislike of normality. I've always thought a macho image really boring.' Perhaps unconsciously he also wanted to highlight the sexual content of his songwriting at a time when his new relationship was inspiring him, pointing out that 'Seventy per cent of our songs are about, or touch on, sex. Personally, I find it amazing when I talk to people and they consider it a secondary thing in life. For me, it isn't something that's very secondary.'

As Gore's confidence in the band grew he was also enjoying the chance to subvert Depeche Mode's pop status: 'We are in a position where we can influence to a certain extent – not to get everyone wearing a skirt, but it does open people up to that sort of thing slightly, especially if they're some of the macho types who like our music. A lot of people think I'm gay which doesn't offend or worry me in the slightest. People can think what they like.'

Nevertheless, Gore also treated his cross-dressing with Christina as a vaudevillian sexual joke, revelling in the extreme theatricality of his stage and club wear with the showy enthusiasm of a childhood glam-rock fan. Wilder quipped of this self-made, fragile-looking Lady Stardust, 'Martin does enjoy it when we go through Customs and they ask him if he wants to go into the Men's or Women's cubicles to be searched. The more you laughed at Martin's outfits, the more outrageous he would make them. He's very stubborn that way.'

Furthermore Gore's transvestism was sweet and camp, rather than threatening or genuinely deviant: 'Occasionally when I buy a new article of clothing and present it for the first time I get a few laughs,' he remarked. 'Sort of "You can't wear that sort of thing!" Like when I got some rubber leggings recently. That's all I've bought recently apart from a dress or two – nothing exceptional.'

Of course, the British media had a field-day with Gore's gender-bending, eventually forcing him to dismiss this phase as ' … insignif-icant. It was totally blown out of proportion. I probably will regret it in years to come when my daughter can look back and see pictures. Try explaining that!' Even so, Gore's growing sartorial adventurous-ness would define his look for the next couple of years.

Meanwhile the highly anticipated *Some Great Reward* appeared on 24 September and became the band's most successful album at that point when it reached No.5 in the UK and No.3 in Germany. It also garnered some of the best reviews of their career. *Melody Maker* highlighted Gahan's 'deeper, mellow croon' and concluded, 'I do believe we are talking about a sparkling '80s version of The Jam.' The singer himself enthused to the press, 'I'm very pleased with the vocal sound on this one – it's a lot to do with being comfortable with the engineer [Gareth Jones]. Also, I took a couple of lessons with Tona deBrett, scales and things, and although I didn't see much appli-cation to singing pop songs, I wanted to learn more about breathing control.' In fact, privately Gahan's first experience with a voice coach hadn't been particularly rewarding and it festered into a taboo subject for many years, until they employed a coach for the *Ultra* sessions in 1996. According to *Sounds*, ' … the lyrics look trite, often naïve and frequently cliched when printed out in industrial grey and white. Yet Depeche Mode have the right balance and necessary gauche to pull it off.' In *Record Mirror*, Eleanor Levy awarded the album four out of five: 'Depeche Mode come of age, Martin Gore comes clean and the result is as an addictive an album as you'll hear all year.'

Smash Hits' Peter Martin gave it eight out of ten: 'Opening with what sounds like an overheating brain scanner, the LP ends with a human breath. What lies in between is a complex interaction between a metallic, computerized rhythmic core and more organic sound ranging from spanking to spinning tops.'

Some Great Reward is a more sophisticated album than the band's previous releases. The textured work in the studio creates a feeling of concealed emotions and private obsessions on tracks such as 'Lie To Me' and 'It Doesn't Matter'. The tone is more weathered and the music demonstrates a developing emotional edge, absent on the brave but inflexible *Construction Time Again*. Arguably the highlight of the LP is the closing 'Blasphemous Rumours', which claims that God has 'a sick sense of humour' because of the apparently random horrors that happen to people every day.

'I was going to church a lot at the time, not because I believed in it, but because there was nothing else to do on a Sunday,' explains Gore. 'I found the service very hard to take seriously. The whole set-up is quite handy but I'm not sure that's what God intended. Particularly a part of the service called the Prayer List, when the preacher rattles off the names of those sick and about to die. The person at the top of the list was guaranteed to die, but still everyone went right ahead thanking God for carrying out his will. It just seemed so strange to me, so ridiculous and so removed from real experiences.' Musically 'Blasphemous Rumours' remains one of the band's most chilling songs, as a slow-dawning synth line rises out of rattling metal percussion and eerie sound-effects, ranging from the snip-snip of scissors to scuttling, insectoid noises. The track also features a music box-like interlude which is very pretty but in this context possesses a nightmarish quality.

Almost the only dissenting critical voice was David Quantick in the *NME*: '*Some Great Reward* suffers from too many missed grips on good ideas. It ought to be an intelligent chart contender, a mix of commercial class and magpie manipulation of the unconventional; it isn't. Depeche Mode can be one of the few acts worthy of the name "pop group". It's just that they should be so much better.' Quantick also remained unconvinced by the album's mixture of pop and industrial soundscaping, commenting, ' ... they failed to produce anything from the two styles, other than add the odd bonking noise and clatter.'

Depeche Mode's 29-date autumn tour was their biggest so far, including four sold-out shows at Hammersmith Odeon. The stage set was designed by a new ally, Jane Spiers. It consisted of a tall riser, four ramps, two in the middle and one on each side, so Gahan could run into the back while dragging or twirling his microphone stand. The overall effect was very stark with lots of striplights along the front and parts of the structure would move by hydraulics to give it a 'Close Encounters effect'. There were also sheets of metal on stage, hung alongside the keyboards, although Wilder admits, 'They were pathetic bits of corrugated iron and it looked a bit silly. Every now and again I'd hit it but we weren't exactly Neubauten. We did it in such a stupid twee way it just looked comical.'

In contrast to the heavier thwack of the music, Gahan was every inch a hyperactive 'close-cropped, fresh-faced pixie who would bunny-hop around the stage and gamely lead crowd sing-a-longs as the rest of his band poked sullenly at their synths' (*NME*). His style of performance was becoming more exaggerated every year, frequently interjected with yelps as he rolled up the sleeves of his fashion-challenged jackets and wriggled his backside. The audiences loved it.

At the end of October, Mute released 'Blasphemous Rumours' as the third single from the album, accompanied by a promo-video filmed during the recent tour. Radio stations were scared off by the challenging content of the song and the single stalled at 16, despite an attempt to market it as a double A-side with the ballad 'Somebody'. Martin Gore was disappointed by the media's moral condemnation of the song: 'Neither this, nor "Master and Servant", had any shock value, they weren't intended to shock people. They both had good meaning.'

Gahan: 'I think the problem arose because it had the word "Blasphemous" in the title, so the record itself must be, whereas it's just the thoughts of one man looking for some kind of reason in the goings on in the world. We did get response from Christian Associations saying that they understood what we were trying to say.'

More surprisingly 'Blasphemous Rumours' divided the music critics. Neil Tennant was dismissive in *Smash Hits*: ' "Blasphemous Rumours" is a routine slab of gloom in which God is given a severe ticking off.' On the other hand Martin Townshend of *No 1* magazine recognized the progression of this new material: 'Depeche Mode are becoming a very important band indeed. Thought-provoking stuff.'

The year ended with 25 dates across Europe, taking in Denmark, Italy, Switzerland, Holland and, at last, a return to Paris at the Omnisort D'Bercy. 'At this stage it was all great fun,' reminisces Balmonte. 'There was less pressure on the *Some Great Reward* tour because I don't think they knew what they had at that stage, so they just said, "Oh fuck it." They weren't scared at all.'

Dressed In Black Again, 1985–6

'Everything about Depeche Mode grew from year to year – it was gradual, constant growth,' says friend and crew member Daryl Balmonte, who signed a full-time retainer with the band in 1984. 'I remember in January or February 1985, Dave Gahan came round my flat and told me that their show at the Hollywood Palladium had just sold all 5,000 tickets in an hour. That was when we realized it was getting really big. There seemed to be this domino effect going on and now America had cracked. To celebrate we had a beer and watched *The Bill* on Dave's telly.'

On 14 March Depeche Mode opened a 13-date tour of America and Canada at the Warner Theatre, Washington DC. On the second night they played to 2,000 people at the Beacon Theatre, New York, followed by huge dates at the Bronco Bowl, Dallas and Irvine Meadows in Laguna Hills, California. The previous year's success of the single 'People Are People' had kick-started the band's momentum again in America after 1983's *Construction Time Again* failed to ignite, despite 'Everything Counts' being a popular track on college radio.

Over the years they'd gradually developed a large cult following through the support of the Los Angeles radio station K-ROQ which had been playing their records regularly since 1981. By 1983 the station had an audience of 1.3 million and averaged 115,000 listeners during any 15-minute stretch. K-ROQ were also supportive of electronic acts, OMD, Pet Shop Boys and America's own reinvented electro-pop duo Sparks. But Depeche Mode were bursting through to another level altogether. Richard Blades from the station remembers, 'Their breakthrough was in 1985 when they played the Hollywood Palladium and they did a great show and got such good word-of-mouth that when they came back they sold out two nights at the Forum with a capacity of 17,000, which Duran Duran couldn't sell out once.' Depeche Mode's success in America was a remarkable achievement because they'd done it completely on their terms. They'd refused to dilute their sound by getting in a live drummer or guitarist and this now strengthened their appeal because they were seen as a radical, alternative band.

According to Balmonte there was a fantastic atmosphere on the American tour as band and crew 'had one big party. Depeche Mode always had a great sense of fun and at this point we were a relatively small, close-knit group of about 20 people who'd been given the chance to travel around the world together. Later it got so big and you had to question how things were being done but in 1985 there were no real problems.'

In May of the same year, off the back of their recent tour which finished on 3 April, the band released a U.S. only compilation of their singles, entitled *People Are People*. In England Depeche Mode enjoyed a modest success when their next single 'Shake The Disease' peaked at No.18. Gahan wasn't too keen on the song which he felt lacked a big chorus but in retrospect it's a strange and subtly arresting single which has stood the test of time. Alongside Gahan's aggressive croon, Gore's vulnerable plea 'understand me' touched a nerve with the band's adolescent audience. The complementary mix of their voices (Gore usually on backing vocals and harmonies) is one of the underestimated pleasures of Depeche Mode's records.

Meanwhile, the band were still travelling around the world through spring and summer, playing four Japanese dates (three in Tokyo and one in Osaka) and then setting off in early July for a tour of Europe. On 13 July, while many of the biggest bands in the world were playing Live Aid, Depeche Mode supported The Clash at a festival in Brest, northern France. Ticket sales were so poor that for a while it didn't look as if anyone was going to get paid until the promoters turned up with the money, which they gave the band in little bags...it was quite a small fee. There was a torrential downpour on the sparsely populated crowd who saw Depeche Mode at one o'clock in the morning. Meanwhile, Martin Gore was pretty scathing of the Live Aid event: 'If all these bands really care so much, they should just donate the money and let that be it. Why can't they just do it without all the surrounding hype?' To this day the band have refused to do Live Aid-type benefit festivals or events, which they view as manipulating people's good intentions for the sake of television exposure.

On 26 July Depeche Mode played in front of 80,000 people in the Panathinaiko Stadium, Athens, Greece. Culture Club headlined the event, which also included The Cure, The Stranglers, Talk Talk and The Clash. However, the festival didn't exacty run smoothly, as Boy George describes in his autobiography, *Take It Like A Man*: 'From Tel Aviv we flew to Athens where Culture Club were to play as part of a government-sponsored all-day festival, featuring a host of mismatched acts – Depeche Mode, The Cure, The Clash. I was spat at in the street and Dave Gahan was punched in the face. As we were about to leave for the show, word reached us that riots had broken out outside the Panathinaiko Stadium. Two hundred anarchists were demanding free entry, even though the fee was only 50 pence.'

The band's July tour also included their first-ever dates behind the iron curtain – Budapest, Hungary's Volan Stadium, where thousands of fans sung 'Happy Birthday' to 24-year-old Gore, and Warsaw's hangar-like Torwar Hall. 'The lack of resources in Poland was unbelievable,' says Balmonte. 'In Warsaw it was weird because you couldn't take any money out of the country so the band gave the crew half their earnings to spend. I went to an art gallery and bought some paintings, a solid-brass jewellery box and a hand-carved cuckoo clock for my mum. We were going to go to Russia but we blew it out when Dave got married.'

At the start of August Depeche Mode arrived home feeling absolutely exhausted after playing over eighty gigs in nine months. They agreed that sessions for the next album shouldn't start until November, allowing Martin Gore time to write some more songs and for them all to take a short break. Dave Gahan and Joanne had other priorities and on 4 August they had a quick registry office wedding, followed by a party in a marquee on the lawn of a country hotel. The couple moved into a three-bedroomed detached house in Essex, which Gahan described as 'grey and white and matt – I hate anything flowery'. They both wanted to have children, with Gahan commenting, 'I just think it would throw a whole new perspective on life. Having to bring up a child totally puts aside all the things that were important to you before. Things like being in the band would become secondary.'

It was obvious that the pair were very close and that Joanne, who had given up nursing to become a business college student, gave the 22-year-old Gahan stability in his life after a troubled childhood and an increasingly warped life as a rock star. 'I've met a lot of girls in my time,' he swaggered, 'and have been with a lot of girls, and sure, I've been in love but Jo's the only girl I've ever met that I could live with. I just get on with her. We have lots of arguments, just like anybody else but somehow ... we cross over, there's something about it that's special. We've been going out for six years and I just got up one morning and asked her and she sort of said, "Yeah, all right." It was that casual.'

Ominously for the future of their relationship Gahan sometimes described Joanne as more of a friend than a lover: 'I don't know why we got married, it was something we both fancied doing. Jo's the only person I feel completely at ease with and when you feel you can do anything in front of someone and it's totally natural, then that's the person you should stay with.' He also seemed to have rather chauvinistic reasons for having a wife: 'When I go away, which is quite often, Jo needs to sort things out for me, and it helps if she can say "I'm Mrs Gahan" rather than "I'm his girlfriend".'

Chris Carr believes that Gahan was trying to grow up and take responsibility for someone else: 'Dave wanted to move forward and leave his teenage years behind. He was looking down his nose at the others, especially Martin who was having this delayed adolescence. As a youth Dave had a police record but after that he went through stages of sobriety where he would look at the band with disdain as they went out to get drunk or go clubbing all night. I remember that was very much the case around the time he got married.' Gahan did indulge in the youthful flash of a metallic-grey Porsche, clothes, a big house, a motorbike and, of all things, fishing – but, as Balmonte confirms, he didn't go out much. 'He tended to stay at home more, but the others were all full-on, everyone wanted to go out.'

While Gahan was trying hard to conform and settle down, there were also warning signs of the rock 'n' roll extremism to come. He simply wasn't at home enough of the time to properly tether his life to a secure, domestic routine with Joanne. For most of the time, he confessed, 'I never just feel all right, I'm either extremely happy or I'm extremely depressed. There's no one that can really understand that unless they're in a successful band.'

At the other end of the spectrum, Martin Gore was in the middle of his Berlin phase. *NME* writer Danny Kelly painted an endearing picture of the Basildon fetishist: 'His tiny, girlish frame is armoured from head to foot in creaking black leather. His platinum quiff has been squeezed, like toothpaste, through a hole in his otherwise shaven head. His make-up is ghostly white and thick, his nail varnish iron-cross black and chipped.' Gahan took sarcastic amusement in the 'experiments' of a man who was a year older than he. 'Personally, I just think Martin's doing all the things I did when I was 16,' bragged Gahan. 'All that stuff about boredom is exactly the attitude that I went through. I went to clubs with people much older than myself. I wore tons of make-up and dresses too. But now if I go to a club I just want to have a good time, not to shock. Nothing shocks any more. Shocking is over, unless you cut your head off, or something … But Martin says that he hates going into the street and feeling normal. As soon as he gets into a normal situation, he gets scared.'

The insightful Chris Carr points out that, 'Dave is insecure in his relationship with Martin. Martin is as guilty as fuck but he's also an innocent. He has the ability to go through day-to-day life and push the envelope but he does it in such a way he doesn't damage other people. I think you'll find very few people who have had an experience with Martin Gore that has damaged them. And through that Dave feels a matey-ness but there's also a detachment because Martin just keeps being himself and can get away with murder, whereas Dave has to regulate himself all the time. Dave is constantly changing or responding to situations, whereas Martin just goes straight.'

Meanwhile Andy Fletcher and his girlfriend Grainne moved into a new flat in London, which he described as 'a cardboard box with lots of plants'. Alan Wilder: 'Fletch has started investing in things like wine-racks, you get the drift? He's even got a couple of books on caring for plants.' However, whenever Gore was around he got his friend out of the flat for long drinking binges, which Gahan thought of as 'childish'. 'Fletch is my best going-out partner,' said Gore, rather touchingly.

They all got back together with the more reclusive Alan Wilder (who was living in London with Jeri, his girlfriend of the last five years) for a new recording session, during which they completed 'It's Called A Heart' at Genetic Studios, owned by ex-Human League producer Martin Rushent. Arguably their weakest single, according to Gore it's, ' ... about the importance of the heart in a mythical sense, as the part of the body where good and evil are supposed to start. I'm not sure whether I believe in it but it's a nice idea.' The band had resolved that they wanted to release a pacey dance track and this was the closest thing they had to that. Unfortunately it's a rather characterless song and after charting at No.18, the single was swiftly forgotten by the band and their public.

'It's Called A Heart' was the only new track on their first hits collection, *The Singles 81–85*, which reached No.6 in autumn 1985. Inevitably the release encouraged critics to take stock of the band's career to date. One noted that the album was 'a savage indictment of the British record-buying public, who've shelled out for this naff tat'; while Stuart Maconie of the *NME* recognized Depeche Mode's rightful status as a great early '80s singles band: 'As the tracks rolled by, every one a hit, every one a miniature crash course in how to "do" pop properly and every one different, from the ingenuous but accomplished Casiotone juvenilia of "Dreaming Of Me" to the opaque gothic extravagance of "Shake The Disease", the truth became apparent. It was only when you heard their career in this way, compressed into nuggets of excellence and strung together like pearls that the truth hit you. Depeche Mode are one of the great exponents of the pop single on the planet.'

During the recording of "It's Called A Heart" and the promotional work that followed the release of the compilation album, the band were a more fractured bunch than they were 18 months previously. At opposite poles were Gahan, who was married and judgemental, and Martin Gore, a decadent resident of Berlin, absorbing new influences into his private life and songwriting. As *NME*'s Danny Kelly concluded, 'Actually, cowhide couture, miserabilism and consolatory sex aside for the moment, Berlin has been important and good for Martin Gore, leaving him more outgoing, confident and having absorbed a lot of music he wouldn't necessarily have heard on Radio Basildon, a better writer. So Depeche Mode, though it's hard to believe that the band's internal cohesion has been helped by Martin's lifestyle transformation, have benefited too.'

The 'Best of' project had brought them together at an awkward time when they recognized they had no idea which direction they should go in with the next album, especially as 'It's Called A Heart' had been a disappointment after the creative high of *Some Great Reward*. 'If we were ever going to split up the band, it was at the end of 1985,' says Gahan, who was really pushing hard for the band to take a more ambitious, risky musical direction. 'We were really in a state of turmoil. Constant arguing. Very intense. We weren't really sure where to go after *Some Great Reward* so we decided to slow things down. But it left us with too much time on our hands. So we spent most of our time arguing. Sometimes, it seems incredible that we came out of that period with the band and our sanity intact.'

The tension freaked Gore out and he disappeared for a few days, turning up at the German home of an old friend he made on a school exchange in a rural part of the country, 150km north of Hamburg. The songwriter spent a week there trying to relax but it wasn't a great success as crowds of local teenagers followed him everywhere: 'Yeah, yeah, I freaked out,' he later admitted. 'This business did my head right in and I had to go away for a few days.'

In late 1985 the band started work on the new album at Westside Studios in London, which Gore planned to be 'a lot heavier, harder and darker'. Daniel Miller suggested that they record the LP in one continuous session, stretching over four months, including a spell in Hansa, Berlin. 'I was very influenced by the German film director, Werner Herzog,' he says by way of arty explanation. 'They were all historical films, and people really lived the films, and it was a very intense way of working. We didn't have any days off and it was a method of working that I encouraged at that time. Partly as a direct result of that it did become very tense.'

The LP's co-producer, the jumpy, energetic Gareth Jones, recalls, 'Sixteen weeks is a very long time in the studio and a very stressful one. We did that without time off, because we decided we were going to live the album. In fact the only day off we had was when we flew from London to Berlin. This was seven days a week and for all of us, it was a long and gruelling experience. Making *Black Celebration* felt like a mammoth process and with the experience I have now, I'd never do anything like that.'

Chris Carr remembers lingering days in Hansa, where people would sit around smoking dope. 'There was a lot of black consumed in the control room at Hansa during the making of that album, although I don't think the drugs necessarily influenced the music. But they obviously contributed to the atmosphere in the studio and maybe that filtered into the recording. The band may have suffered from cabin fever by the end but I remember people not wanting to leave the studio because they were focused on work, or they were chatting and smoking while Gareth worked. Dave was still in his abstinent phase but he was very funny about it, taking the piss out of all of us, basically. I saw Alan come out of his shell a lot more. He wasn't always very open but I saw a looser side of him during those recording sessions. He seemed very much part of the fold by then. Fletch would sometimes worry when things started to drift too much. He was very much the butt of everyone's jokes but it was still funny at that stage. It wasn't until later that things started to get a bit more hurtful. Daniel was around as the quality controller, keeping an overview on the music.'

However, Miller was becoming aware of a subtle change in his contribution as he, Jones, Wilder and the songwriter Martin Gore occasionally disagreed over sounds and the direction of the album's dense, agitated production. 'Alan had become very well versed in studio techniques but I think we agreed on less during the making of that album than we had in the past,' confesses the Mute label boss. 'Part of the problem was Martin hadn't completely determined which way he wanted his songs to go either. It wasn't a very poppy album and there was some concern about whether it was the right direction and is this something we should be doing? The lines of our roles grew a lot more blurred during the making of that album because now Gareth was more involved in production. We were together every day and we were starting to step on each other's toes. It hadn't been like that before. For the last few years I was the one who used to make it all work and come up with ideas. From my perspective, Vince had a love of working in the studio which none of the other original members had. They didn't like tinkering around and experimenting. By the end of *Some Great Reward* and certainly *Black Celebration*,

Alan was becoming very adept in that studio-bod role which I'd filled in before. It tended to be us who worked late at night, while the others played pool or read the papers next door. That left my own position less defined but I still had a very strong point of view. So I think that created a lot of tension.

'In addition to that we were going nuts because of the cabin fever and I was running a record company as well, so I was always up early on the phone, making calls to London. That added to my own stress, and of course I could get a bit temperamental in the studio. Music is meant to be emotional and you're bound to get temperamental about it. I think that's a positive thing. If you're not emotionally involved in it, you're not connected to it.'

Chris Carr: 'Daniel can be an awkward character. One minute he's very shy, another he's very opinionated and bolshy; generous or tight. He's a very contradictory character. I've never seen Daniel say, "That's not happening" or "You can't do that". But within his relationship with Depeche, somehow or other they feel he's either with them or against. If it's the latter then they evaluate that. He's more older brother than dad.'

Alan Wilder feels some of the clarity of opinion was lost during the making of the darkly ambient *Black Celebration*: 'When too many additional voices were brought into the equation, problems seemed to arise. I hadn't immediately had a lot of power in the group, it took a long period of time. It was also a question of getting to know Daniel, which wasn't a quick thing, and then it was more a case of Daniel relinquishing control rather than the rest of the group, or me, stamping their mark. He just gradually started letting go over the course of these albums. It was probably quite conscious on his part, to allow us to take a more active role as we became more experienced. But on this album it was a bit difficult because I guess we were at a transitional stage in terms of Daniel's studio role.'

Perhaps it was a clue to future artistic highs and personal lows experienced by Depeche Mode that *Black Celebration* is one of the best albums of their career, certainly a creative zenith in 1986. The adverse conditions of its birth created a feeling of panoramic claustrophobia – as if the whole of someone's world has been compressed within a very small space. It's the aural equivalent to Wolfgang Petersen's 1981 movie *Das Boot*, which is set in the interior of a

German U-Boat, patrolling the Atlantic. As one critic put it, ' ... the filming's unfailing (and paradoxical) sense of spectacle is rendered even more dynamic by appearing to burst at the seams of its own claustrophobia.'

While Miller and Jones admit to the agonizingly slow progression of the record, in the end their experiments with sound and textures did break new ground. Miller: 'When we set up the studio in Hansa, Gareth was doing amazing microphone techniques and getting these big, textured effects by playing the synthesizers very loud through a PA in another studio.'

Again it's probable that, even if only osmotically, the atmosphere of the Hansa studios influenced the sound of the album. Its ambience derived not only from its location in an almost derelict part of the city (right by the wall with East German guards looking on from their towers) but also from the scale of the building and Studio 2 with its special big recording room and staircase. Wilder: 'Even though we were predominantly working at the very top of the building in Studio 4, we hired out the main recordings room of Studio 2 and set up a 2K PA system to send individual sounds through – effectively to beef them up and get the atmosphere of the room. This was done much to the annoyance of the Hansa café owner, who had to endure 4's on-the-floor pounding directly above his head for three days on the trot – something akin to a road drill placed six inches from your ear. God knows what he used to put in our food as retribution.'

Jones recalls the band's focused pursuit of mood and texture: 'We were trying to do loads of reverb on *Black Celebration*. The band had decided that reverb equals atmosphere and we went for it big time. That was the only kind of brief from Martin.' 'We were always pushing the technology beyond the way it was meant to be and when you do that it usually breaks down,' recollects the technically-inventive rule-breaker Miller. 'So you have to really persist and work out different ways of doing it, which can take a long time.'

Alan Wilder shakes his head as he remembers the torturous process of searching for great sounds in mid '80s studio equipment: 'The Synclavier was a state-of-the-art sampler/synthesizer that sounded great but it was also an overpriced beast which took four grown men to assemble because of all its additional boxes. It was also, quite frankly, a bit of a bastard to use. It was so expensive that hardly anyone could afford one apart from one or two top producers – Dan Miller being one and also Trevor Horn, who produced Frankie Goes To Hollywood.

'Daniel's a technical wizard when it comes to synths. He also has a lot of good production ideas concerning song structures, especially on a commercial level. He might say, for instance, "This middle eight is very good, perhaps we should start the song with it." And he's very good at building sounds. We might start off a song with a single sound on a sequencer and as it progresses, bring in more sounds just to make it richer. We did that a lot on this album – making layers of sounds all play the same part to get a full and warm effect.'

Despite the tensions, the sampling technology once again created an unusually democratic artistic set-up within the band. 'We're all programming and finding samples,' enthused Gore. 'Even David is now joining in with that, which is good because he used to be just "the singer".' The technology was also opening up the possibility of using more guitar, with the band sampling individual notes from the live instrument. He added, 'We'd get those chugging guitar parts by hitting a spring, and part of the bass sound by hitting the end of a hoover tube with my hand, and then these sounds would be processed through guitar amps to add character and weight. We often sample guitars, and then we've used them on a few tracks but it's a bit boring to go back to guitars. It's like the next step, all the electronic bands seem to do it don't they?' Gahan, who had thwarted ambitions of being a rock guitarist, explained, 'We just prefer to find new sounds in the studio. Though most of the music we listen to as a band is guitar-based really.'

This painstaking process of generating original sounds for every song, or creating 'combination sounds' where vocals and metallic sounds were mixed together on Daniel Miller's Synclavier, set the band apart from most '80s music.

They also made it a point of principle to avoid synthesizer presets. Daryl Balmonte recalls recently tuning into Virgin Radio, ' ... and they were playing a lot of '80s retro stuff. I said to my wife, "Isn't it weird that some Japanese studio engineer could sit in a factory in Japan writing all these preset sounds for Yamaha or Roland keyboards, and they were defining the sound of a whole generation!"'

Like their two previous albums, *Black Celebration* was mixed in

Hansa but after all the prolonged tension of the recording, this proved to be another excruciating process. 'I haven't listened to *Black Celebration* since we finished it because the mixing was a bit tense,' remembers Jones. 'The mixing was such a big deal for us that we were a bit nervous I suppose and so we'd get the tune up and spend days on it. Then after working on it for hour after hour, we decided, No, we didn't like it. After that went on for four or five days all the band got together and had a proper meeting with Daniel, Alan and myself and said, "Look, guys this can't go on."'

Alan Wilder: 'Not surprisingly we ran well over our deadline which did add a bit more stress at the end of the session. But I do think the album's claustrophobic feel was probably down to the tension. I think it did add a chemistry to the sound of the record more than any others we've done. It's certainly one of my favourite records that we've ever made.'

Daniel Miller took stock as *Black Celebration* was finally given its last tweak and allowed to leave the studio for the final cut. 'We were late with the record and I wanted to go back to London and see where the record company was. By that time Yazoo had broken up, Vince Clarke wasn't doing much, and I wanted to make some moves and get some new music on the label. So after that I certainly felt that they should work with someone else in the studio.'

Black Celebration was the darkest album of their career so far, an atmosphere that had been originally set by Gore's songs and then thickened by the studio tension. 'There's definitely a dark feeling to both the songs and the production,' says Jones. 'Stripped', the first single from it, is an inspiring mixture of euphoria and gloom. Released on 10 February 1986, it reached No.15, despite or perhaps because of a leathery appearance on *Wogan*. 'We kind of subtly corrupt the world,' laughed Gore. 'Basically if you call yourself a pop band you can get away with anything.' The press were guarded. *NME* described 'Stripped' as 'a morose tidal wave wearing away at the eardrum, perversely soothing but try getting up after listening to it', which hardly reflected the song's hugely anthemic lift.

One of the most striking aspects of 'Stripped' is the mechanized introduction that sounds like an engine revving up beside a railway track. In fact, the entire backbone of 'Stripped' was based around an idling motorbike sound generated from the original Emulator and a bass drone that was eventually fed through a Leslie cabinet. Additional sounds such as the ignition of Dave's Porsche 911 and an array of fireworks were recorded by Gareth Jones in the studio car park using his assortment of unusual microphones. In the case of the fireworks, the mics were placed at varying distances and heights with the rockets being let off at the appropriate angle to create a full stereophonic effect.

One song sometimes led to the conception of another and consequently 'Stripped' spawned the B-side 'Breathing In Fumes', which was achieved by speeding up the backing track and adding a new bass-line, new vocals and different musical parts.' According to Alan Wilder, 'This was quite a radical reworking for its time and perhaps the forerunner to a remixing style that would become much more commonplace in the '90s.' In fact there were several remixes on the 'Stripped' 12", including a first-time contribution from Mark Ellis, better known as 'Flood', who would become an important collaborator with the band in the '90s.

'Remixes were devised as a marketing strategy and instigated almost solely by ZTT and Frankie Goes To Hollywood's 'Relax' in the early '80s,' recalls Wilder. 'Depeche Mode's attitude was that we had to make remixes in order to compete, although Mode tracks were always recorded with the LP version in mind. From there we would either edit down for a 7" or expand for a 12". To make a 12" involved running off differently mixed sections on to the two-track tape until we had enough pieces to edit the new version together. The tape-editing process was much more limiting and took longer than current digital methods. The mere fact that it was so much harder to create a totally different and new version of a song probably contributed to the style of those earlier mixes and accounts for a lot of their charm. They were usually thrown together fairly quickly with time running out at the end of a mixing session.

'Around this time, it became the thing to do, to farm remixes out to other people who might perhaps have a fresher approach to the job in hand. We were always very drained by the end of a record so it actually suited us. However, having witnessed the attempts of some of the remixers over the last ten years, I'm now of the opinion that we were right the first time and it's probably better to do it yourself.'

The song's other B-side, the catchy 'But Not Tonight' was released as the single in America, with 'Stripped' on the flipside, but the change was not a success and the band didn't even make a video for it. Meanwhile, the video for 'Stripped', which was shot just around the corner from Hansa, was the last to be directed by Peter Care (who had previously directed the films for 'Shake The Disease' and 'It's Called A Heart').

Black Celebration reached No.3 in Britain after being released on 17 March 1986. In spite of the noir-ish, gothic surface tension of *Black Celebration*, Gore, who by now had moved back to London with his girlfriend Christina, insisted the album and title track had a life-affirming theme – albeit a cynical one: 'It's got nothing to do with black magic like most people seem to think – it's actually about how most people in life don't have anything to celebrate. They go to work every day and then go down to the pub and drown their sorrows. That's what it's about – celebrating the end of another black day. I think it's tragic that you have to compensate by just getting drunk, though I don't think there's anything unnatural about it. After all, we do it all the time.

'I'm quite a pessimistic person and I see life as quite boring. I want to reflect life's boredom. If you take things to absurd extremes, you're not really reflecting life. Real life is not extreme, so we're not, and nor is our music. So I kind of see our stuff as ... love and sex and drink against the boredom of life.

'When I write love songs people think they're really soppy, but I see love as a consolation for the boredom of life. And drink and sex ... Personally speaking I think we're quite decadent. When we're on tour, which is usually very boring, we, or some of us, tend to go out every night, have a lot to drink and generally have a good time. Consolation, see? I know it's all expected of rock bands, but going out is enjoyable, drinking is enjoyable and collapsing is enjoyable.'

Gore pointed out to *NME*'s Danny Kelly, that his past offered him easy inspiration for songs which reflected the boredom of life: 'What I do when I write songs is often to draw upon past experiences like when I worked in a bank for a year and a half dealing with standing orders – that was total boredom.'

Dave Gahan has contested certain aspects of what Gore was saying: 'I think Martin does think life is extreme. It's the darker side of those extremities that appeals to him. That's a lot more interesting. It involves a lot more. That side of things expands your mind more.'

One thing that Gore was very clear about – he didn't want *Black Celebration* to be interpreted as a band wallowing in self-indulgent misery. 'I know people in England say we're really pessimistic, or manic depressive. We don't see it like that. We're just trying to get some feeling, warmth and realism across in our songs. We like to think our songs are more reflective of life than most of the music that's around in the charts these days. A lot of it is just up, up, up all the way ... What we try to do is present a different kind of pop music to the masses. So we go through the routine of glossy magazines and TV shows. But that doesn't mean our music has to be like everyone else's music.'

Meanwhile, Gore wasn't immune to the artistic, literary influence of his adopted town Berlin, and it's clear that in the mid-'80s he was enjoying a diet of European writers who were shaping his view of the world. 'I am influenced by existentialism,' he said foppishly. 'I'm probably as influenced by Camus, Kafka and Brecht as I am by pop songs. Like on *Black Celebration* where the positive element is the idea of celebrating the end of another grey day.'

As for the reviews, Chris Heath of *Smash Hits* wrote: '*Black Celebration* doesn't only see them go a bit weirder with lots of dark, mysterious percussive episodes snuggling up against sweet, fragile and rather sinister ballads but is also the first time they haven't had to throw in any second-rate stodge. Their best album yet (8 out of 10).' In fact Gore's sweet falsetto features on four ballads, the sensual, vulnerable 'A Question Of Lust', the piano-led 'Sometimes', 'It Doesn't Matter Two' and 'World Full Of Nothing', which collectively establish a strong Kurt Weill influence on the album. Heath's reference to the 'mysterious percussive episodes' is also well observed, particularly on the slinky, reptilian-cold 'Fly On The Windscreen', which scuttles with atmospheric sounds used as rhythm.

Meanwhile, *NME*'s Sean O'Hagan argued, 'They continue to provide a soundtrack for the up-to-date, matt-black bedsit: dark yet faintly ridiculous.' Steve Sutherland at the *Melody Maker* was still complaining: 'It's depressing, though, that in their own small struggle for personal and artistic dignity, Depeche have only managed to trade in one set of cliches for another – white for black, bright for bitter, tunes for twisted chants ... *Black Celebration* finds Depeche even more over-anxious than they were on the depressing *Some Great Reward* to shock for the sake of it, pussycats desperate to appear perverted as an escape from the superficiality of teen stardom.' However, Sutherland's scan for a positive message was rewarded with the album's last song, 'New Dress', where Gore writes the politicized lyric: 'You can't change the world/But you can change the facts/And when you change the facts/You change points of view/If you change points of view/You may change a vote/And when you change a vote/You may change the world.'

DJ Shadow, one of the pioneers of hip-hop and sampling culture in the late '90s, names *Black Celebration* as one of his all-time favourite records. 'They were always the only group that I really felt comfortable listening to outside of hip-hop,' he says. 'They always seemed to make interesting, well-planned music. They seem to have the knack of bringing in all of the instruments you want to hear at the right time, building the tracks really well – so you're waiting for this one part to come in. It's very hard to do that and they never let you down.

'I know they don't get the same respect in the UK but I guess I don't have the same cultural hang-ups as you guys. Things come in and out of fashion but I think Depeche Mode manage to ride this. I try not to take notice of the musical climate when something comes out. I'm more interested in the music itself and I guess it was Depeche Mode that gave me my interest in synth music. I think they've got an amazing body of work.'

Spring 1986 also witnessed the UK opening of the *Black Celebration* tour, their biggest so far as they concentrated on arena-sized venues. The 13 dates included two nights at Wembley Arena, two at Birmingham's NEC, Glasgow's SECC, Brighton Conference Centre and Whitley Bay Ice Rink. Set designer Jane Spiers constructed the on-stage structure, loosely based on Leni Reifenstahl's film of the 1936 Olympics, out of inflatable plastics which were blown at the start of every show, then let down and folded away. These big inflatable 'balloons' were painted with fluorescent, ultra-violet paint, along with the microphone stands and other parts of the set, so that at various points it would all light up in strips. There were also projections behind the band. 'It was all very effective actually,' recalls Daryl Balmonte. 'I think the idea was that by having an inflatable set it would make it very easy to take around the world but the bloody things were always getting punctures.' Despite the best-laid plans, sometimes the stage curtain didn't fall down either.

The arena audiences included a lot of fans who'd grown up with the band, but they were also attracting a more mainstream, predominately male crowd who wanted to see a big show. 'After the teenybop thing, in the mid-'80s they did harness a real bloke audience and pretty normal-looking blokes as well,' remembers Daryl Balmonte. 'I think that's a sign of mainstream appeal. It is weird when you suddenly don't get all the fans in make-up and now you're being watched by builders and estate agents. I would've thought that the leather skirts of the '80s would have put some of those blokes off but maybe they were getting in touch with their feminine sides.' Martin Gore had taken to singing the track 'A Question Of Lust' in a black, short-legged romper suit complete with studs, buckles, suspender belt and black stockings.

Carr also recalls a very male crowd at these gigs. 'They've got such a strong following. One of the things with them is that they've never lost contact with their heartland, which is Essex, basically. At a certain peak in 1986 I remember watching them at Wembley Arena and being appalled by certain aspects of it. I was watching Dave Gahan orchestrate that audience and if he'd said to those people, Let's ransack the place, they would've done. Having just come from Berlin, it was reminiscent of a German rally – just that sort of feeling of control over people.'

John Foxx: 'I wasn't surprised that Depeche Mode started playing arenas and stadiums because I expected synth-pop to become a major part of pop music. I thought a few people would become major stars. They always had a good business person – Daniel Miller. I think he made a tremendous difference. He's honest, intelligent, consistent, and he also has vision. That's a very rare combination. You're lucky if you don't have a manager who's trying to rip you off.'

Radio 1 DJ John Peel reviewed one of the Wembley Arena shows in the middle of April, 1986: 'During the first song, "Black Celebration", the net screen fell to reveal the band and a fine, uncluttered stage-set that had to it something of the look of a Japanese interior. The musicians and their synthesizers were mounted each on a small platform, leaving a considerable expanse of stage for singer Dave Gahan to prowl.

'Visually this is a story of four haircuts. Gahan's is black, angular, inflexible. Alan Wilder is the rock 'n' roll rebel, all grease and quiff, while Martin Gore is the post-punk fetishist, a '30s health and strength haircut over crossed leather body-straps, black miniskirt and leather trousers. Andy Fletcher looks like one of the hipper children's television presenters – smart, modern, friendly, exalting the audience to clap along. The wholly electronic music remains a deal harder than you might imagine from the records. I left Wembley a bit of a fan.'

On the *Black Celebration* tour the band's fondness for booze shocked a few people who still imagined them as sweet young boys from Basildon. Balmonte: 'Harvey Goldsmith's people were a bit taken aback when they saw them. They all had an amazing capacity for going on binges and they'd never miss a show or a TV appearance. They were a big band all around the world, everything was becoming available to them and yet none of them let it affect their workload. They'd be out all night but you knew they'd be on time to do whatever they have to do. In those circumstances, why restrict yourself? I don't think Martin was ever sober when he was on stage, not for years anyway. It was like a big party working around the world and the crew were very much included. Everyone in the business wanted to get on Depeche Mode tours because they had a reputation of being good fun and people were well looked after. I've gone through different phases with the band members but in the mid-'80s Dave and I were definitely partners in crime.'

The thoughful Chris Carr, who worked the press campaign on the album, muses: 'Dave used to be fairly sober in his private life. However, it was different on the *Black Celebration* tour. That was part of his Jekyll and Hyde personality, the adrenalin rush of being on stage and the excitement of the band reaching bigger audiences – naturally it's very hard to come down from that. By the end of that tour he was getting up to high jinks with certain people in the crew. Both him and Martin overcame fear through fun. All the band were really up for fun on tour and some of it was a way of coping. No one realized it in England, but they had become an enormous band and there are pressures that come with that. You've got to remember they were a democracy – there was no leader to hide behind.'

Chris Carr also recalls that during this tour Depeche Mode seemed older, cooler, more mature: 'They were even starting to look very different. By now they were dressing in big coats, lots of black leather. They were growing up.' (As a side-note, one fresh-faced young man who joined the tour as acccountant was 22-year-old Jonathan Kessler, who would later become the band's first-ever manager.)

Shortly before they left the country for a 24-date arena and stadium tour of Europe in April 1986, they released a second single from *Black Celebration*. 'A Question Of Lust' achieved a modest No.28 in the UK but in Germany it was another Top 10, peaking at No.8. According to Alan Wilder, the song includes 'a castanet sound created by dropping a ping-pong ball on to the table and a string "twang" that originated from a traditional Hungarian instrument like a zither (also used on "Master and Servant" and "People Are People").'

'A Question Of Lust' was also one of the songs that featured Martin Gore's falsetto on lead vocal. According to Wilder, 'It was usually fairly easy to predict whose voice would suit particular songs. Generally speaking, Martin's voice tended to suit ballads and Dave's usually featured on the more raucous tracks.' The promo was directed by Clive Richardson during the *Black Celebration* tour in Dublin, Ireland. He'd also directed earlier videos, including 'Everything Counts' and 'Blasphemous Rumours'. Apparently the song 'A Question Of Lust' was a favourite of George Michael who planned to cover it but his version has never been released. Meanwhile *Melody Maker*'s Steve Sutherland liked this one: ' ... it's gorgeous, an Almondesque torch vocal mounting a simple electronic code worthy of The Human League'. *Smash Hits* thought the song was all a big tease: 'Once the black electro clanks of the intro have settled down, we are presented with a floating, melancholic tune and a wheezing, breathy voice that's singing about "love" not "lust" (a word employed solely to rhyme with "trust" and "dust"). Moody and pretty but entirely sauce-free. What a swindle.'

Depeche Mode arrived in Oslo on 24 April for the start of their European tour and following their Scandinavian gigs they played mostly in Germany at huge stadiums. Daryl Balmonte recalls: 'From this tour onwards they seem to grow out of their teeny-pop phase in

Germany and sort of merged with bands like The Cure. They started getting a much heavier, more gothic audience in Europe. That's not to say they haven't had rough rides from the press in Germany and Holland but they don't care. They've always been popular without being fashionable.'

Coincidentally The Cure, while being much more fashionable in Britain, were Depeche Mode fans. The band's singer Robert Smith enthuses, 'I think they have great style. From their innovative use of unusual sounds, through their often weird juxtaposition of lyrical emotion and musical precision, to their instantly recognizable graphics and visual image, they are one of a select group. A unique band. And they've also made some fantastic songs!'

Less than a week after finishing the European shows Depeche Mode opened their American and Canadian tour on 1 June in Boston Wang Centre. It was another big tour, consisting of 29 dates including three in New York's Radio City and two at Irvine Meadows, Laguna Hills. They also played Red Rock in Denver, made famous by U2's performance there in the early '80s. There was a celebratory feel to the concerts, as the huge stadium crowds sang the words to every song. 'I think most of the people who know the songs do understand them,' said Gore, 'but when they come to the concerts, it's a kind of celebration.'

Gore's love of a big party extended to flying his old mates from Basildon to some of these overseas shows. Alan Wilder: 'You'd be playing in some of out of the way place like Austin in Texas, and suddenly a planeload of spanners from Essex would turn up. All these big geezers would arrive. Martin and Fletch would pay for Big Ray or Big John to come out – they were all Big something. Dave couldn't stand all that crowd. I think Dave has a bit of an aversion to England in general, so much so that he eventually moved to America.'

All the band partied hard on the U.S. tour, to the point that Chris Carr remembers, ' ... we thought they would need a long break afterwards, which thank goodness, they decided to take.' Alan Wilder: 'When you're travelling abroad, you're really let off your leash. You know what it's like when you're in someone else's town, you've got an added bravado. No inhibition at all. Compound that with the effect of being in a big gang and having your arse wiped all the time. I think

Ozzy Osbourne said that this is the one job which you're expected to do off your face and it is very easy to live the life. By the time you come off stage it's 11 o'clock at night and you're absolutely awake, as awake as you'll ever be in your life. You've then got at least a couple of hours where you're changing and chatting and having a beer or two. So it's one o'clock in the morning and you want to go out partying. Before you know it, you've been out drinking all night, it's seven o'clock in the morning and you still feel you've only just started but you know you've got to go to bed. Over the course of a tour that tolerance level builds up and before you know it you stay up all night drinking and you don't even feel drunk. So that lifestyle became very normal for the band on tour, for several years really, and it didn't feel as excessive as it must have looked.'

Behind the all-night-until-morning euphoria, Wilder felt that his relationship with Martin Gore was friendly but a little superficial. 'Martin was always a big drinker. I couldn't always deal with Martin when he was off his tree, even when I was off my tree as well, and normally when you're pissed you can talk to anyone. When he's drunk he's the exact opposite to the shy person he is in everyday life, so you can imagine how extreme that is. He says the most bizarre things and it's also a physical thing. He jumps about, jumps in the air and you have to pin him down if you want to talk with him. He's your best mate in the evening but the next morning he's back to quiet Martin again. He won't remember things, he won't acknowledge how you've been together and the bonding fades in the morning. Martin would regularly go on three or four-day benders. I like Martin a lot but he obviously had a need to be excessive as much as Dave, but in a very different way.'

Chris Carr, who often spent time with the band on tour, concedes, 'Martin would often be quiet again after a heavy session. But that's the other side to him. He would hide away in his room listening to music or sometimes he invited me to his room to listen to CDs. He'd always have an acoustic guitar in there and sometimes he'd obviously been playing something. It's funny because almost every rock band I've been on tour with, the guitars are stored until the gig. Martin Gore is the only guy I know who would travel with a guitar and he was in what the rock guys would call a synth band. He had his acoustic guitar everywhere he went, in his hotel room, on the tour bus, everywhere. And yet the decision to actually put guitar on the record was absolutely agonized over.'

Meanwhile, the dissolute nights were a necessary distraction from the monotony of a long tour. Gore revealed his state of mind at this stage of the *Black Celebration* trek, 'When you're in your fifth month of touring you can't enjoy every night any more. It's getting to the point already now where I can almost go through the motions half-asleep. Now I automatically change disks at the right moment, without even thinking about it. It is quite boring but we owe it to the fans to play live because the concerts always go down really well. The audiences love it.'

As the only man on the tour who was physically active on stage Gahan would sometimes be close to collapse before the night of revelries began: 'After a concert I'm often close to exhaustion. Not long ago two roadies had to carry me to the dressing room. It took half an hour before I could say a word. After a tour I'm several kilos lighter and sometimes I feel sick to death after a concert. There is an extensive medicine box in the tour bus.'

After completing the last American date at Irvine Meadows on 15 July, the band flew to Japan for three gigs in Osaka, Nagoya and Tokyo. These were followed by a second European tour consisting of eight dates in 12 days. Chris Carr attended some of these shows and observed the fanaticism of the band's following in Europe, which had been quietly building up since the early '80s: 'I've seen audiences all around the world and they know every word. I've been on the road with them in tiny places in Italy, where we had problems getting the bus down country lanes. We'd arrive at some small village football team pitch and the stage would be constructed. Then all of a sudden thousands of young kids would appear from all over the place and I'd stand there amazed, because they knew every word of the songs. I couldn't see any record shops in the vicinity. Where had these fans come from?'

The band's date at Copenhagen's Valby Stadium on 16 August was their 76th and last of the tour. In the same week, they released the urgent, disconcerting 'A Question Of Time' which was written to an under-age virgin threatened by sexual corruption by an older man. Gore: 'It was written about a person in particular. Full stop, no comment.' Gahan offers a little more explanation, 'I think it's just looking really, observing. Rather than just writing about what would happen to that person – a very young attractive girl who was very innocent and obviously once us lads get our hands on them, they change.' The song was enhanced by an inventive video by Dutch rock photographer Anton Corbijn, who wasn't a great fan of the band and only agreed to do it so he could do some filming in America: 'I thought they were sissies,' laughs the gangly, slightly stooped Corbijn. 'I had no connection with what they were doing. It wasn't until 1986 when they asked me to do a video for "A Question Of Time", and I fancied doing a video in America. I had this idea of a road movie – an old guy on a motorbike with a sidecar, he goes down the road and finds these babies. So we shot it and I didn't hear from them for nine months. I thought they must have really hated it.' In reality the final element of the band's artistic vision had just slotted into place.

See The Stars, They're Shining Bright, 1987–9

After the *Black Celebration* tours the band resolved to discover a new musical style, so they broke up the production team by not calling on Gareth Jones for the next album. A further change was forced by Daniel Miller's decision to concentrate on developing the roster at Mute Records. Alan Wilder claims he tried to persuade the record company boss to co-produce the forthcoming sessions but Miller declined. The ever-cautious Depeche Mode actually grasped the nettle and hired engineer, mixer and producer Dave Bascombe, to work on the LP, and Wilder also took a big step forward in terms of his influence on the new project, *Music For the Masses*. Bascombe's previous credits had included work with Peter Gabriel and Tears For Fears but *Music For the Masses* was his first major production assignment. 'Dave Gahan had liked some of the Tears For Fears stuff I'd done,' remarks Bascombe, who wasn't particularly familiar with the band's previous output.

One of Depeche Mode's reasons for taking on the producer was that he was keen for them to move on from the industrial sound of their previous three albums. 'I think they all felt it was time for a change,' recalls the drafted-in studio boffin. 'When they first got involved in the industrial thing I thought it was very clever and inventive but then they started overdoing it a bit and I thought they needed a more natural feel.' Alan Wilder had also calculated that it was time to break away from the austere structures of *Black Celebration*: 'I think we had used up our quota of metallic sounds by that stage. There are only so many ways you can hit a pipe with a hammer.'

Martin Gore played Bascombe some of his demos before they all

ABOVE: The original line-up experiments with cravat, trilby and braces. The 'look' doesn't last long. From left to right; Andy Fletcher, Dave Gahan, Martin Gore, Vince Clarke. ©HARRY GOODWIN/ALL ACTION

BELOW: Depeche Mode on *Top Of The Pops* in 1981 during their original leather phase. ©LONDON FEATURES

ABOVE: Who needs a drummer when you have a reel-to-reel tape machine? Depeche Mode on *Top Of The Pops* in 1981. ©LONDON FEATURES

BELOW: Martin Gore flies in the face of New Romanticism in a white M&S jumper, circa 1981. These boys influenced techno, house and trip hop. ©LONDON FEATURES

ABOVE: Martin Gore and Andy Fletcher brush up their pool skills, probably during the making of another album. ©LONDON FEATURES

BELOW: Alan Wilder joins the band in 1982 but doesn't solve their image problems with a brown, bum-freezer jacket and green pleated trousers. ©LONDON FEATURES

RIGHT: Martin Gore, the synthesizer pioneer who is never without his guitar.
©LONDON FEATURES

LEFT: Alan Wilder, studio boffin and 'underrated' band member from 1982-95.
©LONDON FEATURES

ABOVE: To combat boredom in the studio band members used to hide Andy Fletcher's spectacles. ©FAMOUS

RIGHT: Dave Gahan as a City wide-boy in 1982, when the band decided that suits were the answer to Depeche Mode's sartorial nightmares. ©REDFERNS

ABOVE: 'The Man In White', leather jacket discarded, takes Depeche Mode to the masses in 1987.
©LONDON FEATURES

LEFT: The Depeche Mode's leathery, *Black Celebration* image of 1986 which survived until Gahan discovered grunge in the early 1990s.
©REDFERNS

RIGHT: Gahan's mid-1980s flirtation with blond streaked hair. ©LONDON FEATURES

ABOVE: Gahan as rock's
Messiah 'living the life'
on tour in 1993.
©LONDON FEATURES

LEFT: Martin Gore after
discovering Berlin,
European literature and
'cowhide culture'.
©LONDON FEATURES

RIGHT: Martin Gore on-
stage in 1993, when he
wore his glam roots on
his sleeve and
exchanged keyboards
for bluesy guitar.
©REDFERNS

ABOVE: On being released on $10,000 bail, Gahan is driven away from custody by his manager Jonathan Kessler. ©ALL ACTION

LEFT: Gahan shadowed by his 'dark side' during 1993's Devotional Tour. The imagery was created by Anton Corbijn, whose use of retrospective flashbacks in the video to 1994's 'In Your Room, expressed his belief that it might be the last promo Gahan would ever make. ©REDFERNS

RIGHT: Dave Gahan as self-styled, tattooed 'Rock God' during the *Songs Of Faith & Devotion* period. ©FAMOUS

ABOVE: Gahan living on the edge of his nerves during the insane Devotional Tour of 1993. ©LONDON FEATURES

ABOVE: Stripped to three for the *Ultra* album. ©ANDY EARL / RETNA

BELOW: Smashing Pumpkins' Billy Corgan joins the band on-stage at the K-ROQ Christmas bash of last year. The Pumpkins have covered the classic Depeche Mode track, 'Never Let Me Down Again'. ©LONDON FEATURES

'Visual director' Anton Corbijn creates a stark, peepshow-styled set for 1998's
Singles Tour. ©REDFERNS

Gahan's change of life after kicking heroin addiction is reflected in a new, clean-cut image for the Singles Tour. ©JON SUPER/REDFERNS

went round to Alan Wilder's home studio in Willesden, north-west London to work on pre-production. 'Martin had these demos, which were fairly sophisticated, although not finished, and we all went round to Al's place and basically deconstructed them and rearranged them,' reveals the producer. 'Martin wasn't really involved in that side of it much. In those days he really wasn't interested in studio work at all. Anyway, I felt that this intermediate step wasn't really necessary and I've read that on later albums they've gone straight from Martin's demos and into the studio, which would have been better.'

The full album sessions began in Studio Guilliame Tell, Paris. As a creative, communal starting point, for their first few days in the city the band wandered around bashing objects and buildings in order to collect lots of different sounds. Although they wanted to move into more organic styles the careful, inhibited group weren't ready to ditch tried-and-tested methods just yet. As a new experiment, however, they hired a few amps and snare drums and made some noise. Guilliame Tell was a great studio for an impromptu jam because it was a huge, old cinema with lots of space. This time together also allowed Bascombe to observe the individual contributions of the band members: 'Dave was buzzing, always full of ideas, and Martin made it clear he didn't want to be there. Alan was in the studio all the time and I think he was really growing in confidence. As for Fletch, I don't know why but I'd always had this image of him as an incredibly literary, studious guy – maybe it's because he wore glasses! Instead he has this most brilliant Essex voice and he's not bookish at all! Fletch has an odd role really. He had an overview of the whole thing. He was also very close to Martin and I might be wrong but I always had the impression that Fletch would sometimes act as Martin's mouthpiece if he wasn't around.'

According to Gore, one of his mate's jobs was to question the musical ideas and present a layman's view: 'If the rest of us get carried away, if we're all sitting around the computer going, "uhm, that's really it" he'll come in and go, "That's terrible, I don't get that!" He's no worse at music than your average fan, so if he doesn't get it, no one's going to get it!'

At this stage Fletcher's comments were indulged by Wilder although it's easy to see how the industrious, quick-to-learn keyboard player would find Fletcher's boisterous, well-intentioned but occasionally tactless opinions distracting or even irritating.

When Vince Clarke left the band in late 1981, Fletcher had stepped into his shoes as the band's main organizer. He'd been vigorous and opinionated in this task for several years, making phone calls, having meetings, keeping some of the 'boring stuff' away from the other, more creative band members. 'We don't actually have a manager, so we manage ourselves,' he explained. 'We have always done that ... It goes back to the whole independent scene, when indie labels started in England in the late '70s, after punk, it was basically a do-it-yourself attitude.'

However, in reality, the band's scale of operations by 1987 required the diligence of tour accountant Jonathan Kessler, soundman/tour manager/assistant J.D. Fanger, as well as Mute boss and adviser Daniel Miller to make things run smoothly. Fletcher helped out by communicating with everyone and checking over minor details but Depeche Mode were now a multi-million pound concern with a very professional infrastructure. In 1986 Mute and the band even entered into their first ever written agreement, although the terms remained exactly the same as the 50/50 verbal contract that had been agreed on in 1980. Martin Gore remembered what happened: 'We did sign a very small agreement with Daniel because it was pointed out to us, what would happen if Daniel died? He was very overweight at the time, and if he died we wouldn't be paid a penny. So there's a sheet of paper which says we're to be paid on a 50/50 basis. In England we pay 50 per cent of all our costs and get 50 per cent of all our profits. In Europe we get 75 per cent of our profits through licensing deals.'

In essence by this stage Fletcher's uncategorized role was to pursue the interests of Depeche Mode above those of the individual band members. Chris Carr describes him as ' ... the conscience of the band. He's part of the driving force. His job is limited on the musical side in terms of his own physical contributions but his ability to rationalize and direct is massively important.' In particular his friendship with Martin Gore has been fundamental to the band's continued success. 'He's the one who pushes the songwriter that little bit further – to come up with another track, play the others his new demos, and so on.' According to Daniel Miller, 'In the early days Fletch used to be the outspoken half of Martin but since then he's had much more of his own point of view and quite often he's been persuading Martin to do things – always with Depeche Mode's best interests in mind.'

Meanwhile, the next phase of recording at the Paris sessions was an endurance test. 'For every melody we needed to find the right sound so there was tons of blending all these various noises,' says Bascombe. 'That was quite a time-consuming process. We'd have five or six sounds layered on every sound. By doing that we created these otherworldly noises, so that the listener knows there's something very odd going on. The band were also obsessed with getting all the beats perfect, almost robotic. The rhythms had to be absolutely spot on. This was before drum loops, so it was very slow, painstaking work.'

Before the album was completed, Depeche Mode released the disappointingly inflexible 'Strangelove' as a single on 13 April 1987. The song, which didn't break much new ground, crept in at No.16 and then quickly fell out of the charts. The band's dissatisfaction with the track led them to reworking it for the final LP version. According to Bascombe, 'The single was released before the final mixing of the album and then during this late phase Daniel Miller, who'd contributed a 12" version (Blind Mix) of the song, visited the studio to assist. When we came to mixing "Strangelove" for the LP we incorporated elements of this 12" mix, so it was difficult to piece together and actually ended up consisting of lots of little parts.'

On the 'Strangelove' single there was also a mix by Bomb The Bass's Tim Simenon, who would work with the band more closely a decade later. Anton Corbijn shot the song's accompanying promo in Paris using his girlfriend Naseem as an extra. The new visual direction – black and white, erotic, surreal, humorous – actually brought out the internal atmosphere of Gore's songwriting, in contrast with previous directors who concentrated on metal-banging, funny haircuts and leather-gloved pop-star posing.

Fortunately on *Music For the Masses*, Depeche Mode didn't stick to their self-imposed rule of no conventional rock chords. This change immediately created a more dynamic style from the one-note symmetry of their electronic LPs, reaping huge dividends with the song, 'Never Let Me Down Again'. 'That's the track I'm most pleased with,' enthuses Bascombe. 'I just loved it. As the basis for the rhythm we used "When The Levee Breaks" by Led Zeppelin, which has a fantastic drum sound. Martin put guitar on the backing track to give it a richer groove. We then heavily processed the guitar sound with lots of different effects. There are also some real orchestral sounds, strings and horns on there, and we restructured the song to emphasize the chorus, which really seemed to open it up.

'I remember Dave was very pleased with his vocals on that song and felt it was a bit of a breakthrough. Maybe he just found it easier to sing to a more organic groove. If so, it must have been very subliminal. Previously in their whole industrial period everything was so separate in terms of sound. The mixes were very processed and unusual sounding, all these millions of effects going on. I don't think that helped the songs and it probably didn't help Dave's singing.'

After Paris, Gahan recorded most of his vocals at Konk in London, which meant he could spend more time with his wife, Joanne, who was expecting their first child in October. 'I'm pretty excited about it,' he said. 'We've wanted one for quite a long time. The thing is we had a good go at it for quite a while and nothing happened. Then the minute we stopped trying so hard, she became pregnant. Typical!'

Music For the Masses was mixed at Puk studios, in the middle of a field in Denmark. It was at least 15 minutes to the nearest town and there was only one club there. 'The band always made their own fun,' laughs the genial Bascombe. 'Even in this little town in Denmark girls would hang around, and that's the main thing. As long as there's some nice girls around, who cares, you know?'

Alan Wilder: 'I enjoyed Puk. It's a well-equipped, well-run studio with a vast control room, nice accomodation, good recreational facilities and top breakfasts (Lars the chef). The problem was that there wasn't much to do around there – probably a good thing actually. Luckily, I'd just passed my driving test and as we'd hired a car, when things got tense in the studio, I'd go off for long drives in the Danish countryside. As for nightlife, I remember one occasion when we ventured out to the local town (having been climbing the walls for a few days) and returned, rat-arsed, in the middle of the night. In our desperation for food, we crow-barred open the huge industrial fridge that was securely locked. Lars' breakfasts were never quite the same after that.'

On 24 August 'Never Let Me Down Again' (backed by the excellent 'Pleasure, Little Treasure') was released as a single, climbing to

No.22. It was a significant artistic breakthrough for the band, with the giddy, blood-rushing chorus – 'We're flying high/we're watching the world pass us by/Never want to come down/Never want to put my feet back down on the ground' – and compelling groove expressing the dizzying vertigo of an unspecified drug – fame, sex or a Class A. Gahan gets right inside the whirling, buzzing, vaguely narcotic mood of the song, almost as if Martin Gore wrote the words for and about him. Chris Carr: 'People have said that Martin writes songs for Dave. What people don't understand is that Martin writes his things for himself. Dave thinks they're for him, but if he was honest ... it's that weird thing, who's living who? If you strip it all down, the main heartbeat is Martin but what he's experiencing, Dave is experiencing at one extreme and Fletch is experiencing on the other.'

Gore's lyrics also flirt with sexual ambiguity as Gahan sings, 'I'm taking a ride with my best friend ... /Promise me I'm as safe as houses/As long as I remember who's wearing the trousers'. New York's *Village Voice* interpreted these words as a 'travelogue which becomes a metaphor for drugs or gay sex'. Depeche Mode have always had a sizeable gay following, initially spawned by the early '80s popularity of the band's first few singles in American gay clubs. A few years later, Gore's taste in cross-dressing, leather bondage straps and lyrics about ritualistic, faux-spiritual S&M struck a chord with adolescent males experimenting with their sexuality. But as Wilder points out, ' ... you couldn't get a more un-gay bunch of lads. Despite Martin's cross-dressing and gay club clothing, he'd sometimes get quite upset when people kept thinking that he was gay.'

Although 'Never Let Me Down Again's failure to breach the British Top 20 was a disappointment, the band found compensation in Germany where it only missed the top spot by one place. Anton Corbijn's video for the song is one of his best, featuring a very cool '60s bubble car driving through fields of yellow rapeseed. The images of travel and cinematic sense of space expressed Corbijn's feel for the music as 'very touchable and filmic'. Wilder: 'This is one of my favourite Anton films. It has a very definite feel and a mood that compliments the song perfectly.'

Although Depeche Mode had successfully loosened up their style from the stringent electronics of *Black Celebration*, neither producer nor band were completely satisfied with *Music For the Masses*.

Martin Gore's rigidly sequenced, over-sophisticated demos had curbed some creativity by not leaving enough room for experimentation. Once in the studio Bascombe felt the band were still imposing strict, over-used techniques on themselves, pointing out that the DJ remixers were allowed a lot more freedom with tracks such as the darkly submissive 'Behind The Wheel', than either the band or producer. 'I wasn't allowed to have a hi-hat on that song, which made it very hard to get a groove going,' he says, wistfully. He then concedes, ' "Behind The Wheel" has got a kind of claustrophobic, unique sound to it because of the limitations.' Although Bascombe was pleased with individual recordings, such as 'Nothing' and 'Little 15', he says, '... the problem for me is that the sound of the album is doomy and dark but it's not ballsy enough'.

Gahan was enthusiastic about the dynamics of the new record: 'We had become aware of highs and lows. We were more conscious of building up atmospheres, heightening the songs to an absolutely massive feeling and then bringing them down again. We had discovered dynamics. It was our first truly arranged album.'

'It's a bit more conventional and traditional than some of our other records,' concedes Wilder. 'But the rest of the album doesn't quite match the standard of "Never Let Me Down Again". The songs on *Music For the Masses* actually stayed closer to Martin's orginal demos than those on *Black Celebration* and after that we said to Martin, "Leave the demos a bit less finished to give us more freedom in the studio". In retrospect, I think the other problem was that perhaps Dave Bascombe was not an adventurous enough route to take. He's a very nice bloke and he did a very good, professional job but he wasn't a dynamic person who could stamp his authority on the album. I think he felt stuck in a position somewhere between engineer and producer.'

Music For the Masses reached No.2 on its release in Germany at the end of September, while in Britain it peaked at No.10. *Melody Maker*'s John Wilde was seduced by the dynamic range of the album: 'Sumptuously produced, it shows Depeche working within their limits, no longer straining for effect. The songs are now full of big flashes, tantalizing refrains, voluptuous flushes. They have discovered beauty in the balance of their parts.' *Gay Times* ignored the gorgeous, fragile 'The Things You Said' and picked up on the oblique lyrical kinks and velvet-dark mood of tracks such as 'To Have And To Hold', describing it as 'Suitable stuff for a dungeon, leather sex party.' Blitz's Mark Corderey echoed Gore's feelings about the band when he described them as 'one of the most subversive pop groups of all time'.

Sounds' Damon Wise awarded the album four out of five but had some reservations: '*Music For the Masses* is a missive from the designer doldrums, which nonetheless betrays the broadest clues so far given of the Depeche Mode predicament, the schizophrenia that sees high-art pretensions chafe commercial considerations. Depeche Mode: great pop, bad art. Get the balance right.' Wise may have reacted to the arty nihilism of 'Nothing' but he missed the humour of 'Sacred' with its pseudo-religious references to sexual positions – 'I'm a missionary' and the phallic one-liner, 'I'm a firm believer'. Most of *Music For the Masses* is about the power-games of sexual relationships, unfolding moments of vulnerability, beauty, manipulation, domination and submissiveness. 'There are a lot of recurring themes in my songs,' says Gore. 'One thing that always reappears is disillusionment and lack of contentment. A lot of the songs also deal with a search for innocence. I've got this theory that as you get older you get more disillusioned and that your happiness peak is when you're in your teens. As you grow older and learn more, the corners are rubbed off your life.'

Jane Solanas at the *NME* wrote: 'The lyrical content, in Gore's hands, may have got progressively more weird since "New Life" and "Just Can't Get Enough", but the music is sharp and accessible as it ever was ... If you still think Depeche Mode are beneath adult consideration, consider this: their music has been turned into tape-loops by experimental underground Soviet groups and hi-jacked as backing tracks by Chicago House producers. In Britain, Depeche Mode will probably always be seen as nine-year-olds from Basildon who make pretty tunes on lots of keyboards. The critical respect and mass adulation they command in Europe, the Far East and parts of America escapes them here. But they should worry.'

As soon as the album was completed, Alan Wilder worked on the laborious process of programming all the keyboards for the tour and Dave Gahan spent as much time as possible with Joanne who was expecting their first child any day. Jack Gahan was born on 14

October 1987, eight days before his father walked on stage at Madrid's Pabellon. 'Becoming a dad is, I think, the most fantastic thing for anyone,' he swooned. 'I only question myself if someone who never knew his father can become a good father. I wish I could discuss this with Len.'

Martin Gore had always insisted that the title of the band's new album was a joke. He told journalists, 'I think our music never crosses over to the general public, hence the album title, it's a joke. It's only the fans who buy our stuff.' However, *Music For the Masses* took on a very different feel when applied to their biggest tour so far. Opening in Spain on 22 October 1987, the touring juggernaut finally rolled to a stop, after *101* gigs, at the 70,000 capacity Pasadena Rose Bowl in California on 18 June 1988. According to Daryl Balmonte, who worked as the band's personal assistant, 'The big stadium set was based on Martyn Atkins' ideas for the album sleeve – the megaphone speakers and so on. The stage had flooring like a racetrack and these strange, ambiguous emblems on big flags. It was done like a concrete Rome amphitheatre, or like an Olympian stadium.' Dave Bascombe, who went to one of the early European shows in November 1987 at Paris's Omnisport D'Bercy, remembers the sensory overload of the 'fantastic opening'. They used 'Pimpf from the album', ' ... which is really Gothic and Wagner-like as the intro music and they had these orange megaphone speakers on top of the speaker stacks. It looked like a stadium rally and kind of took your breath away really.'

Gahan quickly turned 'Never Let Me Down Again' into a show-stopper, encouraging fans to wave their arms from side to side in time with the pumping, heightened music. Wilder: 'The song has a very definite anthemic quality which is especially demonstrated when the song is performed live and the whole audience wave their hands in unison – a Depeche high-point, I think.' The European dates included a huge, high-profile tour in Germany, with shows in eight major cities.

Martin Gore also flashed back to his childhood by singing Sparks' 'Never Turn Your Back On Mother Earth', which he covered on his low-key solo mini-LP, *Counterfeit*. The six-song minimalist covers record, released in 1989, also included versions of Durutti Column's 'Smile In A Crowd' and 'Gone' by Comsat Angels. Meanwhile,

Sparks' singer Russell Mael recalls that, 'We've met Martin a few times, and we went to a sushi restaurant in LA with the rest of the band.' 'He was very soft spoken,' interjects Ron Mael, the brother who writes the duo's songs. 'He's not a man of many words.' Sparks exerted a formative influence on Gore, who names their '70s LP *Propaganda* as one of his all-time favourites. They've contributed to his love of pop songs, a taste for bizarre lyrical ideas and Russell Mael's falsetto finds an echo in the upper level of Gore's singing range. Interestingly, Vince Clarke is also a Sparks fan and Erasure contributed a version of 'Amateur Hour' to the duo's 1997 LP, *Plagiarism*. Ron Mael is also an admirer of Gore's craft. 'There are very few writers who can compose electronic pop songs. It's an increasingly rare art form as synthesizer music is usually dance tracks these days. But Martin does it, so that you can't see the join between traditional elements and the electronic parts.'

After playing 19 dates in Europe, Depeche Mode had a short two-week break before blasting off on the first leg of their American tour on 1 December 1987 in San Francisco's huge Cow Palace. Most of the 11 shows, including two nights at Los Angeles' Forum, were sold out, underlining Depeche Mode's entry into the big league as an international act in 1987. 'We were big news in America when we arrived with the *Music For the Masses* tour,' remembers Wilder. 'And then later it became a press-worthy hype that we were big in America! Our live success happened a long time before our records started selling a lot, and then suddenly with *Music For the Masses* it spilled over into sales.' The album sold over half a million on its way into the American Top 40, eventually stalling at 35. After climaxing with a concert at Madison Square Gardens, New York, the band returned to England for a Christmas break.

On 28 December they released a new single, the oppressive, tech-noir track 'Behind The Wheel', backed by a cover version of Bobby Troup's 'Route 66' (a Nile Rodgers remix of this song was included on the soundtrack for the Julien Temple movie, *Earth Girls Are Easy*). Depeche Mode maintained the theme of motor travel from the opening sample of a spinning saucepan lid, which sounded like a hub-cap, into the flipside. The single followed a familiar pattern, reaching No. 21 in Britain and 6 in Germany, boosted by their recent performances. 'It was actually quite predictable – the pattern for

Depeche Mode releases has been the same for many years,' says
Wilder, arguing the case for Gore's misunderstood *Music For the
Masses* title quip. 'The fans are so dedicated that they rush out and
buy the records in the first week of release resulting in a very high
chart position (usually higher if it's a single pre-release of the album).
This position is difficult to maintain or improve upon in the second
and third weeks and the record doesn't have time to cross over
before it's dropping down the chart. As soon as the single starts to
drop, radio stops playing it and the cycle is complete. Everything is
over within three or four weeks.'

On 6 January 1988 in Newport Centre Depeche Mode opened
their 11-date UK tour, which included two shows at Wembley Arena
where the British press gathered to dissect the event. Once again the
ghosts of Basildon haunted the reviews, as the journalists collectively
tried to prick the band's growing importance by rounding on Dave
Gahan, described by one writer as, ' ... prancing about all over the
place, sticking out those buttocks, swinging around with the mike
stand and yelling, Hey, at every opportunity.' The British media have
remained exasperated by Gahan's frontman persona, which is an
exaggerated, stadium-esque version of his arm-flailing, hip-wiggling
antics of the early '80s. Critics felt the band's increasingly dark music
was at odds with this hyperactive, crowd-pleaser at the front. In reality, Gahan's performances were very much driven by the fans'
responses, which turned Depeche Mode gigs into celebratory sing-a-
longs even when most of the material being performed was bleakly
atmospheric and introspective. This was certainly confusing for
onlookers who'd retained an earlier, more one-dimensional image of
the band.

Danny Kelly in the *NME* reminded his readership that Depeche
Mode are, when it comes to it, Essex boys: 'Dave Gahan treats us to his
fabby new Essex Sex Act; we marvel at his totally convincing pelvic
thrusts (complete with authentic, permanently erect, radio-mic acces-
sory); we gape at his mastery of the Freddie Mercury ain't-piles-murder?
stance; and we stare gobsmacked as (combining the contortions of an
arthritic battery hen, a B-movie stripper and Mick Jagger's grandma) he
unveils the second worst dance routine on earth ... But most wondrous
of all is the sight of Martin Gore as he agonizes through those of his
hilariously doomy poor-little-pervert numbers that even the galloping

Gahan is embarrassed to sing ... And yet when these lads do return from
their imaginary TV slots and slip into the tried and tested groove of their
Fisher Price electrofunk, they are quite brilliant.'

Writer Andy Darling also concentrated on the four personalities:
'Dave Gahan is the youth club show-off, the lad who dared wiggle his
bum at the disco; Fletch is the tall kid with ginger hair who kicks his
legs up a bit and kids everyone he learned karate; Martin is the little
one who got hold of a book about the Bauhaus, liked the pictures,
and did A-Level Art at the tech.' Nancy Culp in *Record Mirror*
recoiled from the spectacle but enjoyed the music: 'Depeche Mode
are awfully and unintentionally hysterical. From Dave's manic pelvic
thrusting and bum wriggling; to Martin's fetching leather jockeys,
motorcycle boots and black bondage harness which all make him
look like Hooky's little brother; to Fletch's curious knee-jerks and
arm-waggling mid-song, Depeche Mode are even funnier than Spinal
Tap in their New Romantic period and it's all totally unselfconscious
to boot ... yet, by and large Depeche Mode have matured immea-
surably into a fine but still criminally underrated all-round group. My
feet barely stopped moving for more than half a second all evening
and the grin on my face will have to be surgically removed ...'

Melody Maker's Adam Sweeting enjoyed the fact that, 'Gahan
brings a fraction of Marc Almond's cheek to a dollop of Gary
Numan's bleak monotone' but didn't find his voice so engaging.
'Even in almost joyful pieces like "Just Can't Get Enough", Gahan's
voice is like being wrapped in a wet, grey blanket and then soundly
beaten with pillows.' Meanwhile, Gore was singled out as 'the Aryan
toy boy of the group', in his silvery outfit, strips of PVC leather and
lots of silver dangly bits. 'There's something a trifle unnerving about
the Mode's version of sexuality. Gore and Gahan look unnaturally
adolescent, as if they've been cloned from a fetishist's catalogue.'
The Times' David Sinclair was swayed by the lightshow: 'The drama
of the performance was the product of the manifest ingenuity of the
lighting designer and of excursions such as "Stripped", where the
musicians bashed raised drum pads to produce the sampled sounds
of an industrial scrapyard in crashing, rhythmic waves.' Another
writer observed, 'For "Never Let Me Down Again", a backdrop
resembling a shopping precinct from 1936 Berlin was wheeled
across the stage!'

The British tour finished on 24 January after which the band disappeared for another quick escape before they set out on the next phase of the *Music For the Masses* marathon. On 6 February they returned to Germany to play two shows in Hamburg, followed by a further 18 stadium and arena shows across Europe. On 7 March they arrived in East Berlin to a play a very rare gig on the other side of the Wall. The gig had completely sold out and there were 10,000 fans out in the street that afternoon, hours before the band were due to go on stage. This was followed by two concerts in Budapest, one in Prague and one in Vienna. Gahan: 'In Hungary there are actually groups of fans called "Depeches"! They're like the Mods and Rockers we get in Britain. Our hotel was surrounded by literally hundreds of them and they all looked like one of us. We're huge in Eastern Bloc countries. Even in Russia they did a survey on the streets asking people what film of a rock band would they most like to see. First it was The Beatles, then The Police and then Depeche Mode.'

They took almost a month off at this point, allowing Dave Gahan to spend some time with his son and for all the band to chill out briefly before the next leg – four dates in Japan, in Osaka's Festival Hall, Nagoya's Koseinenkin Hall and two shows at Tokyo's NHK Hall. By now the band were in full swing, and a week later they were back in America, where they'd scheduled 31 shows leading up to the Rose Bowl, in Pasadena, California. This was their biggest tour of the States so far, playing to a total of 443,012 Americans in 1988.

They wanted a visual record of this achievement, so just before they set off on the dates they hooked up with D.A. Pennebaker, who'd made his reputation by documenting Bob Dylan's 1965 British tour in the movie *Don't Look Back*. Pennebaker accepted Depeche Mode's commission to make a movie of the tour, adopting a fascinating approach to the band: 'I don't think of this film as a documentary,' he said. 'I find the word misleading. Most people are bored with documentaries. To me, if you are making a documentary, you are telling the viewer everything about the subject that you think they ought to know. With a regular movie, you try to tell them as little as they need to know. I prefer the latter and feel this works on that level. I wanted to make a film about real people in real life.' Gahan: 'We saw what he had done with Dylan and Monterey Pop, and the

Kennedy documentary – they're very factual. Too many bands make totally scripted, cliched films, as glossy as possible.'

Pennebaker wanted to capture a 'certain edge' he sensed in the band. Nothing was scripted, no scenes were engineered. He started with a blank page. 'I knew nothing about Depeche Mode when they approached me,' he admitted. 'My kids did and they told me something about their kind of music. But that's not really important to me. I wasn't a Dylan fan when I made *Don't Look Back* – my job is to transfer the music and the band on to film.' His method was to get to know Depeche Mode through the camera, an endeavour that ended up sprawling across 150 hours of film. He scythed through all these reels to what he saw as the heart of the story – the band's daring, entrepreneurial independence. 'That's the kind of drama I grew up on – things like Errol Flynn, that whole American sense of adventure that it's all there for the taking. I wasn't trying to indict anybody for making money or making fun of the process because it's much more complex than anybody imagines. When they decided to go into the Rose Bowl, they stuck their heads out a little, and like any entrepreneur or anybody who hunts for treasure, they take a chance. I applaud if they win; I don't look on that as the process of a foul capitalist machine. I'm not looking to propose an answer, just showing what I see, which is complex and contradictory.'

Alan Wilder offers his view: 'He just made a film about four lads from England on tour in the Wild West, playing to these millions of people. He didn't pretend to understand it but he wanted to show it. He picked up on the rape and pillage as the band arrived in each town. There wasn't any pretence to it.'

The director recognized that Depeche Mode had mobilized, ' … an enormous cult audience that somehow came out of the backyard. Here's a band that doesn't get played a lot on the radio, they go into town for a concert and there isn't a lot of advertising, most people don't know who they are but suddenly the place is full to capacity. And the people aren't just there because it's a place to get away with smoking pot. They've really thought a lot about the music; they know the words and are right into it. For the band, this must be a kind of wonder.' According to a spokesperson for Los Angeles' main alternative rock station, K-ROQ, the band's airplay is driven by demand, not record company promotion: 'One out of every three requests we get is for Depeche Mode. We play them round the clock, both new ones and oldies.'

Pennebaker argued that in the mid-'80s Depeche Mode had connected with 'a strange angst [which] has mid-America by the tail ... all these children of the middle class all wanting to revolt against something and there's nothing to revolt against'. Daniel Miller defines the group's core U.S. following as, ' ... basically white, middle-class kids from the suburbs who are a bit fucked-up – post-puberty with a lot of problems. They are part of America's suburban sprawl.'

A cross-section of Depeche Mode fans form an important part of the build-up to the final event in the movie, titled *101*. The director worked with Long Island's 'new music' college radio station, W-DRE, who sponsored a dance contest at the 'Malibu Disco'. Eight teenage winners and a film crew were then put on a chartered bus which took them along Route 66 to the Rose Bowl. However, all the tittle-tattle reveals very little about the band's relationship with their fans, or vice versa and Wilder is sceptical about the device: 'I could have done without the fans on the bus but I guess it showed something about our audience.'

Orchestral Manoevres In The Dark, who also received a lot of airplay on K-ROQ, supported Depeche Mode on the American tour. This was an experience that OMD's singer Andy McCluskey recalls with mixed feelings: 'At one level it was good to be playing to 15,000 people a night but it was slightly galling as well because Martin Gore told us how much he loved our early single "Electricity" and that it was a big influence on Depeche Mode all those years ago. We were earning $5,000 a night and losing a fortune because of our over-heads – by the end of the tour I think we owed our record company over £1 million in total – and they were earning enough to retire on every single night!' McCluskey affords himself a wry grin, as he recalls, 'We did that tour in order to build up a following and we had some success but before we could really capitalize we split up. Depeche Mode built themselves up with that tour and then delivered their best album *Violator*, so I have to hand it to them really. Most bands crumble in that situation.'

Meanwhile, encouraged by the prospect of six weeks in the fantasy land of a major and very exciting American tour, the band's appetite for fun was indulged through all-night drink binges, lots of cocaine and ... cricket matches. Wilder: 'We played OMD at a cricket match on that tour, and I got Andy McCluskey out. I was really pleased about that because I didn't like him, he seemed a bit of an arrogant fucker.' The OMD frontman claims he was dismissed by Wilder's keyboard tech. 'I think we played in a park in Long Island, New York. We had a big picnic and Depeche Mode had imported all the gear, so we had proper stumps, bats and cricket balls. They absolutely thrashed us.' 'I think OMD were all out for 11 and we scored 12 without losing a wicket,' gloats Wilder, rekindling the moment with a grin. 'We've actually played a few games of cricket on tour over the years. I remember one time in Nashville, there's Dave on the tourbus, sitting under this big hat, and someone said, "You're in next Dave", and he hoovers back this massive line of coke and strolls out. Of course he lasted one ball.'

Andy McCluskey also confirms, 'There was a lot of partying on that tour. It was funny because we were a couple of bands who had quite clean-living reputations at the time, and we were all behaving like animals.' Daniel Miller was growing concerned about the flipside of this debauched, unreal on-the-road lifestyle. 'I started feeling nervous for them because I saw the potential for damage. There were a lot of people around, friends and crew members, who wanted to party and have a good time and they all probably influenced each other. I felt the self-control slipping but there was very little I could do about it. The boredom, the routine, the adulation, it all fucks you up. I didn't see the drug-taking for myself. They were really trying to hide that side of things from me. I've never once seen them take drugs, apart from smoking a joint. Obviously I've seen them when they're on drugs, but they'd never get them out and take them in front of me – ever. I think it was an uncle-type relationship and they felt a bit embarrassed.' Wilder: 'I'm lucky in that I don't have that addictive streak. I love drinking and I love being excessive at times but I don't have the kind of personality where you must go to the ultimate extreme. I have quite a stable background and I think that's stood me in good stead.'

However, Dave Gahan was very emotional and easily led astray on tour. As the band's frontman he was always a focus for attention from fans, media and assorted hangers-on. While there is a side to him

which is very much a loner, Wilder points out that Gahan's ' ...
natural instinct is to be funny, witty, very charming and very open,
but obviously this vulnerability which makes him a very attractive
personality, in lots of ways it is also the cause of his problems. It's
part of his edge as a performer and there's definitely a sense about
him of someone who is constantly looking for something.'

At the time of *Music For the Masses*, Gahan was in a mess: 'I had
everything I could possibly want but I was really lost. I didn't feel like
I even knew myself any more. And I felt like shit, 'cos I constantly
cheated on my wife, and I went back home and lied, and my soul
needed cleansing badly. I had to figure out why.' In 1993 he told
Vox: 'Over the years I think I was a pretty shitty person. I didn't like
what I was creating ... in my own life.' He also agonized that he
wasn't pushing his personal and artistic boundaries far enough. The
philosophical Chris Carr recalls a chillingly prophetic conversation he
had with the singer during the *Music For the Masses* tour. 'I had a
conversation at Dave's behest where he said to me – I didn't make
much of it until later – he said to me, "There aren't any rock 'n' roll
people any more." I said, "What do you mean?" And he replied,
"People that do it because they really believe in it." I said to him that
Guns N' Roses were around, and there's Iggy Pop and Neil Young,
the "true believers" if you're going to fall for all that stuff. By now
Dave had this fixation with Nick Cave, I think through Martin, who
had started listening to music in a much more serious way. Perhaps
more importantly Dave now found himself facing massive audiences
and he didn't really know what to do. He felt he had to become
something more. Dave decided to take it upon himself to make sure
that rock 'n' roll continued in its purity, so he pushed it as far as he
could.'

Oddly enough, Axl Rose of Guns N' Roses was a big Depeche
Mode fan and he invited them to join him at a heavy metal night-
club, the Cat House. However, when he went off to a friend's
Beverly Hills barbecue and allegedly shot a pig, Depeche Mode were
sufficiently shocked to issue a statement: ' ... as strict vegetarians,
the band were appalled by Rose's behaviour and do not wish to
associate themselves with anyone who goes around shooting pigs
for fun.'

Meanwhile, backstage tensions between the band members were

starting to flare up. While Gahan and Fletcher kept up their semi-affectionate verbal warfare, the latter did end up scrapping with Alan Wilder backstage in Salt Lake City when Fletcher criticized Dave Gahan's performance. 'Yes, that's true,' says Wilder. 'I thought that was a bit rich coming from him, and a physical brawl did ensue between us. Punches were thrown, some landed, some missed and I heard that a few tears were shed. The worse thing was that we all had to go straight back on stage to play "Just Can't Get Enough". In fact, all of the physical encounters that have taken place over the years have included Fletch although the predicted big one involving the most aggressive member [Gahan], has strangely, never gone off – I'd like to see it when it does.' Andy McCluskey vaguely recollects being told that Fletcher had given Gahan a pep-talk at one of the shows: 'I heard that he gave Dave Gahan a dressing down because he felt Dave was partying too much and was struggling with his voice. That was a shock to us because in most bands the singer is the dominant force who calls all the shots but Depeche Mode seemed more democratic.'

As the American tour drew closer to its climax in Pasadena, the gorgeous, string-laden 'Little 15' was released as a single in France. Amazingly enough British fans bought it on import to push it into the UK Top 75 at No.61. The promo for 'Little 15' was directed by Martyn Atkins in London. Depeche Mode also released a linked collection of Anton Corbijn videos, entitled *Strange*. Corbijn's taste for European art movies and opaque, noir-ish imagery is given full vent in this mini-movie, which established the band as 'The Frank Sidebottoms of the avant-garde' according to *Sounds*' Damon Wise.

Depeche Mode's concert at the Rose Bowl was a very daring move, clearly designed to show them off as a huge international act and effectively silence all their critics – especially in England. Daniel Miller: 'I think the Rose Bowl concert had a huge influence on people's perception of the band and to be honest, we made sure that it did. It was a massive leap of vision for them to make the decision to play there and the fact that it sold out instantly was incredible.'

Gahan was keen to prove a point in their home country: 'The problem with the British is that Depeche Mode have always been underrated artistically. Earlier in our career we felt we had to be in every magazine, the more the better. We were very naïve and because of that we were taken totally the wrong way. We've always had to justify ourselves to the press in Britain and that really offends us; that's why we've avoided talking to them in the last few years. We don't feel we really have anything to say when the line of questioning is, Why do you exist? That's another reason to make this film; we wanted to be portrayed as we really were, and if we're still considered dickheads, then fair enough.'

When Depeche Mode played this 101st gig of the tour, they sold 66,233 tickets and generated gross receipts of $1,360,193. Tour accountant Jonathan Kessler is caught on Pennebaker's *101* movie as he tells everyone, 'We're getting a lot of money, a load of money, tons of money – $1, 360,192 and 50 cents. The paid attendance was 60,452 people tonight at the Rose Bowl in Pasadena, June 18, 1988.' Gore: 'The film is supposed to be an honest, candid look at a band on the road and what happens backstage. Every night the accountant is backstage talking to the promoters, hassling them about money and money is a big part of the music business, which is very capitalistic.'

Gahan: 'When you tour America, suddenly things like merchandising are far more important than ticket sales. Merchandise finances tours. People talk about million-dollar deals with merchandisers. Before you know it, you may as well be running a chain of T-shirts. To tour in America you need to sell T-shirts. We like the idea of being quite open about these things, and we hope that people take it the right way. It's something that's always taboo with bands, though everybody knows that bands make lots of money, sometimes far too much for what they do. But you must never talk about that because it detaches you from your audience who are supposed to be on the same level as you.'

In all the *101* movie, which premiered at the Berlin Film Festival, cost a relatively modest $600,000, compared to the $5 million chewed up by U2's film, *Rattle and Hum*. However, Pennebaker's stark observational technique did leave some people frustrated, in particular the alert, questioning Alan Wilder who was disappointed that the film made no attempt to dissect the reasons for Depeche Mode's huge success. 'I was a bit disappointed with it in the end because I felt it was a bit lightweight,' confesses Wilder, whose biggest speaking part in it is when he explains how his keyboard works. 'But I think from Pennebaker's point of view he could only make a film based on what he saw and I do think it was a very honest film. I think maybe if it had tried to go into more depth it would have fallen flat on its face. And *101* was a nice antidote to U2's *Rattle and Hum* which was around the same time and was highly pretentious.'

There are some funny, candid highlights, such as the pre-show conversation between Gahan and the band's tour manager:

GAHAN: 'I don't think I should say "Hello, Pasadena", I think I should say, "Hello, the Rose Bowl" ... I don't know.'
FRANKS: 'Why don't you say "Good Evening, Welcome To The Concert For The Masses"?'
GAHAN: 'I'm not fucking Wordsworth, you know.'

The most intense glimpses into the unadorned, turbulent side of the band are through Gahan, who claims he'd be happier stacking shelves in supermarkets than touring because, 'You lose your friends, you're away from home doing this. But you get more money.' The singer also rants about a bust-up with a local taxi-driver, revealing his pent-up aggression as he admits he'd been looking for a fight for a while.

As for the performance itself, Wilder nerdishly asserts that 'it wasn't actually one of the best, due to monitoring problems'. Daniel Miller concedes, 'I had very mixed emotions. It was scary. When you see 70,000 people doing the same thing at the same time. The power was really scary. It was incredibly satisfying to see them succeed, against all the odds really. They proved a lot of people wrong. To go from nothing to that in seven years was amazing. I just wandered around, watching the audience more than the band. It was a very emotional experience.' One final element of Depeche Mode folklore was created when there was a freak rainstorm during 'Blasphemous Rumours', which contains the line, 'Then came the rain/And once again/A tear fell/From her mother's eye'.

The concert was also documented with a *101* live album and a single, 'Everything Counts' (which was an encore and reflected the fiscal theme of the *101* movie), released on 13 February 1989 and reaching No.22. Wilder: 'I can't remember who really pushed for "Everything Counts". I think it was fairly unanimous. It has been a very popular live track for a number of years.' In Britain the *101* album actually charted higher than *Music For the Masses* when it reached No.7 in March 1989. Gore remarked, 'I don't know if the double album marks the end of a period for us as a band, but it certainly marks the end of an era, the end of a decade. We started in 1980 and this album is coming out in 1989 and our next stuff won't be out until 1990 when we will be moving into the next decade.'

World Violation, 1989–90

'Techno is technological. It's an attitude to making music that sounds futuristic: something that hasn't been done before,' says Detroit electro/techno pioneer Juan Atkins. The term 'techno' was originally applied to a specific form of dance music developed in the mid-'80s out of repetitive, minimal melodies and subtle textural modulations by the likes of Atkins, Derrick May and Kevin Saunderson. In the late '80s and early '90s, alongside house and garage, techno became part of an explosion in dance music in Europe. As Jon Savage explains in his book, *Time Travel*, 'Acid house – acid being a Chicago term for the wobbly bassline and trancey sounds that started to come in from 1987 onwards – coincided with the widespread use of the drug Ecstasy.'

John Foxx, who in the late '80s worked with Bomb The Bass's Tim Simenon as the underground act Nation 12, enthuses: 'Most of the '80s was a vile period for anyone involved in electronic music – at least in this country. In the '80s I carried on recording abstract stuff with beats but I didn't release anything. I think there was mutual disdain between myself and the music scene. We really didn't care for each other, I hated everything that was happening and I felt in a complete void. Then I suddenly felt at home again when I first heard an acid squelch in 1987. At last electronic music was creating something new and exciting again.'

Depeche Mode were recording their next album *Violator* when *The Face* magazine contacted them with the idea of flying to Detroit and hooking up with one of the techno innovators, Derrick May. Several British synthesizer acts of the late '70s and early '80s had been credited as influential in electro, techno and house music, including The Human League, Gary Numan, Soft Cell, New Order and Depeche Mode. In truth, Kraftwerk were more important than all of these acts put together but, that said, the bizarre, fascinating musical path from Basildon to Detroit was certainly worth exploring.

The cream of America's dance pioneers have at various times credited Depeche Mode as playing an important part in their style of music. Derrick May, whose Rhythm Is Rhythm project is arguably his best known, argues: 'They've set a standard in what they do. In America they've been able to please almost everyone, from a guy like me who's a hardcore dance addict, to the stadium crowds. They're right on time, right in sync, and they can't even help it. They have dance in their blood.' Kevin Saunderson of Inner City has claimed that 'Get The Balance Right' was the first ever house record – not bad for a song which the band weren't happy with at the time. 'I used to play Depeche Mode as a DJ,' reveals Saunderson, 'before I even knew the name of the group – their music was very hot at that time, records like "Strangelove". We were influenced a lot by their sound. It's real progressive dance and had this feeling that was so European: it was clean and you could dance to it.'

Juan Atkins of Cybotron and Model 500 has declared, 'I liked Depeche Mode. "Get The Balance Right" was a great dance record and was influential amongst musicians in Detroit. They were part of that wave of European music which was played by an early '80s radio station, W-LBS.'

Another Detroit techno hero Carl Craig, whose *Landcruising* LP is a fine example of the genre's clean, cityscape sound and pulsey sense of movement: 'I remember hearing "Lie To Me" for the first time. It completely blew my mind. Together with bands like Yazoo and Visage, Depeche Mode had a major impact on a lot of the techno guys here.' Frankie Knuckles, DJ at the original Warehouse Club in Chicago, where the term 'house' was born, used to play 'Just Can't Get Enough'. The commercially infuential Todd Terry talks about them as his favourite dance group.

Dave Gahan, who prefers Marvin Gaye or Al Green to underground techno music, was somewhat incredulous when he heard all this praise at the end of the '80s: 'I don't think there have been many occasions in pop music when black music has been influenced by white, and that's something we're very flattered by but don't quite understand, because our music is as white as it comes, very European

and not made for dancing.' John Foxx whose debut solo LP,
Metamatic, is a cult classic in techno circles, muses on this bizarre
twist of pop culture: 'It's interesting, no one could have predicted that
synthesizer pop would become part of black music. In retrospect, it
doesn't surprise me in some ways because I always saw it as white
urban blues. I think the American black audience picked up on it,
because they were all trying to kick out American sounds. This music
was very European and alien to them and it struck a chord.'

Like Dave Gahan, the recently rehabilitated Gary Numan is flattered but puzzled by the connection between electronic pop and
techno's minimal, repetitive rules: 'These people seem to have taken
the purely electronic, futuristic aspects of my albums and then used
them as a very small part of their overall style and approach.' Daniel
Miller believes the link is a shared forward-looking 'technological
sound', echoing Atkins' definition of techno as 'an attitude towards
making music'.

Gore: 'I think it's a testament to the diversity in our music over the
years, that we are cited as influential by techno people, by house
people, and by industrial people. We had a lot of different elements
in our music. I think the most important thing for the techno and
house people was the way we made music. The fact we were an electronic band and one of the earlier ones.' However, the songwriter
also points out: 'Half of every album is made up of atmospheric
ballads. We've been labelled a dance band throughout our career, and
I find that funny, because I would like to see somebody dance to half
of our records – you can't do it. I like to dance and I enjoy dance
music; we always try to use interesting people to do remixes of
singles but to me it's not the most important thing.'

Despite their slightly bemused attitude towards techno, the band
did agree to *The Face*'s feature idea and they were interviewed with
Derrick May in Detroit. 'We were badgered into it,' grimaces Alan
Wilder. 'The remit was, You lads fly over to Detroit and meet Derrick
May, pretend you're old buddies and talk about techno. Our press
guy said "Yes, OK, that's an angle." So I was like, "Who is Derrick
May?" I didn't want to go halfway across the world to pretend to be
buddies with this bloke but that's exactly what we did. We all went to
May's flat and pretended we were part of this scene. Derrick May was
horrible, I hated him. He was the most arrogant fucker I've ever met.

He took us into his backroom where he had a studio and played us this track and it was fucking horrible.'

Nevertheless, Detroit's stylish, non-alcoholic club life was a revelation to the band. 'When we actually went to Detroit back in 1990, Derrick May took us to the Music Institute [a legendary, now defunct techno club],' said Fletcher of the experience. 'We walked in and it was completely black people. But they were the most beautiful people we'd ever seen.' Gore interjected: 'They all looked like film stars.'

Fletcher: 'Well dressed, handsome men and beautiful women. There were no drugs at all, not even alcohol. And they all wanted our autographs ... But downtown Detroit was desolate. Absolutely empty. Empty houses, massive houses and big avenues. Everyone has fled the city, to the suburbs ... Being in Detroit was one of the most amazing memories about being in Depeche Mode. Suddenly you feel you hit an almost alien social group, that you'd never expect to like our records.'

For most of 1989, these freshly heralded 'dance pioneers' kept a low profile as they toiled on a new album, *Violator*. They asked Dave Bascombe if he was available to work on the record but he was in the middle of recording the Tears For Fears album, *Sowing the Seeds of Love* and so they had to look elsewhere. Daniel Miller suggested Mark 'Flood' Ellis, who had been working with Mute acts as an engineer and producer since the early '80s. His credits included Nick Cave, Cabaret Voltaire, Soft Cell and Renegade Soundwave but his only previous association with Depeche Mode was a 12" mix of 'Stripped' three years previously. 'I was a young whipper-snapper and they were at the top of the pile,' laughs Flood. 'I was a big fan. In fact when I first got the call from Daniel Miller about working with a Mute band, the first thing I thought was, he wants me to work with Depeche Mode! But it turned out to be Nick Cave.'

Wilder describes Flood as a 'normal, trainspottery sort of bloke', who was very skilled at operating all the studio equipment and creating cool sounds on their synthesizers. 'This scruffy, bespectacled, rather unlikely looking bloke rolled up,' grins Wilder, 'raided the fridge a couple of times, slouched down on the sofa, pontificated for a bit and thus – a new production team was born.' The pair forged a very successful, complementary working relationship, with Flood able to provide the technical know-how, while the band's best musician worked on the arrangements and song textures. 'That's how we made the group work at that time,' clarifies Wilder, 'by accepting that we all had different roles and not actually all trying to do the same thing. So we ended up with this unwritten agreement in the band, where we'd all throw together a few ideas at the beginning of a track. Then Fletch and Mart would go away, and they'd come back after we'd worked on it for a while to give an opinion.'

Miller has observed this method of working for years, noting the personal dynamics between the group members in the studio. 'They all have different takes on how things are going at any one point. Martin will go, "It's OK, I suppose", Dave and Fletch tend to be a bit more distanced from the process but when they come in they'll make a much stronger point – usually, "I'm really worried, it's not going very well." Fletch in particular is like that. He's Mr Man In The Street. Dave's quite good at vibing people up, especially in later years, even though privately he might say, I'm really worried about it. Of all of them Dave spends the least time in the studio.'

After the rigid, limiting effects of handing over almost-finished demos for *Music For the Masses*, Gore kept them less complete this time around. Several of the basic recordings consisted of vocals over a simple guitar or organ part, with the odd percussion loop but definitely less sequenced material this time around. Daniel Miller heard these rough sketches at Gore's flat in Maida Vale, west London and was immediately excited by the quality of the new material. As a further change of tack, the band also decided to cut down on the amount of pre-production – to keep things fresh before they went into the studio and stop certain band members from becoming more bored than was absolutely necessary. They spent three weeks with Flood in Mute's WorldWide programming room and then flew to Milan for the new sessions in Logic studios.

'Milan was a vibey start,' recalls Flood, whose credits include engineering U2's *Joshua Tree*. 'Martin and Dave were there most of the time. Everybody was feeling each other out, because they wanted to try working in a different way. I think we spent six weeks there. The idea was to work hard and party hard, and we all enjoyed ourselves to the full. We didn't do a substantial amount of work, except for the song "Personal Jesus", but it was absolutely crucial in setting the tone for the album.' Fletcher: 'It cemented the spirit of the whole album. He also remembered Flood instigating different methods of working, including some new elements of live performance. 'Once in the studio with Flood (who co-produced the album) we jammed, I suppose. Instead of just perfecting songs, we worked on an overall sound, and this suits us because we're still not strictly technical, we'd still like to remember being 15 and inspired by punk. We could never be Emerson, Lake and Palmer.'

The bluesy, rootsy strut of 'Personal Jesus' emerged fully formed from the sessions with the main, stompy beat originating from a recording of two or three people jumping up and down on flight cases. Various guitar-based components of other songs were also laid-down in Milan. The band had a strong aversion to conventional rock-guitar playing but on *Violator* they were happy to run Gore's guitar parts through synthesizers and studio devices to bend them into something that sounded like high frequency radio waves or a chugging, metallic riff which retained the original thrust and power of the instrument.

Gore's sparse demos allowed the band to take creative liberties with the songs. 'Enjoy The Silence' started out as a slow ballad but at Wilder's suggestion became a pulsing, up-tempo track, perhaps unconsciously born out of the band's frantic, Ecstasy-fuelled Milan clublife. 'There were no hard and fast rules – sometimes the songs drastically changed from the demo and sometimes they were pretty similar,' reveals Wilder. 'Martin didn't like to explain his songs to anyone and knowing that, the other group members would rarely ask him what they were about. It's clear to me that he enjoys the ambiguity of his words and the subversive quality of some of them (with their possible dark meanings) is probably what makes them interesting. It is also probably right to say that from *Violator* onwards, the final music bore less resemblance to the original demos than ever before.'

Meanwhile, Gahan was his usual full-on, energetic self during their time in Milan but in private moments he admitted he was having problems with his marriage and had taken to phoning up the band's American publicist Teresa Conway for female advice. The singer was often drunk when he rang up, pouring out his heart in conversations which would sometimes last for hours. It was hard for him because the other band members were in stable relationships. Although Gore and Christina had split up after living together in Berlin, then London for two years, he'd met a Texan girl, Suzanne Voisvert, in Paris. The couple are still together.

After Milan's 'vibey' mix of experimentation and city nightlife, the band knuckled down at Puk in Denmark, where most of *Violator* was recorded. Wilder and Flood toiled for weeks, trying to texture the electronics to give them a human rather than mechanical feeling. The organic, 'live' elements had definitely added a new feel to the music but the art was to make the join between man and machine invisible, so that you couldn't detect where one started and the other finished. 'I found myself sitting in a field in northern Denmark where all you could do there was work,' remembers Flood. 'That was a very creative session, although Fletch was going through a difficult period in his life and he had to leave to sort himself out.'

In the middle of the decade, Andy Fletcher had lost a sister when she was only in her early twenties. Karen had died from stomach cancer, leaving behind a child and a husband. Four years later the nervy, emotional Fletch slipped into a depression which he now believes was rooted in his grief over Karen's death. 'Andy's anxiety problems really started to surface very seriously in this period,' confirms Wilder. 'He would come into the studio and say, "Oh, I feel really bad"', and he'd have this very long face. So you'd go, "What's up Fletch?" And he'd say, "Oh, I don't feel right and I've got this lump." He started to imagine he had these weird, horrible illnesses. Some days Fletch wouldn't appear at all and Mart would say, "Oh, you know Fletch is really bad today."'

During the band's stay in Puk they were living in two residential cottages. Gahan, Wilder and Daryl Balmonte shared one, while Gore, Fletcher and Flood stayed in the other. Wilder remembers hearing from Flood and Gore that their live-in mate was moping around the cottage all day. Eventually it got so bad that everyone suggested he should fly back to London and get some professional help. According to Wilder, 'He saw a specialist psychiatrist but nothing really changed for a long time. He went to various doctors and got different tranquillizer prescriptions and so on. He also went to stay at a place called the Priory but he didn't really seem to improve. He certainly changed because the drugs he was taking made him manic. I don't know what they put in that stuff but he was very speedy, so he'd be talking a mile a minute. You could tell it wasn't his normal self. I don't think he really got any better for several years. He seemed to go up and down, and he was regularly checking himself in and out of the Priory until I left the group in 1995.'

Although Wilder was sympathetic about his colleague's problems, he was often impatient with Fletcher in the studio environment where he felt the latter had a very minor role – to keep Gore company: 'Fletch wasn't really involved in making the records. He was there or thereabouts but he wasn't actively involved. He's not a musician, he doesn't have much of a musical angle on things at all. He may have been at various recording sessions so that Martin had someone to go out with in the evening after the session. Studios can be incredibly claustrophobic places – even more so for those who perhaps don't play a big part in the nuts and bolts of the process. Boredom is an especially powerful and destructive force. For example, one of the most annoying things is if I'm working on a complicated sample (which I want to cut into many pieces and reconfigure into something new) the process is inevitably complex and until the procedure is complete, things will usually sound chaotic and meaningless to anyone listening in. If someone who doesn't fully understand this procedure interjects at an unfinished stage and makes negative comments like, "Oh, that doesn't sound right", it can be really irritating.'

As Wilder took greater responsibility in the studio, the last thing he wanted was for a non-musician to unwittingly distract everyone's attention by becoming the butt of the others' jokes, talking at a break-neck speed, complaining about his illnesses or criticizing what Wilder was doing. 'I don't think Fletch had enough confidence in himself to make judgements on the music but when he did, we didn't pay much attention to them,' is Wilder's rather hardline reading of the situation, although he concedes: 'To be fair, he understood his role wasn't really a musical one.'

The pair's inability to communicate on the same wavelength would become a growing problem over the next few years and throws some light on the power base of the band. Although Depeche Mode work democratically in their decision-making, Martin Gore is the backbone of the group because he writes all the songs. Gore's relationship with Fletcher is crucial to the chemistry in the band, because his friend acts as foil for him in his relationship with Gahan and, at this point, Wilder. It diffuses the pressure of responsibility and allows Gore to avoid direct confrontation, which would be inevitable if he was in a duo with Gahan.

Flood is sympathetic to both Wilder and Fletch's views, recognizing that they're 'very different people'. He argues that the band did listen to Fletcher's thoughts on the music but, ' ... sometimes he said the right thing at the wrong time, and on other occasions the manner in which he expressed himself would wind certain people up – but I took note. I interpreted his opinion as the view of the ordinary person. Good or bad, Fletch's views were certainly black or white. But it was difficult for Alan. He was bothered by things Fletch said about music because I think he found it difficult to take advice from someone who isn't particularly musical.'

Daniel Miller also noted how the pair were incompatible in the studio, observing a growing gap between them which would become irreconcilable: 'Alan didn't really understand Fletch's role, and if he did understand it, he didn't acknowledge it. He was like, "Well, Fletch isn't contributing to the music, he's hanging around the studio playing pool or football and distracting Martin." That was his attitude and view of it. He was happy for them to do what they did and then not be around, which may well have been a practical approach to take but it didn't do much for band solidarity.'

Gore's take on Wilder's uncompromising views was to dub him 'a control freak'. The songwriter's view was that as the band's musician Wilder was there to be directed and manipulated, and that although it was healthy to encourage him to come up with his own ideas, the keyboard player certainly wasn't the man in charge. 'Alan tended to really focus on the production and it's something that really didn't interest me as much,' Gore says casually. 'Obviously I cared about what was going on and what the end result was; if I liked what he was doing then I would let him get on with it and if it came to a point where I really didn't like something then I would say, "I don't think that works, maybe try something else," which is like you're sort of a background producer.'

At any rate, Fletcher's disappearance at this stage of the recording didn't affect the record. The songs were some of the best of Gore's career; the initial Milan sessions had thrown up a fresh musical direction of mixing new organic sounds into the electronics, and Flood was making a more dynamic contribution to the band after the likeable but laid-back Dave Bascombe. Wilder: 'The Puk period was much more prolific and although some tracks like "Clean" and "Policy Of Truth" went through many guises before the final versions were settled upon, we had the most productive and enjoyable time. There was a song called "Mother Me" which we also recorded during this period but never finished, and for a long time "Happiest Girl" was going to be on the LP.'

In August 1989 they relocated to The Church in Crouch End, north London, where new band associate Steve Lyon helped out with the engineering. 'When I was first offered the session I said no,' recalls Lyon, 'because at the time it wasn't my sort of music at all. I still had an image of them as a teeny-bop band at school although I knew that I liked certain stuff off *Music For the Masses*. They called me back and said, "Just come in and do it for a week," because Dave was doing his vocals.' This latest studio combination hit it off very quickly, with Lyon completely reversing his opinion after hearing a mix of 'Personal Jesus' by Francois Kevorkian, whose credits included classic remixes of Kraftwerk's 'Radioactivity' and 'Tour De France'. 'I heard "Personal Jesus" on my first or second day in the studio and I realized this was something special. There was a great atmosphere in the studio, very vibed up, we knew we working on really good material.'

Francois Kevorkian helped out with the mixing of the album but it was a slow process. After a month's work, the irritable perfectionist had only finished four songs. Worse, the band were only happy with one of his mixes. 'The problem was he was making everything very electronic,' explains Flood, 'and giving it a disco style which worked for one track but not for the others. So from then on the band asked me to go into the studio for an hour or two every day to check how things were going and make suggestions. Basically I was trying to complement the supreme electronic craft that he was putting in with a dirtier, edgier approach.'

Lyon comments: 'Kervorkian was quite a twitchy character, I remember him totally destroying the tape operator one time. He had mountains of equipment and definitely shaped the clean-sounding side of *Violator*.'

A quick glance at the credits reveals that the album's mix is credited to Kevorkian, with the exception of 'Enjoy The Silence' which Daniel Miller vetoed. 'He made us recreate the way it was on the rough mix,' says Flood, who worked with the Mute boss on the final version of the track.

On 29 August 1989 'Personal Jesus' was released as a single, charting at No.13 in the UK. The band were more than a little relieved as initially they'd been convinced it was destined to be a complete commercial flop. It's actually one of the best songs of their career, built around a bluesy, glam-rock stomp which had a subliminal effect on most people, because, as Gore says, 'people still think of us as a synthesizer band'.

For once Gore reluctantly agreed to talk about the lyric, which was inspired by Priscilla Presley's portrait of her ex-husband in the book, *Elvis and Me*. Gore: 'It's a song about being a Jesus for somebody else, someone to give you hope and care. It's about how Elvis was her man and her mentor and how often that happens in love relationships – how everybody's heart is like a god in some way, and that's not a very balanced view of someone, is it?'

The song took six months to reach the Top 40 in America, eventually selling over one million copies and becoming the biggest selling 12" single in Warner Brothers history. There were U.S. record company executives who were nervous the song would be blacklisted as blasphemous but bizarrely some radio stations interpreted it as 'a religious tribute'. Gore laughs at this: 'It seems you can get away with anything if you've got nice pop tunes.' There was also a beautifully executed sexual subtext to Anton Corbijn's spaghetti western-styled video, as the band arrive at a desert bordello and disappear with various different women. 'Dave has said I have a twisted sexual mind,' laughs Corbijn, 'but all I say is it takes one to know one. I am Dutch, so it's not so surprising.' Daniel Miller, not an American censor, insisted on the removal of a section of film featuring a horse's backside because it coincided with Gore's 'o-ooh ooh' backing vocal and could be interpreted as bestial innuendo. MTV America loved the promo and played 'Personal Jesus' on heavy rotation.

By now Corbijn's creative relationship with the band had blossomed to a point where they let him have complete freedom with his ideas. As the frontman and therefore the band's visual focal point,

Gahan in particular was grateful for Corbijn's input: 'I hate to think where we would have ended up without him. Chicken-in-the-basket by now! New Romantic Night at the London Palladium! God, no, please. He gave us credibility, that's the bottom line. I'd rather be misunderstood than understood, and with him you can do that, you can escape into his photos and videos. He gave our music a filmic look, big landscapes, panoramic, really uplifting.' Chris Carr comments, 'Dave needed an image and identity. He kind of fell in love with Anton who saw a gap and went for it. Dave was very much in the hot seat at that time and they all went with him.'

Flush with the success of 'Personal Jesus', the band finished off *Violator* for release in March 1990, six weeks after a second single, 'Enjoy The Silence'. This became the band's first Top 10 hit in Britain for six years when it reached No.6 in February, and it also gave Depeche Mode their first American Top 10 single. It was also voted Best British Single of the Year by Radio 1's listeners at the 1991 Brit Awards. Propelled by a New Order-ish guitar line and a flowing dance rhythm, the song's sense of motion echoes the effects of some techno travelogues. It's feel is very electronic, even Kraftwerk-like, and yet there are organic elements to the recording which would have horrified the synth purists.

Anton Corbijn completed a seamless package with his most famous promo video for the band. He came up with the idea of portraying Dave Gahan as a king walking across silent, deserted landscapes, carrying a deckchair. According to the Dutchman, ' ... the idea was simple – you could have peace anywhere without money – but the band just couldn't see it. Eventually, Depeche said, "Go ahead, make it." We shot it at Balmoral in Scotland, Portugal and the Swiss Alps. I wanted snow but it was so warm that year we rented a small helicopter to get to the top of a mountain, 3,000 metres high.' Gahan: 'It was freezing up there. I thought, I'm not dressing up in this silly outfit, I'm going to look a real prat here. One shot I finally refused. The robe weighed a ton, snow up to here, carrying this fucking deckchair, the crown was freezing, I said to producer Richard Bell, You fucking do it! So in one of those long shots it isn't actually me. I hated the idea. I was like, Anton, I want people to take it seriously!' Corbijn was absolutely right in the end. 'It was the most successful video they ever had,' grins Corbijn.

In March 1990 the band turned up at the Wherehouse record
store, La Cienega Boulevard, Los Angeles for a signing to launch
their new album. Some 5,000 fans had camped outside the store for
four days, creating a queue which extended for two miles. By the
time Depeche Mode showed up at nine o'clock, there were 17,000
hysterical fans outside, some climbing trees, others invading the
Beverly Centre opposite in order to get a better view. The Los
Angeles Police Department closed down the event after 90 minutes
because they felt the band's lives were in danger. A staggering 200
police units, including helicopters and mounted officers in full riot
gear, tried to calm the fans down as the police moved the band out
of their hotel under escort. The Police Chief reportedly commented,
'This is our biggest police operation since the Presidential visit.'
Fortunately only seven people were hurt in the scuffles.

Violator was released on 19 March 1990, missing the top slot by
only one place in Britain – at that point, their highest chart position
in this country. Gore has claimed that the heavy metal-ish title was
supposed to be a joke but most people just assumed Depeche Mode
were trying to be 'pervy' and 'weird' again. *Sounds*' Damon Wise
criticized the album for its one-dimensional take on the dark side of
life: 'If William Burroughs wrote for Gahan, Depeche Mode would be
terrifying. But he doesn't. Martin Gore writes for Gahan and
Depeche Mode are hilarious. The charm of their doggedly glib plati-
tudes is wearing thin.' He concluded, 'Their guile has saved them this
time, but Depeche Mode aren't 19 any more. Their technology
supports them, but they need to progress. More to the point, they
need to read. Their lyrical naïvety may seem endearing in its childlike
artlessness, but when Gore plays up to darker obsessions the end
result is plain embarrassing. What a load of Ballards ... three-and-a-
half out of five.'

Wise's views are fairly typical of the British media's levelling
sarcasm towards music which is 'dark', 'arty' or 'theatrical', rather
than commonplace. This is commendable in many ways but rather
unfair in Depeche Mode's case – *Violator*'s intricate music more than
makes up for the occasional glitch in Gore's lyric-writing. It's a darkly
beautiful, cinematic album, ranging from the alluringly anthemic
'Sweetest Perfection' and 'Halo', to the menacing travelogue of
'World In My Eyes' and 'Clean's hysterical oppressiveness. As for

Gore's lyrics, they're brought to life on *Violator* by Gahan's rich, crooning vocals and the subtle atmospherics cast around them. Guilt, immorality, black magic, voyeurism, power and faith are all explored on *Violator*, not with the random, cerebral flair of Burroughs but as pop songs. It may be the stuff of adolescent self-aggrandisement and fantasy-making, but, as *Spin* magazine stated in 1990, 'Violator caught the American nation's mood of dread, doubt and uncertainty' with an immediacy which is now almost impossible in any other artform other than pop music.

Melody Maker's Paul Lester did at least recognize that, 'Violator, their seventh studio album, contains Depeche Mode's most arresting work to date. While their more dashing, radical peers have fallen prey to the vagaries of fashion and floundered on their own erratic brilliance (League, Heaven 17, Cabs et al), Depeche Mode have hardly succumbed to contemporary dictates, rarely innovating but always managing to coincide with current tastes. Surprisingly, they are presently judged by Detroit and Chicago's house cognoscenti as prime movers in the new dance culture ... "Policy Of Truth", one of the five potential singles on *Violator*, is based around a sadistic, cynical electro-riff and oozes with genuine danger. Best of all is "Halo", a dim-lit, menacing slug-funk dirge that achieves the impossible by being both grimly oppressive and gloriously uplifting.'

Francois Kevorkian's handling of the band's synthetic sounds and rhythms made *Violator* feel sufficiently dancey and electronic for critics such as Paul Lester to link it in with house styles. However, as Dave Gahan says, ' ... there's a lot more rootsy stuff on *Violator*. We've managed to marry a bluesy type of feeling to hard electronics; hard technology.'

Vox were even more positive, declaring that, 'From the opening chill of "World In My Eyes" to the relationship power games of "Personal Jesus" and "Enjoy The Silence", this is a stark, very sexy record.' Helen Mead of the *NME* was also impressed by the album's sparse, minimalist approach after the power chords of the previous album: 'You'd expect to hear a leap in musical logic between *Music For the Masses* and *Violator* but instead it seems almost a step back. In fact, it's cleaner, sparser, more clinical. Lyrically, they're still dealing with raw emotions ... big subjects that can be hard to capture in a three-minute pop song ... Then there's the kinky song – "Blue

Dress" – breaking you gently into the knowledge that fetishes make a man's world go round, not love – all in waltz time. Isn't that nice and proper? – 8/10.'

Gahan was sufficiently buoyed up by these up-beat, complementary reviews to remark, 'As far as people in England are concerned, we've always been part of the furniture. We've been out there niggling away, refusing to go away. But that's all changing now. Attitudes towards us have turned around, mainly because we've paid our dues. There's no longer a taboo attached to Depeche Mode.'

While Gahan publicly basked, in early 1990 Alan Wilder and Steve Lyon spent long days in Mute's studio, programming the music for the upcoming World Violation tour. They made it harder for themselves by incorporating some different arrangements and remixes into the set, but it was a vibey period during which Gahan, Fletcher and Gore 'popped in' nearly every day to see how things were going.

Behind the band's success, Dave Gahan was going through a traumatic time as his marriage to Joanne continued to unravel. The pair had been friends since they were teenagers but he confessed, 'That had deteriorated, mostly on my part ... you tug away until you lead separate lives. I decided the only way I was going to get a focus on my life was to crush everything down. I had to regain perspective on what I really wanted to do.' During the rehearsals for the World Violation tour he met up with Teresa Conway again, and realized he'd fallen in love with her: 'You look at yourself in the mirror one morning and suddenly everything's very, very different and the whole perspective has suddenly changed. Before I just wanted to get laid – I didn't want to be that person any more. Teresa brought out some emotions in me that I hadn't discovered, like love,' he said, rather cruelly. 'I think I was just denying my true feelings a lot of the time, having to lie my way through a lot of my life with people I was supposed to respect and love and care for. So I blew that completely.'

Understandably he was in a very intense, extreme state of mind as the band set off on their American leg of the World Violation tour, opening at Pensacola Civic Centre on 28 May. Like the other band members he felt on top of the world, flushed by renewed success in the UK (where the LP's third single, 'Policy Of Truth', had just reached No.16) and another step forward in America, where

Violator peaked at No.7. It went on to sell over six million world-wide, including double-platinum in the States. But his personal life was all over the place; a mix of infatuation for Conway and guilt at the way he'd walked away from his wife and son. 'I think he just felt that performing was the only thing he could do right,' says Fletcher. 'He was very emotional with all of us. I personally tended to steer clear of him.' Gahan: 'The Violation tour was really intense, I actually thought that was probably it. I was trying to flee from something, but it wasn't the band, and it took me a while to realize that. I have this chance to make lots of people feel really good, and I feel like if I really push ... it's a great feeling. Oh God, I'm starting to sound like Jesus!'

The 31 American dates were a triumph, with Gore enjoying the moment as he told the press, 'Here in the States, we've been working on it for years and years. I think in a way we've been at the forefront of new music, sort of chipping away at the standard rock-format radio stations. And I think with this record, we've finally managed to bulldoze our way through.' They'd become a glamorous, big-name act with the celebrity guest list at their New York show at Radio City on 18 June including Bono from U2, Eddie Murphy and Sylvester Stallone. Electronic, the supergroup formed by New Order's Bernard Sumner and ex-Smiths guitarist Johnny Marr supported them at the Dodgers Stadium, Los Angeles.

For New York's Giants Stadium 42,000 tickets were sold within four hours; Dallas's 24,000 Starplex Amphitheatre sold out instantly, as did the World Music Theater in Tinley Park, Chicago. Within one hour of going on sale, 48,000 tickets were gobbled up for their last scheduled night at the Dodgers' Stadium. This was two months in advance of the show and they decided to add another show which also sold out. Yet at the height of their artistic and commercial success, Dave Gahan was feeling uncertain about his future and Andy Fletcher was only a few months into an erratic, difficult recovery after a nervous breakdown.

Craig Schmidt of *Sounds* understood the band's genuine connection with the audience which was rooted in their own insecurities: 'The electronic existentialists' greatest asset is their ability to lend a melodramatic importance to a quiet suffering endured by much of this adolescent audience. Fractured families, indifferent parents and a general high anxiety for their futures is the driving force for much of the crowd's fanaticism.' This emotional connection was complemented by Anton Corbijn's evocative imagery, projected on massive screens behind the band. In contrast to the bombastic media-scan of U2's Zoo TV, Corbijn's visuals were more erotic, mysterious and almost tackily vulnerable. The *Guardian*'s Adam Sweeting picked up on this aspect of Depeche Mode's presentation when he reviewed the band's show at Wembley Arena a few months later: 'We see the group in shadow, whirling sparklers, or gape open-mouthed as little blond Martin Gore flutters past in an angel costume, peering doe-eyed into the camera.' Freelance journalist Spencer Bright was also 'impressed by the stage set, which included a series of pyramid arches which, by a trick of lighting, could look like apartment windows'.

The tour was also a dissipated, riotous party on a major scale, with Depeche Mode now able to travel by a 15-seater private plane for the internal flights, while their gear was shifted in 11 articulated lorries by a crew of nearly 100. This rock 'n' roll juggernaut, according to Daryl Balmonte, 'opened the door' to the bigger, more physically and mentally destructive Devotional tour in 1993/4. 'Dave summed it up later when he said that in 1990 everybody's life was changing. The difference between Violation and Devotional was the length – Violation stopped before people got into real trouble. Plus everyone was a little bit younger and fitter. It was very compact and it was the end of a more bonded era and the opening of a more fractured period. The hedonism had started in the early '80s but it picked up momentum with Violation which was on a plateau with the Devotional tour.'

Gahan admits that the Violation tour was the last time he had a great time on drugs – 'Ecstasy was the thing and you'd pop an E after every show.' The band and crew's consumption of the drug Ecstasy added to the feeling that this was one big party spinning around the world. 'They all love to have a good time,' says the analytical Chris Carr. 'Ecstasy was a big thing with the band. Martin used to have parties, both on and off tour, and he'd come over and say, "Are you on one?" I'd go, "No." "You're fucking boring, get on one. Go and see such and such, he's got 'em." That is the most aggressive and demonstrative side of Martin but purely so that you were having as mental a time as he is. Fletch would indulge heavily but he would feel the guilt. That's where the band's conscience would usually come from. Martin is ... if it's out there and he wants to see what it's like, he'll try it. He's not a dilettante, he's a liver and his liver puts up with a lot! He's not an addict like Dave, who goes out there and does these thing and knows by doing it he's going to be punished. Martin's not like that because he has this innocent attitude so that things are done for pure experience and fun. It would be interesting to be his wife or girlfriend because he's such a loving person but there's a side of him which is too open.'

'Martin gets very loved up when he's off his trolley and he'll commandeer complete strangers and give them his life story,' recalls Wilder. 'But, unlike Dave, he has been excessive without leaving a trail of destruction. Maybe Dave needs to cause problems to humble himself a bit, whereas Martin keeps quiet and a lot of stuff never comes out. To be honest I think alcohol has had more of an influence than anything else over the years but there was a lot of drug-taking in the *Violator* period – Ecstasy, cocaine, everything except for heroin. Then Dave started taking heroin on that tour. I think it comes down to that personality thing where he always had to push things to the ultimate extreme.' Daniel Miller recalls, 'I knew they were doing a lot of Ecstasy and cocaine on that tour but I didn't hear that Dave was dabbling with heroin until later.'

Gahan: 'I've been drinking and using drugs for a long time, probably since I was about 12 years old. Popping a couple of my mum's phenobarbitones every now and then. Hash. Amphetamines. Coke came along. Alcohol was always there, hand in hand with drugs. Then all of a sudden I discovered heroin, and I'd be lying if I said it didn't make me feel, well ... like I've never felt before. I felt like I really belonged. I just felt nothing was gonna hurt me. I was invincible. That was the euphoria. But the euphoria was very short-lived.'

In Teresa Conway, Gahan found a 'companion in doing everything it took to be a rock 'n' roll star – I wanted to lead that very selfish lifestyle without being judged. Teresa was joining in. I'd actually played around with it back in Basildon. From the moment I first injected I wanted to feel like that all the time and ... you can't.'

The American dates ended at the Dodgers Stadium, LA on 5 August, and three weeks later they played their first Australian show in Sydney's Horden Pavillion. A second night in Melbourne was cancelled when Gahan badly strained his vocal chords during the previous performance, the first time they'd ever cancelled a concert due to health reasons. This was followed by six dates in Japan, and then their European and British tour which stretched from 28 September (the week that their latest single 'World In My Eyes' gave them another Top 20 hit in the UK) to 27 November 1990. They decided to cut the Eastern Bloc countries out of their itinerary this time around to keep down the expense and there were no gigs in Hong Kong or Singapore. In total World Violation was a marginally less demanding 75 dates, as opposed to the 100 they played on *Music For the Masses*. They'd played to over 1.2 million people around the world.

Lead Me Through Babylon, 1991–3

In 1991 the only song released by Depeche Mode was a ballad, 'Death's Door', for the soundtrack of the Wim Wenders film, *Until the End of the World*. The various band members spent most of the year apart from each other, starting families and indulging in their own projects. Both Martin Gore and Andy Fletcher had their first kids within two months of each other. The first to arrive was Suzanne and Martin's Viva Lee Gore on 6 June, followed by Grainne and Andy's Megan Fletcher on 25 August. For Gore this year was a chance to recharge the creative batteries: 'I put everything on hold as I was completely burnt out and empty. I didn't have a single idea in me. I also spent some time wondering if I should do a solo album, but then my girlfriend got pregnant and I went straight back into the eager father mode. In the end it was my little daughter that gave me the inspiration back. You see a life being born and growing, it's just wonderful, it moves you.'

Always a generous host, he also held a few parties in his Hertfordshire home. Chris Carr: 'Fletch and Martin have a group of friends that they stick with. They know they've gone above and beyond them on a financial level but when it comes down to it, it's like things have never changed.' The most celebrated of these gatherings was his 30th birthday on 23 July. He formed a glam-rock group The Sexist Boys, especially for the event, starring Wayne Hussey from The Mission. 'I first met Martin Gore when The Mission and Depeche Mode were playing the San Remo festival in Italy,' notes Hussey from his home in Los Angeles. 'There were lots of bands there and everyone was having a good time. The Alarm were playing some blues with Curiosity Killed The Cat and Sinead O'Connor was at the party. The Mission did this glam-rock tribute thing, The Metal Gurus, and Martin remembered this when it was his 30th birthday. He phoned me up and said he wanted us to play at his party. So we did it in a marquee in his back garden. We all dressed up and he played guitar, doing these very dodgy glam-rock covers – 'Twentieth Century Boy' by T-Rex, some Abba and Gary Glitter. Martin is a big glam-rock fan and for his wedding present I got him a signed photo of Gary Glitter. What do you get for the man who has everything?'

Hussey was impressed by Gore's knowledge of music and checked out the songwriter's 'fantastic '50s jukebox in his Maida Vale flat'. According to The Mission singer, the Depeche Mode man has it ' ... stacked with old seven-inch singles. His record collection is enormous. That's the common ground we had – we're roughly the same generation and into a lot of the same sort of music. He's a big fan of the blues and Led Zeppelin, and that's come through the last few albums from *Violator* onwards. He's become a good guitar player, certainly more than adequate for what he has to do in Depeche Mode.'

'I'm not passionate about anything other than music,' asserts Gore, who over the last few years has added Kurt Weill, Leonard Cohen (Gore contributed to the Cohen tribute LP *Tower of Song*: *The Songs of Leonard Cohen*), Velvet Underground and Neil Young records to his Sparks collection. 'I bore my friends to death with music! I often invite friends to come and stay with me, and I get drunk and I play them every one of my favourite records. At the end of the night, everybody is crawling to bed, and I'm still left saying, "But you have to listen to this one!"' The music fanatic's infectious enthusiam even turned his girlfriend from someone who "wasn't particularly interested in music", into a budding musician.

Meanwhile Andrew Fletcher opened up a restaurant, Gascogne's in St John's Wood, London. Now he could pour over the books of a slightly more manageable operation – that was if he wasn't hanging out with his girlfriend and baby, which, understandably, was most of the time. As for Alan Wilder, he kept himself extremely busy by following up his two previous Recoil releases (a collection of solo demos *1+ 2* in 1986 and 1988's *Hydrology*) with a new Recoil album, *Bloodline*. Described by Nitzer Ebb's Douglas McCarthy as 'Depeche Mode with different singers', the project featured an impressive list of front-people – Moby, Curve's Toni Halliday and McCarthy, who sang the standout track, a cover of the Alex Harvey Band song 'Faith Healer'. Wilder also co-produced with Flood the next Nitzer LP, *Ebbhead*. In August 1991 he married his long-term girlfriend Jeri and he invested in a Sussex country mansion, which Wilder started to fill with art deco objects from the 1920s–50s, such as fridges, hoovers, light-fittings and telephones.

After Christmas 1991 Gore called up Gahan in Los Angeles where the singer was now living with Teresa Conway, and said he had another set of demos ready to start work on. Gahan's first thought was to tell him to find another singer but he waited for the demos before he made up his mind. 'Unless we pushed it a lot further there was no point going on,' Gahan claimed. The first track he heard was the bluesy 'Condemnation'. 'It was a total relief! I couldn't believe it. Then 'I Feel You' came on: that was the moment when I looked into the mirror, grabbed a broomstick and started miming air guitar.' It was this trade-off between Gahan taking things back to his own adolescent fantasies of what being a rock star should be all about, and Gore's bluesier, more traditional-sounding demos that formed the basis of their next album, *Songs of Faith and Devotion*.

By this time the singer was a very changed man from the character on the *Violator* tour. Over the last few years he'd fallen out of love with England, where he was the only band member to be hassled by fans. 'I'd be chasing them down the road with my dog because they'd be singing our songs outside my house at two in the morning.' After his break-up with Joanne he'd bought a riverside studio flat in London's Docklands but he hardly spent any time there. 'I just packed a suitcase and split,' he says. 'Teresa and I went off and rented a place in Los Angeles. My year was really spent doing a lot of soul-searching and trying to find out what had gone wrong in my life, and thinking, to be quite honest, about whether I wanted to come back and do the whole thing – records, tours, fame, Depeche Mode, again. Just tearing myself away from everything that I had really grown up with and known, including my wife at the time, and my young son, Jack as well ... all that stuff was quite painful to me.'

His relationship with Teresa Conway fuelled a lot of these changes: 'I was besotted, blinded. I was in lust. I cut off everyone who

had ever been involved with my life up to that point. I started anew.'
They weren't exactly a good influence on each other. Gahan
described his girlfriend as 'a partner I could play with, in all sorts of
ways without being judged', which is fine except they were rapidly
heading down a slippery slope: 'We made a pact early on that I'd
never use intravenously,' revealed Gahan a few years later. 'But of
course, being a junkie and a liar, it didn't take long.'

Within months of living together both were physically transformed. Gahan's drug-intake thinned him to skin and bone mapped
with tattoos, which he bragged were from some 'truly brutal
parlours'. 'They're my warpaint, man,' he swaggered. 'They all mark
a time and a place.' In one interview he pointed at an elaborately
drawn Celtic dagger on his left arm: 'This one here I had done when
I was using dope really heavily. I kind of meant it to mean I might as
well be stabbing myself, kind of thing.' He also had the letters
'TCTTM-FG' engraved in Indian ink beneath a caged heart on his
arm. 'That was done for my second wife. It means Teresa Conway
To The Motherfucker Gahan, 'cos I'm the fucker who married her.'
He also showed off his winged tattoo: 'It's something that used to be
put on the gates of big houses to ward off evil spirits – that took about
ten hours to do. Apparently, my father – I didn't know this at the time
because he left when I was six months old – was covered in tattoos
as well, so I think it must be something that's in my genes.'

Teresa's taste in long-haired men encouraged him to grow it and
he completed the change into a psuedo-Californian travesty by growing himself a goatee, listening to 'boogie-woogie music' and trying to
learn the harmonica. His partner had also changed, from a vivacious
blonde into a 'thin-cheeked, brunette vamp'. Wilder: 'Their relationship was always apart from us, out in LA, so we didn't see much of
it, but we could observe the effect of it. Teresa changed a lot. She
used to be bright, bouncy, blonde hair, quite full in the face – a nice
Los Angeles girl. Within 18 months she'd turned into this thin, gaunt,
wasted creature in black clothes.'

In April 1992, a month before his 30th birthday, Gahan married
Teresa at the Graceland Wedding Chapel in Las Vegas. The cere-
mony was witnessed by a porky but unconvincing Vegas-period Elvis
lookalike supplied by the chapel. 'My name's up on the wall now next
to Jon Bon Jovi's, in big lights outside,' said an intoxicated Gahan in

1993. 'Of course, everything was plastic, you know, false. They wouldn't even light the candles in the chapel because they were just there for show. We were a little upset!'

The singer wore a dark see-through shirt that exhibited his new tattoos, a hippie OM symbol representing 'every sound of the universe' above his right nipple, to complement the one Teresa already had on her chest. He also had a phoenix stitched into his back, symbolizing his spiritual rebirth.

Rather than just doing one song, the fake Elvis ended up singing a half-hour set, testing Gahan's patience until in the end he said, 'Will someone get him the fuck out of here?' He continues, 'I wanted to get married. And so Teresa's mum, Diane, sort of politely said, "Um, excuse me, Mr Elvis, do you think you could stop now, 'cos I think they want to get married." And so he says, "Well, I've just got one more song darlin'." And he leans over to me and asks, "Have I offended you in some way?" And I say, "No, just carry on with it, mate, get it done and get out!"'

The emotional turbulence of this period was further stoked by the news in late 1991 that Gahan's real father had died. 'In the space of six months everything just piled on top of me,' he later confessed. 'I still think about my dad from time to time. I reckon I could have learnt a lot about myself from him. Somebody told me he used to keep a scrapbook and stuff. He was pretty old though. And I never had any contact with him from a very young age.'

While he was intense about his feelings for Teresa Conway, he wasn't able to shut off his guilt about the way he'd treated his first wife, Joanne. 'I hope that Joanne falls in love and she can be as happy in that area of her life as I am, because then she'll know and understand why I had to do it. It was for very selfish reasons. I have a son as well. It's a heartache. I want to influence him, but I'm not there, so get real, you know? I don't want him to grow up with the same feelings I had when my stepfather died, wondering what was going on. I want Jack to know he has a father.'

Gahan flew over from Los Angeles every three months to see Jack, staying at his flat in Wapping with Daryl Balmonte. The singer would be up one moment, consumed with guilt the next. He was also loaded for most of the time but a year into his heroin addiction, the drugs weren't taking him to the same highs any more. The singer was fighting to feel life at a heightened state. Gahan would twist from intense, almost hysterical and desperate emotions expressed over his family and in his love for Teresa, to narcotic withdrawal and creeping paranoia. Both extremes took him away from a balanced, normal life. The wealth that had come with the success of *Violator* and the last couple of world tours afforded him the luxury of not having to deal with day-to-day chores if he didn't want to: 'Now I've got enough space to really get into music, not thinking about that kind of stuff, like, "Aah, I wonder if I can, like, buy a car or something." What would I want to think about shit like that any more for?'

In stark contrast to Gore and Fletcher who'd kept a firm grasp on their local roots, Gahan shivered in horror at the prospect of visiting Basildon: 'Scary, but yes, I've been back a few times,' he said in 1993. 'In the last six years I've been back about three times. I get my mum to come to London. I'm like, "Mum, bring the flat round with you." I just feel like I'm going to get arrested in Basildon or something. I walk out at the station and I'm like, "I want to go back, I want to go back." I really do, it's fucking horrible. I walk past the taxi rank where I've been beaten up so many times or had a fight. The cab rank after the Mecca. Fucking hell, Basildon. It's scary because you go back there and it's exactly the same, it's just a different generation. Very scary.'

Gahan was absorbed in testing and pushing himself, aggressively hyping up his feelings and then dosing them down into a medicated numbness when he wanted to feel loaded. In 1991 he declared, 'For me at the moment, "average" is no good, "okay" is no good, or "we'll get away with it". I want brilliance out of life, I want the best: passion, sex, love. I want to feel moved by things.'

Carr: 'Dave is a creature of extremes. He won't just go down the middle.'

For two years he was bounced between intoxicated recluse and a party fiend who later bragged, 'I spend a lot of time with my friends. It's something I'd forgotten how to do, I think I sort of really isolated myself, not even intentionally, but ... over the years I had. Now I've made lots of really, really good friends, good people. Mostly women, I may point out as well. Totally cool, especially when they're all really good looking as well.' The scrawny frontman was set on living up to the rock 'n' roll myth: 'I'm in it right up to my fucking neck, and I'm going to remain in it.' Timed with Gahan's self-mythologizing was the new grunge music scene in America, especially in the west, which encouraged him to pursue his goals even more vehemently. 'I was able to go out pretty unnoticed and see bands like I used to when I was 15, 16 years old,' he says of his time in LA. 'I really enjoyed that. When I saw Jane's Addiction's last show at Irvine Meadows (an arena south of LA), I was like, "I can fucking do that, I can do that." I was fucked if I was just gonna go back and just sit around in the corner of a room and mope around about my life when I've got so much I wanna do with it.'

Gahan's transition clearly echoed the conversation he'd had with Chris Carr on the *Music For the Masses* tour: 'I actually consciously thought, "There's no fucking rock stars out there any more,"' he disclosed in 1993. 'There's nobody willing to go the whole way to do this so what's needed? What's missing here? What am I missing? It's one thing singing the songs but doesn't anybody really mean it? So I created a monster. And I made the mistake of thinking that it means you had to take yourself to the very depths of hell. So I dragged my body through the mud, to show that I could do it.'

In retrospect Gahan acknowledges he was on a complete ego trip at the time: 'You know I think I was once again trying to change the destiny of Depeche Mode myself, all on my own and I was like, this is what we should be doing ... and you know, Depeche Mode is a collective group of people and ideas, and I think I was just trying, basically, to boost my own ego, for whatever reason, I don't really know, because it's a bit of a blur. I don't feel like I need to do that any more.'

While the band didn't see Gahan in 1991, Daniel Miller met him face-to-face on several occasions when the singer flew back to London to see Jack. 'The first time I knew about heroin was when he was living in Los Angeles after the *Violator* tour and he came over to London,' recalls Miller. 'This was before they started on their next album, *Songs of Faith and Devotion*. I hadn't seen him for a few months and he looked like a classic junkie. He was skinny, he looked terrible and that was when I knew he was a junkie. He used to do this great impression of a wasted rock star and here he was – he'd become that impersonation, even down to the fact that his problem was so obvious but he was trying to conceal it from me.'

Gahan put a more positive spin on these nights out when he spoke about them in 1993: 'Several times when I'd hit London, mostly to see Jack and I'd go out to dinner with Daniel and he'd say, "Look, I know you're going through a lot of stuff at the moment, but you've got to keep going and you've got to keep pushing." I think everyone knew I wasn't trying to destroy the band, I was just trying to push us a bit harder. I mean, my wife's American, and you know, she's really aggressive, and I've definitely picked up on that. And most of the time she's dead right about what she thinks. She's said things to me over the last year that've completely changed my view about a lot of things I was doing, and she's done nothing but encourage me.'

In early 1992 the band met up with each other again in Madrid where they'd rented a villa and transformed it into a residential studio. Alan Wilder: 'We decided to live together, which was difficult. I think it was Flood's idea because he'd just done it with U2 and so we tried it.' The boffin-like producer owns up, 'I think I was the one who suggested living and recording together, on the back of the U2 sessions for *Achtung Baby*.'

On the surface Spain was an idyllic choice, which had also been suggested by their friend Anton Corbijn: 'They've been totally into my idea of recording in Spain, just because the light there is so beautiful.' After scouting around, they'd found a modern, glass-fronted villa on the outskirts of Madrid. 'It was quite a big organizational exercise,' reckons Daniel Miller, 'because they'd recorded in virtually every country in Europe at that time – France, Germany, Denmark and Italy. They wanted the stimulation of a new country and new city, so we decided on Madrid but unfortunately it didn't really have the kind of recording facilities that we needed. So we rented a house and built our own studio there. It was in this really odd location on the outskirts of the city, like a gated estate, the sort of place where Costa Del Crime people live. Very high security, big houses, beautiful gardens but sort of weird.'

The pseudo-Americanized Gahan was happy they were recording in Europe, rather than back in England. 'Initially we loved the idea of renting a villa in Madrid and setting up our own studio,' says the singer, 'but in practice it was an absolute disaster. We all hated it there because it wasn't really in the centre of the city. It was about

30–40 minutes outside. So every time we wanted to go out, we had to get cabs into town. The clubs there were open until really late and you'd come out really drunk and you've got to take a long cab ride home and the drivers never wanted to take us that far. Also living on top of each other became really difficult. We never had any space from each other, so I think we learnt our lesson there. It's much easier to be living in totally different places and meet up whenever we have to.'

For the last 18 months they'd all lived their own lives and now their differences had hardened. 'I'd changed but I didn't really understand it until I came face to face with Al and Mart and Fletch,' recalls the frontman. 'The looks on their faces battered me.'

Wilder was dismissive of the long-haired, tattooed singer: 'Tattoos are just a bit silly, aren't they?' He adds, 'To be honest, it wasn't too much of a shock when we saw Dave in Madrid, we were all expecting it. We knew, given how he'd seemed the last time we saw him and the fact he'd been living in LA, that he'd come back different. I think Dave's very, very easily influenced. He's a vulnerable kind of character and he goes to extremes. So it wasn't that surprising but it was a bit saddening. For all his faults and his problems, you couldn't dislike the bloke. You just wished he could be a bit more strong willed.'

The band personnel rubbed each other up the wrong way and the only way of papering over the cracks was through the tried-and-tested method of clubbing every night. In the cold light of day, however, they were making absolutely no progress with the album and they avoided each other as much as possible. 'It was really traumatic,' disclosed Gahan in 1993. 'There were lots of little struggles going on. Depeche Mode is a very English set-up and I came back from Los Angles with a lot of aggressive influences, like, "I wanna do this, I wanna do that ..." I came back fully loaded with plenty of passionate ideas and things that I wanted to do to the sound of Depeche Mode and everybody else was kind of like, "Well, actually, we've just been at home with the wife and the kids for the last year, so calm down a bit there, Dave." Now I realize it, but, at the time, I just felt like it was me and them. And I had to keep pushing.'

Although he didn't see them in Madrid, their former press representative Chris Carr [he stopped working with them after *Music For the Masses*] kept in touch with the situation: 'There was definitely a point where the band were one place and Dave was somewhere else, very much on his own.' 'It was obvious what the problem was,' says Daniel Miller, as he recalls this fraught, jarring and uncreative period. 'They'd spent time apart, they'd all gone through quite big changes in their lives, some of them had kids in that period, and there wasn't that natural coming together any more. They just weren't connecting in any way.'

'We found that our personalities clashed incredibly when living together for 24 hours a day, seven days a week,' said Gahan during press interviews for the album. 'I didn't mind so much, but Alan detested it.' Wilder was growing more frustrated by the day as he wanted to crack on with the job in hand – making the new record. 'I've got a strong work ethic and I was fed up with fucking about,' he argues. 'The only way I can complete a project is to know I've given my absolute best. Flood and I found it increasingly difficult to concentrate with some of the distractions we encountered in the villa.' The pair would spend a few hours doing the 'donkey work' together, then Wilder would go up to his room, 'which was tiny' and try to unwind. 'Dave was next to me and I could hear everything he was doing. Dave's main recreation at that time was to have an amp in his room and make feedback noises with his guitar, so I had to listen to that for several weeks [the band did two six-week sessions in Madrid, with a month off in between]. I didn't complain about it but I didn't want to hear it. I guess he was letting off some steam.' 'There was no separation between work space and our own space,' confirms Flood. 'You could drop a pin on one side of the villa and it would sound like a canon on the other side. There was absolutely no privacy. To be honest, the easiest place to be was in the studio, so I spent as much time in there as I could.'

Martin Gore, who rarely shows any hint of anguish, got drunk a lot and killed the slow hours by playing Sonic the Hedgehog; Wilder bristled with irritation as he worked; when Gahan emerged from his room, he was unpredictable – sometimes self-absorbed and truculent, on other occasions vibey and positive. When in this latter mood he would give Wilder and Flood bursts of encouragement, before withdrawing again. 'Dave would stay in his room a lot during that period but by the same token he was really enthusiastic about the record even though he wasn't particularly active in it,' explains Wilder. 'He'd come down and say, "That sounds brilliant Al, well done, you're doing a great job." And he was the only person in that group who ever said that kind of thing to me. At least he cared about the group, whatever condition he was in.' 'I was probably the closest to Alan,' said Gahan. 'He really resented the fact that he was spending 12 hours a day in the studio and Martin would be off somewhere getting drunk and I'd be up to my tricks somewhere else. He pretty much pulled it all together and didn't really get any appreciation for that because everyone was too much into their own ego shit.'

Meanwhile, Fletcher found it hard being away from home and the security of a familiar environment. The tense, pressurized atmosphere was clearly dangerous for someone who'd already had one nervous breakdown, especially as he was trapped inside this stressed-out, claustrophobic villa for the next few weeks. Furthermore Fletcher's rather hammy approach to his self-defined role as a belligerent, common-sense force within Depeche Mode, jarred badly with the others in this situation. When he tried to pep everyone up, nobody wanted to listen, which made things worse for him. He started to fret and wallow. 'From the time Fletch first got this depression thing during *Violator*, he was continually up and down like a yo-yo,' reveals Wilder. 'He was often worse when he was on the anti-depression drugs because he was hyperactive and he'd say all these bizarre things. You'd think, what are you on about Fletch? Then he'd go into a very down period where he would be sitting there not speaking and looking very glum. It was from one extreme to the other. During the Madrid sessions it was hard for him because the tension was building and the pressure was on all of us to get the record done. He just got worse and worse.'

At this point Fletcher wasn't strong enough mentally to deal with Dave Gahan, or the problems he was causing. The singer's emotional extremes were a bit too full-on for Fletcher who was dealing with his own depression, especially as the banter between the two had developed a surly, antagonistic edge. The more sussed, worldly Gore and Wilder were more accepting of the rift in the band and were both happy to let Gahan get on with his own thing for the moment. As a result the singer became completely isolated from the others: 'I'd shut myself up in my room and whenever things got a bit sticky I'd run off to my room, lock the door and start painting. And I ended up paint-ing a really fantastic oil for Teresa. Which I'm really proud of, 'cos I hadn't put brush to canvas for ten years. I'd be up all night painting. I found it incredibly therapeutic, 'cos it was my thing and it was like, well, fuck you lot, you can't tell me how to do anything here.

'I remember when I'd finished, no one had really seen it except Anton and the rest of the band were really quite surprised. Martin, I remember, said to me … "Oh yeah, you know I didn't realize you could paint, I've never been able to do that myself." And he was quite knocked back. And I said, well, "Yeah, that's what I used to do, Mart, that's all I could do. I was in art college for three years, and the only thing I was ever any good at was painting."' Gahan invited Daniel Miller up to his room in Spain: 'It was very dark, and he'd been paint-ing, quite good stuff of a cat. There were candles everywhere, very ritualistic. It seemed to me that when he first came to London, that was a big shock for me and then after that he appeared, if anything, a little bit better than that. And he was singing quite well. He was moody but he was always quite moody with the others. But obviously I was aware that he was the caricature that he'd once portrayed. All his energy and focus were going into drugs.'

This first visit, a week or so into the recording sessions, confirmed Miller's worst fears: 'I walked into this house and it was the worst vibe. Everyone seemed to be in their own little space, no one was relating to each other at all. Alan was downstairs in the drum room, just drumming away to himself; Dave was locked in his room paint-ing; Flood was crawling around on the floor, playing a synthesizer noise; Fletch and Mart were reading the *Sun*. It's not an untypical scene in a studio but usually it's three months in, not one week. You'd expect a bustle of activity but it felt that they'd burnt out before they'd even started. There was very poor communication. They'd recorded a few bits and pieces which nobody was very happy with, and there wasn't a very productive feeling. I stayed for a few days on that occa-sion and I went backwards and forwards from England to the studio quite a number of times.'

Miller also sensed that the pressure of following up *Violator* was contributing to the tense atmosphere. 'Everyone felt that *Violator* was such a classic, and artistically they wanted the next record to be another development, which it was. It wasn't *Violator* Part Two.'

Furthermore, Depeche Mode's commercial success meant that it was harder for them to shut off the world outside when they were working. 'Suddenly you realize there are so many people out there waiting for the next record and I think that just adds pressure,' explains Gore. 'You suddenly realize how big this thing is, whereas before I suppose it never really hit me.'

Three partly finished tracks emerged from this first six-week session – 'In Your Room', 'Walking In My Shoes' and 'Condemnation'. The birthing process was horrific but arguably this adversity and tension contributed to the rougher, heavier feel of the new songs. At this stage, Gore had only written six songs for the album but all of them invited a rockier approach to the production. Wilder maintains that the demo for 'I Feel You' featured 'Martin playing that riff with the most heavy rock guitar sound you can imagine and a stomping beat underneath it. The music insisted on a rockier direction – it's a John Lee Hooker blues riff.' Gore confirmed that he wanted to make a song-based, increasingly organic record: 'Right now there's a lot of dance techno music out there. I think everyone expected us to come up with a dance album but there's so much of it out there right now that the songs are really getting lost. I think I subconsciously tried to rebel against that.'

Gahan had seized on to this traditional blueprint and was anxious for the band to emulate the raucous energy of U.S. acts such as Jane's Addiction and Rage Against The Machine, in the execution of this rock direction: 'I wanted something very different this time – I wanted to feel like I was playing with people. And I wanted that from day one with the record and pushed really hard for it, and I think that's why, in lots of ways, we achieved things like "I Feel You". We'd never really rocked that hard, y'know? Without me bullying everybody to hell it wouldn't have happened. I bullied Alan into drumming and they said, "Dave's gone crazy, he wants drums, next thing he'll want backing singers". And I did.'

Wilder grins at the frontman's exaggerated bravado while reiterating that Gahan's encouragement was helpful. He claims he couldn't get any perspective on the music from Gore. 'Martin wasn't very good at expressing his opinions,' says Wilder. 'He certainly wasn't very good at giving praise. It's part of his shyness. I don't think it's a mean streak, he just can't say what he feels. And if he didn't like something, he wouldn't say anything. So you'd end up in a situation where Fletch would say, "Well, Al, Mart's not very happy with that." But Martin hadn't said anything to me about it so I'd wasted hours, days, whatever.' 'Martin and Alan weren't talking to each much in the studio,' confirms Flood. 'I can see why Alan would be frustrated. Martin was able to articulate his feelings with me more easily than with Alan. He'd tell me what he wanted but he wouldn't say anything to Al. That put me in a very difficult, stressful position obviously, because as the producer I was the only person that everyone was talking to.' However, the songwriter has insisted that, although 'the sessons did put a strain on the whole band, Al and I were still talking'.

Gore felt his demos had defined the new direction of the record and he then allowed everyone their input – Gahan's grungy narcissism; Flood's boffin-like problem solving in the journey towards a mix of organic and electronic sounds, and Wilder's cerebral approach to detailing the sound – while the songwriter remained mostly passive in the studio unless he didn't like something. Up to now the fact that everyone had a well-defined role and the 'leadership' of the band would change at various times, meant that Depeche Mode functioned with a bizarre efficiency. However, in the ego-swamped atmosphere of Madrid, the lack of a clear band leader encouraged factions to form. People were more intransigent over their ideas, digging in their heels and individualizing the sounds rather than blending them into a new overall style.

Gore was unsure about the new recordings – he wanted to push on from *Violator* but was very conscious that the band had originally formed as an antidote to rock music. 'Martin wasn't particularly interested in following a full-on rocky style,' explains Flood. 'That was one of the tensions between Martin and Dave, but also between Martin and Alan. I think Martin wanted to make the record a little more organic than the previous records without forgetting the past. Alan likes big chords and a more anthemic sound and Dave was very influenced by grunge, so they were pushing further away from the band's roots, I suppose.'

The cut and thrust of egos and ideas in the studio made each new track complicated and difficult to create and even harder to edit. One of the first songs to be recorded in the Madrid session was 'Walking

In My Shoes' which is driven by heavy, dirty percussion loops. 'A lot of people in rap music are using the technology in an interesting way to make their records sound dirty,' says Wilder. 'So much of pop music is clean and pristine, and there's an awful lot of bollocks because of it. I like to try and capture both sounds, to make it clear, with a full frequency range across the board, but also to have a lot of grit. On "Walking In My Shoes", for instance, there are different loops in the verse, an additional loop comes in on the bridge, and the chorus brings in a complete change of drum sound and rhythm. Plus there are different drum fills, hi-hat patterns and top percussion parts in each section. The combination of all that gives you the impression of the rhythm changing all the time.' Closer examination of 'Walking In My Shoes' also unfolds a live bass and an E-bow guitar, strings, distorted piano and a harpsichord riff.

Wilder: 'The piano part at the beginning of "Walking In My Shoes" was put through a guitar processor, which distorted it and made it more edgy. We then added a harpsichord sample on top of that. I wanted us to use snippets of performance and different loops, because I found the approach of hip-hop very inventive. You know, DJs coming in and chopping up people's bits of music, all that.' Everyone was excited by the song but Daniel Miller felt the optimistic, almost spiritual uplift of the demo was ground out of the final recording. 'I remember lots of discussion about "Walking In My Shoes". Everyone had a very different view. I heard it as one of Martin's classic pop singles, and I think the way it was finished off on the record was almost a deliberate attempt to not make it like that. A classic record company mistake – never say, "That's the single", because the band will react against it. I personally don't think that song reached its potential. The spirit of the demo got lost somehow.'

Flood: 'There was always a very good dynamic between the four of them. They had disagreements and different ideas but on their previous albums they'd all come together to reach a common goal. On *Songs* their individual desires no longer met in harmony. So it was very tense from start to finish and their differences in approach were never resolved. For instance, I think "Walking In My Shoes" is a fantastic song but we never worked out how to finish it. My feeling about the track is obviously coloured by my memory of the session, but in the end it ended up being several different versions spliced together into one. There's something unresolved about the record which reflects all the contrasting opinions about the direction we should be going in.'

Boosted by Flood's diplomatic encouragement, the song 'Condemnation' started out as a studio jam. 'The idea of that track was to enhance the gospel feel, without going into pastiche,' reckons Wilder. 'We wanted to try and create the effect of it being played in a room, in a space. So we began by getting all five members of the group to do one thing each in the same space. Fletcher was bashing a flight-case with a pole, Flood and Dave were clapping, I was playing a drum and Martin was playing an organ. We listened back to it and it was very embryonic but it gave us an idea for a direction.' The sketchy gospel backing was easier to build up than some of the more loop-based songs. At the heart of the final recording is a strident vocal by Gahan, performed in the white-tiled garage underneath the villa – 'a low-ceilinged place, very concrete and metal and echoey and cold, and it had a great sound and a great ambience,' says the singer. 'When I came out, everybody in the control room went all quiet and turned around, and suddenly Flood said, "That was fucking great," and Alan and everybody said, "That's probably the best vocal you ever did" – and I thought, yes, it was. It was completely breaking me up inside, and at the same time, it was really optimistic and uplifting.'

This was a damaging epiphany of sorts for Gahan, who for a long time afterwards believed he'd achieved this artistic high by putting himself through all the exaggerated, mostly painful emotions of the previous few years: 'I did think I had to be in a place of complete pain to sing a song like "Condemnation". I thought that performance was down to the fact that I could just about stand up and had to take everything in my body to get it out.' Fletcher confirms that Gahan would completely drain himself through his vocal takes. 'Dave would come forward on a real burst of energy, do a vocal, then disappear to his room for a couple of days. It was a bit odd.'

For Gahan to psyche himself up into such a frenzied and exhausting emotional state when he was singing, he had to identify with Martin Gore's songs. He applied the new lyrics to his own life with an obsessive, intense fanaticism which rivalled that of the first row in a Depeche Mode concert: 'With this album I felt that every single song on the album, even the songs that Martin sang were the best things he could have done for me at the time. As a friend to a friend – he kind of helped me to heal a lot of my personal problems and he wasn't even trying. When you've been in a band for 13 years together it's four weird energies, and I think now with Depeche Mode we can really do anything.' Gore in turn complimented Gahan during the LP's eventual press campaign: 'Dave is like another instrument. He's the voice of the band. His voice is particularly suited to a lot of the songs. I can't sing the way he does.' However, Gore also pointed out that, 'David claims he feels that they're almost tailor-made for him, that I was writing from his perspective, which isn't true, obviously, 'cause I don't do that sort of thing. I don't ever try to write from Dave's point of view ... If you start writing and try to imagine what a third person's thinking, the emotions are gonna get diluted somehow. If you write what you're feeling, you know exactly what you're feeling.'

Six songs were at various stages of completion as Depeche Mode arrived in Hamburg's Chateau Du Pape studio to begin their third album session. Fletcher was burnt out by his experiences in Madrid and stayed at home to sort himself out. Although he didn't admit it, this was a relief to Wilder whose impatience with his vulnerable, emotionally erratic colleague was at breaking point. Martin Gore was also having to deal with some strong emotions created by hidden secrets, guilt and finally acceptance. After his 31st birthday, the song-writer was told that his real father is a black American, who'd come over to England in the late '50s. Gore's mother had kept the truth away from the judgements of race-conscious Essex in the '60s. His real father had returned to America and lived in the South. According to a friend of the pop star, when the pair met they shared a similar shyness and nervousness.

Meanwhile, by the time they'd arrived in Hamburg, everyone in the band had witnessed Gahan's drug paraphernalia and there was a series of rather awkward discussions about it. The singer didn't come clean about his using but it just became obvious what he was up to and, after a while, he didn't make much attempt to hide it. Occasionally Teresa Conway would fly over and they'd shut them-selves away for a couple of days. 'Nobody would see them,' recalls Wilder. 'They were completely in their own world.' He adds, 'The drug thing was obviously disappointing – not for any moral reasons but because it adversely affected his personality and more specifically his greatest asset, his sense of humour.'

'I remember we had our first ultimatum meeting with Dave,' recalls Gore. 'We said to him, "You've got to sort yourself out. You're putting youself in danger."' Gahan: 'They were genuinely concerned about my health. Of course, I couldn't see that. I said to Mart, "Fuck off! You drink 15 pints of beer a night and take your clothes off and cause a scene. How can you be so fucking hypcritical?"' The dissipated frontman had a point as Martin Gore was drinking heavily throughout the Hamburg sessions. 'If we had some time off, Martin could easily go on a three or four-day bender where he literally wouldn't stop drinking,' says Wilder. 'And often he would drink just beer. I can't understand why he doesn't put any weight on! I just turn into a fat slob if I don't get any exercise. Anyway, Martin came in one day when we were making *Songs of Faith and Devotion* and we hadn't seen him for a while. He was in a state where he could hardly communicate but he managed to tell us that he'd drunk 67 Weiss Beers – and these are served in big glasses – in 11 hours. He'd counted them! He's probably forgotten he did that. I'm sure his memory plays tricks on him and he doesn't realize that he'd disappear for three or four days while we were making an album.'

Gore and Wilder were still not on the same wavelength in the studio but they had a few good nights out together as the album began to come together a lot more quickly. Sometimes they'd play impromptu versions of the new songs and take requests in a Hamburg bar, or back at their hotel. Wilder: 'We used to take over the piano at our hotel nearly every night and the great thing is that Martin knows the words to just about every song ever written and I can work out the chords to most pop songs, so between us we can do a turn and people love it. Mart can sing you a great Elvis cover. He's very musical. He's not the greatest keyboard player in the world but he's got a better voice than Dave, certainly in terms of being able to sing melodies in tune. But the thing is he used to combine this with taking his clothes off at the same time and some hotel managers used to take offence at that. He does like to display himself!' laughs Wilder, who points out that at the start of the video for 'A Question Of Lust' the director Clive Richardson filmed Gore stripping in a club.

The band had another memorable night out when Erasure turned up in Hamburg to play a show there. 'Vince actually came out with us and had a good time!' says an amazed Martin Gore.

Meanwhile, in the later stages of recording, Flood and Wilder wrapped electronic sounds and textures around the real-time traditional instruments used in Madrid. On the thunderous 'I Feel You' they applied a lot of technology to a performance-based track, in an attempt to retain the dynamics of a human performance without becoming an average rock band. Depeche Mode were still using their Akai and Emulator samplers, along with lots of rack-mounted and modular synths: a MiniMoog, Oberheims, the Roland 700 system, ARP 2600s. On *Songs of Faith and Devotion* there are fewer modern synthesizers than ever before – no DX7s, PPGs, or things like that – because they preferred the roundness and grittiness of the analogues. Plus, the old synths have their own organic quality which bled into the raw, natural sounds of the songs. 'Actually if you listen to that album it's not a rock record at all,' argues Wilder, 'it's got lots of electronic elements on it. I think a lot of the perception comes from the image of Dave with long hair and tattoos.' It seems that *Songs of Faith and Devotion* has been dubbed 'rock' as a broad term meaning 'not electronic', as the influences are quite wide-ranging, including gospel, blues, progressive rock, hip-hop and soul. There's even a psychedelic, trippy feel to 'Mercy In You' and 'Rush', created by Wilder's experiments with reversing sounds which was all part of a determination to move on from the rigid pulse of *Violator*.

The band recorded eight tracks in Hamburg and then moved back to London for the final session at Olympic studios. Flood brought in a gospel trio, Hildia Cambell, Bazil Meade and Samantha Smith for 'Get Right With Me'. They also solicited the help of an Uilleann piper, Steafan Hannigan, for 'Judas' and, having decided they wanted real strings for 'One Caress', the band called on the services of Wil Malone, who'd also arranged Massive Attack's 'Unfinished Sympathy'. 'One Caress' was recorded at Olympic using a 28-piece section, with Martin Gore singing the vocal live. After 13 years without needing an outside musician to flesh out their tracks, Gore was 'very cagey' about this latest development. However, Flood said it would work out fine and the songwriter was prepared to experiment with the idea. 'We got the choir in,' recalls Gore, 'and I was just sitting at the back thinking, "This isn't going to work, I don't know why we're trying this." I was really nervous about the whole thing. But the moment they started singing, for me, it lifted the track on to another level, it was just up there somewhere, and so I decided I shouldn't be so closed-minded about the whole thing.'

The album was eventually mixed at Olympic Studios in London by Wilder, Flood and Mark 'Spike' Stent, the latter knocking them out at a rapid rate which alarmed Wilder. *Songs* ... remained a difficult, troubled album to the end, with 'Walking In My Shoes' mixed out of three different versions and then being ditched as the opening single because they couldn't agree. They settled on 'I Feel You', although Gahan only reluctantly gave up on 'Condemnation' as the first excerpt. Tension also overshadowed the last few weeks as everyone realized they were running so late with the record there was going to be very little recovery time before they set off on a lengthy world tour. The LP was finished on New Year's Eve, 1992.

At the time there was no time for a post-mortem but over the years each contributor has developed their own view of the record. For Gahan, 'We did the best we could. We pushed a lot harder to actually create something more as a group effort and it was really hard at times. I don't think we really fulfilled that as much as we could have if we'd put personal things aside, but they are always there, the problems, the personal things and the outside interests. They are always in the studio with us, if you like, and as you get older the chance to do that seems to get further and further away. I think it's probably an impossible task for the band to make a group album.'

Gore believes they set off on the right direction to make music 'from bodies rather than machines', but 'on a few tracks we may have spoiled the songs by trying this pseudo-rock'. Even so, its one of his top three Depeche Mode LPs. Flood also feels they were right to experiment but adds, 'I don't think we achieved as much as we could have done.' Daniel Miller: 'They figured out a way of making it work. It was like a really difficult puzzle and bit by bit they made it fit. Even at the end when they came to London to mix it with Mark Stent, that was a struggle. Apart from "I Feel You" and "Condemnation", nothing came together very quickly. So there wasn't a clear view of how these songs should end up sounding. It's a good album but I don't think all the songs came out as good as they should have done. There was a lack of the band having one view.'

Even the ever-resilient Flood, who went on to produce 'difficult' albums with Trent Reznor and Smashing Pumpkins, decided he 'didn't want to work with Depeche Mode again' after this LP. 'It was a combination of things – the lack of communication and the feeling that we'd reached a natural conclusion in our work together. I felt it would be better for them to find someone else and explore a new direction. I didn't think our relationship was going to produce anything different. But of course there was a selfish aspect to it, because I didn't want to put myself through all that again. There's a level of excitement, respect and tension when you first work with someone which creates new ideas, but there wasn't that sort of feeling between us at the end of *Songs*.'

Just two months after the album was cut, the throbbing, squealing grunge-electronica of 'I Feel You' blasted into the UK charts in mid-February 1993 at No.8. *NME* got their description about right: 'Depeche Mode positively pulp a backing track while the newly grunged-up Dave Gahan has his nuts tattooed live in the studio. Synths fart, squelch and whine, amps howl.' Gahan's skinny little rock-star persona was thrust on the world through Anton Corbijn's video which showed the frontman stripping in front of English actress Lysette Anthony. On a very different tip, Brian Eno remixed the song into a dreamily ambient affair which Martin Gore had to take off the car stereo a couple of times because it was making him fall asleep.

When *Songs of Faith and Devotion* appeared on 22 March it went straight to the top of the charts in Britain and America. The album also received some of the best reviews of the band's career. *Select*'s Andrew Harrison suggested that, 'The songs of faith and devotion are also songs of lust and corruption and greed, smeared all over with the most viscous, poisonous sound textures Depeche Mode have yet created. Where *Violator*'s clinical, cynical re-gening of house dynamics was calculated to maximize the clamminess of its songs, here the keynotes are curdled sweetness and the same raging noise that opens "I Feel You" – it's not Ministry but it's the nearest they've got yet. Not heavy metal but heavy plastic.' Harrison's assertion that they are 'songs of lust and corruption and greed' was accurate but as Fletcher notes, 'the new songs are a bit more emotional and less pervy'.

The album's tone is harder to interpret because it definitely changed from the demos to the final execution. Gore has attributed a more positive feeling in the original songs to his daughter's birth, coupling his belief that 'man is inherently evil' with the faithful resolve that 'you have to have faith in him'. Although these ideas filter through the LP, the uplifting euphoria of 'I Feel You', 'Higher Love' and 'Rush' is closer to the 'rush' of a chemical high than Gore's tempered optimism. The complex atmosphere around the album has tilted the songs into some weird moods, which reflect the state of Dave Gahan's drug use more than Gore's frame of mind.

Although the singer has hyped up the record as 'lifting people to a higher spirtual level', Gore himself has always remained ambiguous about his spiritual beliefs: 'I do believe in some sort of power even though I haven't really had any particular experience myself. I'm still searching. I really like the idea of belief but I've never found something to believe in. The only Godlike things I know are sex and love. In my eyes God is sex personified, by the same token love is too. Both have something that lasts longer than a moment. Love and sex last forever and therefore bring some sort of reason for our being. Therefore it's no surprise that I write about God, sex and love all the time. As far as I'm concerned they're the biggest mystery of this planet.'

Meanwhile, *NME*'s David Quantick (in an eight out of ten review!) quipped, 'Like New Order only more sort of Essex'. He added, 'Style fans will note that Depeche Mode – nearly out-Depeche Moded by U2 on the Corbijn/Berlin/monochrome/Eno-styled *Achtung Baby* – have returned with an album which out-Achtung Baby's *Achtung Baby*. *Songs of Faith* is Depeche Mode in all-out, moody Euro-art stadium rock, um, mode, and it leaves all competitors spitting ineptitude at the starting gate ... while on occasions I'd prefer the wide-eyed pop cynicism of *Black Celebration* or the dreamy weird rock of *Violator*, this is an album that *every* sane person should own.'

'Walking In My Shoes', remixed by Nirvana and Smashing Pumpkins producer Butch Vig, was released at the end of April and charted at No.14. It was backed by 'My Joy' which didn't make it on to the album in the end. A Johnny Dollar mix of the A-side featured 'additional scratches' by Geoff Barrow of Portishead, tipping a hat to the synthesizer band who'd experimented with loops and samples a long time before 'trip-hop' was invented. Corbijn's video is one of his strangest, recreating an Hieronymous Bosch painting, *The Garden of Earthly Delights* with freakish-looking characters whose faces are further distorted by being squished against glass. Gahan is set in the foreground of an erupting volcano, while skating nuns and a red bird-woman add a surreal edge to the scene. Alan Wilder: 'I remember how odd it was being surrounded by all these people with every manner of deformity – especially at meal times. It brought a smile to my face standing next to a hunchback, dressed like a gothic night-mare and hearing him ask the catering girls, "Have you got any ketchup love?"'

More Than A Party, 1993–4

The delay in completing *Songs of Faith and Devotion* was particularly stressful for Alan Wilder who had to do all the pre-programming for the upcoming world tour. 'Booking the tour upfront was a problem,' confesses Miller. 'They were in the studio for months, straight into rehearsals and promotion of the album, then they had to go on tour. They'd had a couple of breaks in recording but the deadline wasn't set to get the record out, it was all because of the tour. This made things very intense, especially for Alan who had to work on the backing tapes for the shows.'

The Mute originator had a very strong instinct that this would prove to be a 'difficult' tour for the various band members: 'Fletch wasn't in a great state after a couple of nervous breakdowns, and neither was Dave because of his drug problem. Martin was OK, Alan was OK on a physical and mental level but he was not really communicating with the rest of the band. They were all very tired and stressed out. The fact that it was a follow-up to *Violator* had created a lot of pressure. Then they went straight out on the road.'

In January 1993, five months before they were due to set off, Wilder and Steve Lyon finally started work on the 'live' music at Olympic Studios and then at Wilder's own studio in West Sussex. In stark contrast to the more sociable pre-tour work on *Violator*, Steve Lyon immediately noted the absence of the other band members: 'Alan and me didn't see anyone for three or four months. It was a very different situation to the run-up to the World Violation tour. We just locked ourselves away, sampling stuff from Depeche Mode records and basically creating another album.' This pre-tour work was quite complex, as it effectively meant they were re-recording the whole of the new album and rearranging a lot of Depeche Mode's back catalogue. 'Unfortunately, putting the Devotional live show together proved to be more of a handful than either myself or Steve had bargained for,' notes Wilder. 'We knew when we started that we didn't have a lot of time on our hands and it didn't help that our Roland sequencer was giving us continual problems. However, we persevered and had nearly completed the work when disaster struck.

'The machine couldn't handle the sheer volume of traffic we were demanding from it and one day the whole system just crashed – we lost everything – three and a half months of work.' Luckily the pair had backed up all the music on to multi-track but the edits were gone. With the single, 'Walking In My Shoes', due for release in April and rehearsals beckoning, they found themselves with the mammoth task of re-editing everything in about two weeks. They worked night and day and then sued Roland.

While Wilder and Lyon burnt the candle at both ends in the studio, the band's 'visual director' Anton Corbijn was dreaming up the new stage set. He spent four or five months on ideas and execution, with two months gobbled up by the process of actually creating images for the video projections on 11 full-size screens. The set was big enough to recreate a thunderstorm and had elements reminiscent of U2's Zoo TV Tour, toward which Corbijn had contributed some ideas. Martin Gore defended Corbijn against the criticism that he was diluting the effectiveness of his ideas by sharing them across the two acts. 'The people we work with, and U2 work with, happen to be good in their field. I don't think it's that unusual for us to be working with the same people. It's just that both of us happen to use films and screens, which, I think, is a natural progression for shows ... After we used the films and the screens on the last tour, it's very hard to go back to the standard conventional rock show because you really feel that it's lacking. It really does make a big difference to the audience reaction. It really does affect things. There's somehow a very different feeling at the concerts, in a positive way.'

Gore had a valid point, as once a band is exposed to audiences of 10,000 or more, they need to think of strong visual elements. Giant screens were an obvious way for technology-led acts such as Depeche Mode and the reinvented U2 to explore and in the latter's case, Corbijn's work added another visceral dimension to the show. For Devotional, Corbijn came up with some appropriately dark, sexual and religious on-screen imagery which bonded with the music to give the shows a distinctive atmosphere. Gore: 'We are trying to be more abstract, previously we had used lots of images of the band and we wanted to get away from that.' Corbijn also points out the contrasting working methods of Depeche Mode and U2: 'Right from the start Depeche Mode didn't want to be involved so much in the videos. They hate having meetings whereas U2 will have meetings all the time. Martin doesn't have a strong visual sense so he would place his trust in me but U2 direct their whole operation. Alan was the one I used to talk to about videos because he is intelligent and well educated visually. But they couldn't be two more different bands.'

Meanwhile, Dave Gahan was preparing himself by going to the gym every day doing 'three hours of circuits', martial arts and '20 kilometres on a fixed bike'. According to Carr this work-out regime was '... another form of self-discipline to him. It was a way of testing himself and pushing hard. He would lose a lot of weight. He's always been prone to puppy fat and he's very conscious of that.' Gahan also psyched himself up for the tour with his 'winged tattoo': 'It was like my wings, really, for the tour. It was, like my weapon for the tour – if you can do this, you can do anything, y'know? If you can sit under the needle for ten hours, you can do anything, man.' Fletcher put himself into a good, positive state of mind for the impending marathon by finally tying the knot with his girlfriend of 15 years, Grainne, on 16 January 1993.

Meanwhile, when Chris Carr saw Corbijn's stage set he was concerned about the fact that Gahan was on a different level to the rest of the band and had a huge area to patrol. He didn't like the dangling metal shapes at the back either – in fact, very few people did. 'I rate Anton but he uses the same trick over and over with different bands and so being a purist I think the man's a charlatan,' argues Carr. 'My personal feeling was that Depeche were treated the worst by him and so he gave them a stage set which presented Dave with enormous problems. What else could he do but run around and go, Yeah! But that's the fallibility of the democracy, because the vanity appealed to Dave and he was probably in the driving seat at the time.'

Corbijn points out that Gahan had reservations about the Devotional set for completely different reasons. 'Dave had a problem with it because he sees himself as a rock singer and so he doesn't need visuals.' Gahan wanted the audience to focus on him – the ring-leader of a real-life rock 'n' roll show, rather than a diminutive figure in a zoo of hi-tech gadgetry. He felt it was his job to be larger than life, a fantasy figure who pushes life to the limits: 'Personally, I have to take it all the way, otherwise there's no point. At the end of the day it's just a rock 'n' roll band – but if I can make a lot of people really happy for a couple of hours, then that's quite an achievement for someone who most of the time is a real miserable cunt. It's my little time; it's what I do. That's why Rage Against The Machine is fantastic; what a great name for a band. That's what you're doing all the time, you're raging against the machine for about two hours every night.'

In May the band flew to Zurich, Switzerland at the start of 156 dates in 14 months. They had a personal entourage of 15, a road crew numbering nearly 100 and their own therapist. According to Gore the latter wasn't a great success and ' ... although Fletch saw him occasionally, the rest of us never did. After six weeks we knocked it on the head.' Their tour manager Jonathan Kessler was there for most of the dates to oversee the operation, along with an accountant, a press person, personal assistants and security guards. Flash hotels, private planes, limousines and people who provided whatever the band required made this an extremely luxurious round-the-world party. 'From the moment you start on the first day of the tour until you get home it just seems you're living in a total fantasy land,' says Gore of the hedonistic, self-enclosed on-the-road atmosphere. 'Personally I just try to accept it, try to have as much fun as I can in fantasy land and then come back to earth at the end of it.' 'It was like taking a mental asylum on the road,' says Gahan. 'We had 120 people working for us. I didn't even know all their names. A differ-ent city every day. We were on the road nearly 18 months. This lifestyle ... everything is taken care for you. You don't really do anything for yourself. It was really insane on this tour. We employed a drug dealer and a psychiatrist.'

The first leg of the tour was mostly in Scandinavia, opening in Zurich on 21 May, followed by dates in Brussels, Copenhagen and Lausanne. The rest of the European shows ran through June and July, predominantly at big indoor arenas. Gahan commented, 'We prefer playing indoor places, generally, because the atmosphere is really contained and it seems so much more exciting, even if it's not. When the audience screams or sings along, the whole thing gets captured, rather than just escaping off into the air.'

Over the course of these two months Depeche Mode binged and partied. Fletcher confessed to a journalist, 'For us, more workload means more partyload. I know it's a cliché, but wherever you go everyone wants to scream at you, photograph you, take you out. For the night, you're the kings of the city.' Gore: 'When you finish a concert and every door is open to you, it's very hard to say, Actually, I'm off to bed.' At this stage the only dark poison seeping into these indulgences was Gahan's heroin abuse which continued unabated. Wilder remembers the band trying to anticipate and hopefully prevent future problems: 'We had discussions with Dave about his drug use, now it was at a point where it was obvious what he was doing. We had meetings where we said, "You've got to clean up and sort yourself out, Dave, otherwise this tour is going to go horribly wrong." And he would say, "Yeah, I know, I know." But we didn't talk about it much. There's not a lot you can say, really.' Wilder adds, 'I couldn't say for sure but I don't think there was anyone else on the tour using that particular drug. Of course, it is possible to conceal these things but a lot of the time Dave was very much on his own. That wasn't a problem, he could always get company when he wanted it. In a big organization like this, there are always going to be sycophants who can get you what you need and all the rest of it. So he didn't have too much trouble feeding himself or finding someone to talk to.

'But Dave probably felt unable to communicate with us. He must've felt alienated from the rest of us because no one else in the band was using heroin. And no one else was even remotely in the same kind of place that he was, so he was uncomfortable with us and he used to shut himself away a lot of the time on the tour. He created his own world. He used to decorate his dressing room with candles and drapes, à la Keith Richards, and stay in there. He wouldn't come to the hospitality room after the show. I had no problem with that at all. You've got to do what you want to do. But to Fletch it was very important that you come back to hospitality and meet a few people. I never felt that was part of the job. Anyway, the only thing I minded was when Dave used to come down late in the lift every day. So in the end we used to tell him a time 20 minutes before everyone else so we'd all meet at the same time. He never knew that. For the whole tour everyone's meet time was 2.20 p.m. and Dave's was 2 p.m.'

Gahan's on-the-road stamina and professionalism wasn't affected by the drugs: 'I'm very driven,' he said. 'I always showed up, no matter what was going on. Fletch brought that up. It was hard to point the finger at me and say, "Man, you're looking really bad" because I was always showing up and doing the show and giving it my all. I'm a great show-off. I can stand up there and be king for two hours.' On stage he revelled in his elevated, ego-sponging position, boasting, 'I think I started doing that when I was about seven, grabbing my crotch. It's great fun. You get to grab your dick in front of 20,000 people and they all scream.' At the time Gahan insisted that he had a clear perspective on his role as a tongue-flapping, genitalia-clutching aphrodisiac. 'What you've got to be careful about is that there's a fine line between, "Come and look at me, I'm God" and, "Come and look at me, I'll entertain you and make you feel like going home and fucking your girlfriend," ' he explained. 'I definitely fall into the latter category.'

Of course, the drugs and the adrenalin rush of playing to huge crowds meant the last thing the singer possessed was lucid self-awareness, and he easily gave himself away when he started to dream up ludicrous rock-star fantasies and then related them to the press. 'I tell you, I had this idea the other night,' he told *Time Out* with exaggerated excitement. 'I want the security guys to somehow make it so I can walk across the top of the people. What about that, man? Can Prince do that? Ha ha! I've already been talking about this: 'cos I'm fit, right? When we shut "Personal Jesus" down, I wanna run to somewhere up at the back of the arena so they can suddenly light me up when the song comes back in, and I can be like: "I'm here!"'

Wilder is sympathetic about Gahan's interpretation of the fine line between egotistic self-aggrandisement and the demands of entertaining a stadium audience: 'Dave genuinely loved being on stage and it gave him a feeling of power because the audiences would react to everything he did. He got off on it. Sometimes his performances would be a bit over the top but he really involved the audience and that's not an easy thing to do in a stadium show. I don't think the touring destroyed him, because he was in a bad state when we were making the record. And once you're on stage and into your routine, it's almost like a safe haven – no one can touch you while you're up there. It's like being on automatic pilot and you feel like you're in a very safe environment. Dave used to do the same moves every night. I knew when he was going to be in front of my keyboard going, Yeah. It would be on a particular beat, on a particular bar. He wasn't deliberately doing the show every night, he just couldn't help it because it was so routine.'

Wilder's on-stage routine was a little more varied on this tour as he took the opportunity to play some live drums. 'I'm really glad I did because it was very enjoyable. It was prompted by a desire to challenge myself on stage and to try to make the Depeche Mode live show a bit more varied.' Martin Gore also played his guitar on stage more than ever before and at various stages the two backing singers from the *Songs* sessions, Hildia Cambell and Samantha Smith, were also introduced to inject a strong gospel feel into the shows.

All the band members lived their own lives on tour, with Gore and Fletcher sharing one limousine, Gahan would be in another and Wilder in a third. They discussed business and day-to-day work issues with each other only through Jonathan Kessler and, said the now increasingly worried Daniel Miller, 'they tolerated each other on stage.' Gore: 'We did manage to carry that off for 14 months. It was just that at some points separate limos were necessary.' Gahan: 'We didn't get to separate hotels but I think it was on the cards. It did get to separate floors though. We were separate everything; separate security; separate rooms. The room we were together in was on stage and we functioned together well on stage. We all had our roles and knew what we were doing. That was the most comfortable place. The thing you have to remember is that it's not just us. There are 100 people working with us and it's everybody: everybody's emotions all wrapped up together and sometimes there's going to be conflict.' Wilder confirms, 'It's true there was a bit of juggling around with rooms, because of practical things like Martin used to regularly have parties in his hotel room, so I don't think Fletch wanted to be next to him, or underneath him.' Gore: 'It started off as separate floors and then we realized you could still be above or below somebody, so we had to be on separate floors at opposite ends, and it ended up in a zig-zag pattern.'

Despite, or perhaps because of the internal haemorrhaging, Depeche Mode went down a storm every night, connecting with their fans who felt their own frailties expressed. This strong emotional connection froze out the support acts who were given a rough time by the audience. Spiritualized were kicked off the tour almost immediately after going down very badly. A spokesperson at Mute Records, recalls, 'People were booing and throwing things at them. The Depeche Mode crowd can be quite tough.' They were replaced by a Swedish bar band, Spirit, who jumped ship one night early. They were replaced by a jazz-rock fusion act, Cain and Abel, who were the entertainment at Depeche Mode's hotel. According to the Mute spokesperson, 'The band went to them and said, "Do you fancy a gig, supporting Depeche Mode?" and they agreed. They were only used to playing in bars and were suddenly playing in front of 16,000 people. And they went down really well – much better than Spiritualized.'

Then Miranda Sex Garden, who were on Mute at the time, stepped into the fray. Within a few days the band's violinist Hepzibah Sessa had struck up a friendship with Alan Wilder (they actually met on the keyboardist's birthday, 1 June 1993) and this developed into a long-term relationship. Sessa recalls, 'The Mode fans are a vociferous lot and they don't like support bands. I had bags of shit thrown at me, a turnip and rotting meat. But we were enjoying ourselves and the thing about Depeche Mode was they all came up and said, "Hello, nice to meet you." They were a very personable bunch. Martin had tried to be like that with Spiritualized and invited them to the bar and they'd given him the cold shoulder. Then they got very arsey when they were coined every night.'

Ironically after their June date in Berlin, Depeche Mode were banned from their regular hotel, the Intercontinental. There was a party in someone's room and people were getting a bit rowdy, but it wasn't anything serious. Suddenly the local riot police arrived in full gear – helmets, shields and truncheons. They were very embarrassed when they realized it was just guests having a bit of fun but the hotel management didn't see the funny side.

In Britain the fluctuating perceptions about the band improved when *NME*'s Paul Moody saw them at the Garbsen Stadium in Hannover, Germany on 31 May 1993. 'The show is the stuff of Gary Numan's dreams,' wrote Moody. 'An enormous stage looms over a vast green open space on the outskirts of Hanover. It is flanked by two huge mauve Depeche Mode symbols between which three solitary keyboards tower on a platform where the guitar amps should be. It's a masterpiece of subtlety: a stark, Bauhaus reminder that stadium pomp when stripped of the hoary trappings of MTV, can still hold you in awe at its sheer mind-blowing magnitude.' *Time Out*'s Lee Davies also checked out the band in Europe. His view was that 'The show is spectacular. The powerful set, mostly culled from the last two rockier albums and a handful of carefully treated old favourites, accompanied by Anton Corbijn's striking, sometimes tacky, sometimes moving, sometimes bewilderingly arty images, is matched by the audience's complete commitment to the performance, pushing singer David Gahan ever further into his mock-God role, so that he takes the crowd with him on every mood change, every handclap.'

So far so good. The familiar mix of cocaine, Ecstasy and drink fuelled the all-night parties but they still retained a machine-like efficiency when it came to performing. However, Gahan threw a spanner into the works when he pushed his rock-star creation to new highs (or lows) by jumping into the front rows of the crowd at their Mannheim show on 12 June. 'I thought, I'm going to do it as if I'm diving off the top board at Basildon at 16 at Oswald Park swimming pool,' says Gahan of his plunge into the heaving crowd. 'Me and my mate Jay used to dive off the top, get up enough courage to dive off that top board. You just go, YES! Somebody's going to pick you up, they can rip you apart but they eventually will put you back up. You feel it, it's scary, it's a weird thing with all these hands, a million hands all over you, pulling you, and you see faces and suddenly you see someone like one of our security guards and they're like, "Dave, we've got you." They ripped my shirt off, it was really funny.

'The true story of Mannheim is I just went too far, too far to the front of the stage. I could hear it. I just knew I wasn't going to go back. So that was the first time. I thought, fuck it I might as well fly into them, they're going to pick me up. So I just went for it and got one of the biggest charges I ever got in my fucking life, getting back

on stage. They just tear you apart. They want something, like everybody does I suppose.'

A few weeks later *NME*'s Gavin Martin reported that the scratches
on Gahan's arms were 'inflicted by rabid fans who tore their idol
apart in Germany'. However, the *NME* writer also hinted at the
band's 'dirty little secret', and his description of the singer was a
repulsive, yet oddly compelling portrait of a strung-out, wasted rock
star: 'He doesn't look or sound like a well man. His skin is sickly grey,
his eyes sunk into blueish sockets. The insides of his long skinny arms
are all bruised and scratched.

'Gahan's own private dressing room has been transformed into a
darkened coven. Candles burn on table-tops, on flight cases and
other surfaces provided by his makeshift on the road furniture. Loud
music blasts from his hi-fi, Jasmine incense sticks are burned to give
the atmosphere he desires. Behind him there's a red carpet, hung
against the wall, the final touch in this full rock 'n' roll Parnassian set
up. Such are the trappings that befit a Cool Icon, a man playing, or
trying to play the role of A Rock God.'

Gavin Martin also described the numbed hysteria which Gahan
sometimes relapsed into on stage at the MTK Stadium, Budapest,
Hungary on 27 July. 'Gahan's performance was disconnected, flail-
ing helplessly as he tried to brandish and capture a spurious sense of
bigness.' *Rolling Stone*'s Steven Daly also referred to Gahan
'borrowing every stadium-rock trick in the book' in his review of the
Hungary show. The frontman conceded afterward, 'Tonight I felt like
shit. I felt like I've got a fucked-up voice. I'm just borrowing time. But
you go on there and you see all these people and they're all waiting
all day and you can just smell 'em. So you just gotta fucking go for it.
And when you touch them it's just incredible, they'll kill you. They
tried a couple of times.'

Although the band recoiled from these criticisms and closed ranks,
when I reviewed Depeche Mode in Detroit for *Vox* magazine a year
later, I felt much the same way about Gahan's strangely uninvolving
display: 'There's no sign of a physical let-up, as he snakes around the
mic stand and bounds across to the front row. However, he looks
numb and preoccupied in between bursts of melodrama. It's understandable because of the enormous effort of will needed to satisfy a
fanatical following over such a long tour. Furthermore, there's no

way back because the band's set is built for Gahan to roam around and make his stadium-sized gestures.' Gahan's vulnerability was palpable as he thrashed around like a proto-Robbie Williams, but without the jokes. He communicated something to the audience, behind the absurdly over-inflated ego, which was a simple, fragile and basic desire to be loved by absolutely everyone there.

In a lurid but insightful piece the *NME* journalist, Gavin Martin, also picked up on 'the internal struggles, the turmoil played out in their songs, the lavish hedonistic conceit that has grown around them', which the band have worked hard to keep private for most of their career. However, Gahan wasn't ready to spill the beans on his drug habit for a while yet and the other band members tried to shrug off the rumours. Gore countered, 'They're writing these stories at the moment that Dave has AIDS or he's dying or he's on heavy drugs, and it's so funny because it doesn't actually do us any harm, it sells more records. Anyone reading it must think, "That sounds really interesting, I've got to go and buy that!" I think kids would rather buy albums from bands with a bit of scandal than from the boring gits that we really are.'

On 31 July Depeche Mode returned to England where they played to 30,000 people at London's Crystal Palace Bowl, supported by the Sisters of Mercy. They felt dissatisfied with the show from the start as it was still daylight when they came on stage, which undermined their intro-atmospherics. 'To be honest I can't remember much about the performance,' says Wilder, 'but I do remember the party afterwards.' There were girls in conical bras and fishnet tights, and a porn-themed VIP area, but this was light, throwaway stuff compared to what was happening in the band's inner-sanctum. Gahan was in his own candlelit cabal, where one friend remembers, 'Seeing him with his relatives was really weird; seeing him with his son – there seemed to be an invisible wall between them.'

Another insider said: 'I think David does a good job but he has a lot of problems. I think he's looking for something really. I really think what he needs is love, he needs to be loved.' Chris Carr was also there: 'At Crystal Palace I saw something pretty horrendous,' he admits. 'The band called up and invited me and I brought my kids along. There were lots of layers around the band – the big party on the outside with no expense spared and people going mental but backstage it was very weird. It's true there were a lot of women backstage but most of them were friends. It was strange though because Fletch walked up to me and goes, "The cunt wants to see you." And I said, who are you talking about? And he says, "Dave, he wants to speak to you. He's got his own dressing room area and he wants to see you. It's down the bottom there, go and see him." Then Martin comes up and he says, "Have you seen Dave?" and I said, no, and he was like, "Well, he wants to see you. We're not talking to him." Then finally I walk down to the next staging post and Dave was there with his family. His child, Jack, was there. Dave came running up to me, a big hug and everything. He had all these marks on his arms which he claimed were scratches from the audience, you know ... There were a lot of people around him, who as far as I could see were living the party life, and as long as Dave was still up for it and was still standing, he was obviously the centre. It was awful. Anyway, apparently Dave wanted to talk to me about Nick Cave, who'd cleaned himself up and got himself into rehab. I personally felt inept, because I didn't feel that I was in the position to ring up Daniel and say, "What the fuck is going on? How did it get to this point?"'

Gahan later told the press about his son coming to see the band at Crystal Palace, although the singer felt extremely proud and sentimental about the occasion: 'He saw us at the Crystal Palace Football Ground in London and I think he just tripped out completely. He suddenly realized what Dad does and that I wasn't a complete loser. He's got all my moves down and he really enjoyed watching. That made me feel real good.

'I haven't seen him for a while. It's almost impossible if you're on the road for a long time. You can't take kids on the road. I'm going to see him soon and I got a report from his school and he's doing great. That was interesting to read. He's seven this year.'

For the next few weeks Alan Wilder started work in U2's Windmill Lane Studios in Dublin on a live album from the tour, while the others took a break. He also worked on the sound for the forthcoming *Devotional Live* video. On 8 September Depeche Mode launched their Canada, USA and Mexico tour in Canada's Quebec City, where Gahan and Daryl Balmonte were arrested after a 'scuffle' with a hotel employee. A few days later they released a new single, the gospel anthem 'Condemnation', backed by a new mix of 'Death's Door'. Gore's 'dialogue with God', which *NME* described as 'perv gospel', was remixed by Alan Wilder and Steve Lyon at Guilliame Tell Studios during the band's time in Paris at the end of June. Wilder incorporated additional hip-hop drum loops and female gospel voices provided by Hildia Cambell and Samantha Smith.

A month or so later Anton Corbijn shot the video in the countryside surrounding Budapest. Corbijn himself names 'Condemnation' as one of his worst videos, as Gahan is dragged across a field in a messiah-like pose by Cambell and Smith, while the rest of the band are dressed up as monks. To add insult to injury, the American record company didn't want to release 'Condemnation' as a single, insisting the band make a video for 'One Caress'. That was shot just outside Chicago by Kevin Kerslade, on a very cold day which did nothing for the band's spirits. Wilder recalls, 'The only amusing part of the whole event was when half of the creatures used in the video escaped into the trees and the crew had to spend the rest of the night coaxing them down – pretty hard when you're talking about a cockroach ...'

This leg of the tour consisted of a stamina-sapping 49 dates, climaxing in Mexico City's Sports Palace on 3 December 1993. The partying was relentless, although by now Andy Fletcher's fragile mental state was a real problem. 'Fletch was unbearable at that time because he was either so depressed or complaining about being depressed,' says Wilder. 'His initial thing about depression manifested itself by complaints of illness which I think is quite a common thing, not that I know much about the nature of depression. Of course his problems were mental not physical.' Gahan: 'At this point when we're touring, it's very much down to the individual to deal with it their own way. There doesn't have to be much interaction between us except for meetings about what's happening. It's not a particularly creative process.'

Absurd, scary, funny incidents started to pile up through the tour. 'Remember New Orleans?' Gahan later commented on the 8 October show. 'At the end of the gig I couldn't go back for the encore. Mart had to do a song solo while all the paramedics rushed me off to hospital. I'd overdosed, I'd had a heart attack. Next day, we didn't think any more about it.'

Wilder remains sceptical about the frontman's description of the incident: 'There was an occasion, which is a little bit vague to me now, when apparently a medic was called in when Dave was off stage. I was probably back on stage with Martin doing a slowie. Apparently during that time Dave had a bit of a turn and a heart palpitation but I think overdose and heart attack is a pretty shocking way to describe the incident.'

On 16 October there was another scare when Gore and Wilder set off for a short break in the West Indies – it was a coincidence that they'd both decided to go to the Caribbean, so they flew together. 'It's strange but on that tour we had a few flights where things went wrong,' recalls Wilder from the security of his art-deco home. 'On one occasion we had this private jet for most of the travel and we were going between New York and somewhere upstate and there was a terrible storm. The sky outside was a deep orangey-grey colour and we couldn't land in this weather. Then the pilot, just to instil confidence, said, "We're running out of fuel lads!". Cheers, thanks for telling us mate. Eventually we risked a landing and on the third attempt we made it.

'The worst one was this flight with Martin from Dallas to the Caribbean,' says the keyboard player, who has been a nervous flyer ever since. 'After 20 minutes or so, there was a loud bang and I think all the oxygen masks came down. It was some kind of pressurization problem. There was a fair amount of panic and the air hostesses, tearfully embracing each other, didn't exactly inspire confidence. The pilot had to turn around and we sat through a hair-raising 20 minutes as the plane tried to make it back to Dallas. We had a few minutes of serious worry. I was trying to stay calm and Mart was being a doom merchant, you know, "Oh no, we're all going to die." It was obviously a tense moment but it wasn't like we suddenly bonded or anything. Later on, we were reliably informed that had we been at our proper cruising altitude, this would have been a major incident. The telling thing about that was what we did afterwards which was to get completely pissed back in Dallas which we'd flown back to. Martin suggested that we get a private jet to the islands and generously paid the £15,000. He said, "Come on, I'll get a plane and you can come with me", because we were going to different locations in the West Indies. So then we went to a local bar where a lot of people recognized us and before you knew it we were entertaining this little crowd in there. We got rat-arsed and the next thing I remember was waking up in the back of this plane in the West Indies. Mart had given me a sleeping pill to stop me worrying about the flight.'

When they all got back on tour a few days later it was Daryl Balmonte's 30th birthday. 'As I've said they all have an amazing capacity for going on binges,' he says, sipping a pint in a Soho pub. 'My 30th birthday in Chicago was one of the classic ones. It lasted three days!'

Although the band always showed up for gigs, the partying was taking its toll. The first serious victim of the Devotional tour was Martin Gore who had a seizure in the middle of a business meeting in the Sunset Marquis hotel in Los Angeles, at the end of November. Gahan later recalled, 'He keeled over and started banging his head on the floor, making these really weird noises.' Fletcher: 'I really thought the whole tour was over.' Wilder shakes his head as he relates what happened: 'We were all sitting around this boardroom table, when Mart suddenly stood up and then went weird. He shook a bit, his eyes glazed over and then he was on the floor convulsing. I realized it wasn't the first time it had happened. He'd been complaining of memory loss a few weeks before. He came down from his room and said, "I can't remember anything about this afternoon". We were like, "Oh, shut up Mart". He's being mad again. And of course, he must've had a blackout in his room.' Gore regained consciousness within the hour and was told by the doctor it was a fit brought on by stress and alcohol-abuse. 'I think the fact that everyone witnessed it brought home to him the seriousness of the problem,' says Wilder. 'He realized he was over-doing it and so he curbed his drinking a bit.'

The band's songwriter was also suffering from panic attacks, which would send his heart pounding to the point where his 'pulse felt strange' in his arms, and he felt he was, 'going to die at any moment'. 'I can never work out if I'm just being realistic or if I'm a total hypochondriac,' he commented later. 'That probably comes through in the music. Maybe it's not real danger at all and I'm an eternal pessimist but sometimes I think it's based on reality.'

Relief from the excesses was just around the corner when the band returned to Britain for a short pre-Christmas tour, playing arena dates in Dublin, Birmingham, Manchester, Sheffield and London.

Reviews of these shows focused on Depeche Mode's new rock-ist characteristics, which were naturally reviled by the British media. *NME*'s Johnny Cigarettes attended the band's Birmingham NEC concert: 'After 13 years, Depeche Mode have finally embraced ROCK and got it WRONG. They haven't taken individualism, or invention, or drama or emotion: they've taken cliché, pretension, pomp, melodrama and bullshit and flogged its carcass once more ... Reservations of a different kind creep in when the other three are revealed, up on high podiums with cornflake-packet futuristic silver trimmings, mooging away like your mates in a fifth-form talent contest. At first it resembles a goth Des O'Connor backed by Ronnie Hazelhurst's avant-garde orchestra, but then Dave discards his jacket to reveal a black, bushy dress shirt and boogies badly on the catwalk. He is Martie Pellow's evil twin and I claim my £20 entrance fee back ... Of course, that's one thing you can't deny about Depeche Mode. They've never lost the ability to pen a brooding, stirring tune. "Everything Counts" finishes off the evening, reminding us that they can also write a pithy lyric to accompany them occasionally. But it's a cruel world, and even those talents are not sufficient to override the misguided avant-garde pretensions, pomp, shabby cultural baggage, confusion, cliché and bullshit this band are wallowing in. An unholy mess, frankly.'

Melody Maker's Taylor Parkes was even more scathing: 'The emptiness that pours from the stage of the NEC tonight has nothing to do with alienation, just vacancy.'

Songs of Faith and Devotion Live was released on 6 December but only reached a lowly 46. The tracklisting exactly followed that of the original album, a twist on the increasingly common remix LPs, but it was impossible to convey the original flow and atmosphere of the live shows in such a regimented format. Gahan: 'We wanted to do something special. So we put out an album that was a live performance of one of our studio albums. We thought the fans would really get into it.' The British reviews of the live album were typically barbed. Andrew Smith, *Melody Maker*: 'There's nothing wrong with it. It's fine. We just don't learn anything new. Life and live albums tend to be a bit like that, don't they? Oh well.' Clark Collis, *Select* magazine: 'Depeche Mode should not make live albums. On record they have mastered the art of combining technology and emotion with often devastating results. On stage they merely seem to have mastered the art of getting people to use more lighter fuel than is eco-friendly.' However, *Arena* magazine did point out that 'there's real power and urgency in these performances'.

The *Devotional* video was also unleashed on the Christmas market. Ben Willmott conceded in the *NME*: 'Fair's fair, the stage set looks brilliant throughout, but the effect is horribly muted by small-screen viewing, and the Mode's icy music gains nothing in the live arena ... Artistically and musically it adds precious little to what we already know.' Ian Cranna was a voice of enthusiastic sanity in *Q* magazine: 'It's the combination of lighting and design that really impresses, however. There's no attempt to dazzle or be flashy – it's all kept simple and sparing, including the evocative but non-nostalgic images which enhance rather than distract, and are perfectly in tone with the music ... An absorbing experience even for non-diehard fans, *Devotional* is a wonderful, creative example of achieving success without artistic compromise.'

Christmas came and went with Wilder only able to enjoy a short break because he and Lyon had to fly to a studio in Milan for three weeks to prepare a new version of the show for South Africa, Australia, Asia and South America, plus the second leg of the American tour. The opener, 'Higher Love', was replaced by a dynamic version of 'Rush' which sparked into life with a thrilling techno sequence. Wilder also reworked a trip-hop version of 'I Want You Now'.

Meanwhile the band's vote to do a second tour of America in outdoor 'sheds' was not unanimous. Gahan and Wilder had been the most aggressive in pushing for further dates, Gore was also in favour but Fletcher was adamantly against it. He had the support of Daniel Miller, who believed the group were risking ill health and permanently damaged relationships if they put themselves through this relentless, extended schedule. 'The second American tour was where Fletch bailed out and that's where it went really nuts,' explains the Mute boss. 'There was a big split in the camp about the second leg of the tour. I'd gone along to quite a number of dates and you couldn't really speak to Dave because he was locked in his dressing room; Martin was drinking a lot and not enjoying it at all; Fletch was very tense and Al was very distant. There were three limos. They put up with each other on stage and at the occasional record company dinner but that was it. Pretty horrible, really. Then this idea of going back to America came up. I personally was against it and very vocal about it. Fletch obviously couldn't deal with it. But there were a lot of reasons why they did it. The other members of the band felt they were on a roll, a party they didn't want to stop.

'There was also a financial aspect to it. The production had been very expensive up to that point. They'd lived it up in terms of costs – suites in the most expensive hotels, the band paying huge bar bills every night, we're talking about lots of money. I think there was a realization that they hadn't made much profit on the tour and so there was an element of, well, now that we've started, let's keep going and make it more of a financial success. There were some elements who felt that was important. And they did cut down production costs on the American tour. But I was against it, the American record company were against it, Fletch was against it, and everyone else was for it. The American record company and me both felt, they've done America, there's no new product in the market place, they're in bad shape, this isn't going to do them any good from a career point of view. And I don't think it did. If they wanted to make a lot of money out of it and that was the sole purpose of it, then so be it, but they came out of it completely shot to pieces.'

On 10 January Depeche Mode released another single from *Songs of Faith and Devotion*, a Butch Vig mix of 'In Your Room'. Some band members didn't like it but it actually possesses a restrained beauty which the original sacrificed for power. *NME*'s Paul Moody summed it up as, 'a tedious peice of cod-meaningful bilge' which only served to highlight the degree to which the band were still underrated in their home country. Anton Corbijn came up with another imaginative promo for the song, although the S&M imagery of the individual band members each in turn strapped to a chair was not appreciated by MTV America who refused to play it. Linked by the simple image of a lightbulb, the promo also recreated various scenes from old Depeche Mode videos. 'It was the last song off the album and the situation with Dave made me question whether it was going to be their last ever video,' confesses Corbijn, 'so I made it into a retrospective look at the work we'd done together. Did I tell Dave what I was doing? No, I didn't.'

Alan Wilder and Lyon only just completed the new set in time, and the keyboard player flew directly from Italy to South Africa where the next phase of the tour was due to start on 9 February. They played seven dates at the huge Standard Bank in Johannesburg, along with two in Durban and another couple in Cape Town. Gahan was acting no differently from his antics in Europe and America. Wilder: 'Of course, everybody was concerned about his welfare but addicts are notoriously difficult to dissuade from their cause unless they themselves really want to change. At the time Dave wasn't in that frame of mind and therefore any advice given to him fell on deaf ears.' Gore: 'We worried about Dave's health. One of the main considerations for me was whether it would be better for Dave if we ended the band, because the trappings – access to whatever he wanted – were obviously not doing him much good.' Fletch: 'Dave was pretty bad at the time. He was sort of engrossed in his habit all the time, and it was like one big party, which does take its toll.'

However, it wasn't Gahan who was hospitalized in South Africa – the latest casualty of the Devotional tour was Alan Wilder. Balmonte relishes a chuckle as he recalls, 'Alan had decided he had a bit of indigestion and then I went to the lift and I could hear him screaming. So he was rushed to hospital and had to have this thing shoved down his dick.' It turned out that the keyboard player was suffering from kidney stones – 'A definite side effect of all the drinking', claims Balmonte.

Wilder returned to the band after a couple of days and on 1 March they started their Australia and Far East tour at Singapore's Indoor Stadium. Over the course of the next month Depeche Mode performed in Perth, Adelaide, Melbourne, Brisbane, Sydney, Hong Kong, Manila and Honolulu. However, a much more serious problem than Wilder's booze-inflicted innards deepened over the course of these dates. Fletcher's stressed-out mental state was aggravated by a feeling of isolation and homesickness on the Far East tour. The American dates, which he'd strongly objected to, had extended the tour until July, which was a big personal blow as his wife was expecting their second child in the summer. Fletcher was trying his best to see things through to the end of the tour but it was a day-to-day struggle. He was no longer in a state where he wanted to party with the others which meant that he was thousands of miles from home and on a completely different timetable to the rest of the band and most of the road crew. He'd wake up at nine o'clock and often wouldn't see anyone for hours until they started to emerge in the afternoon. 'With the targets, the deadlines, the partying, the excess, I just lost it,' he later acknowledged. 'I had an obsessive-compulsive disorder which made me displace this stress into worries about bodily symptoms. This sounds terrible, but I thought I had a brain tumour. I couldn't sleep, I couldn't think, this headache wouldn't go away. I had tests, it wasn't a brain tumour, it was a breakdown.'

Even luxurious distractions and day-to-day avoidance weren't enough to cushion Wilder and Gahan from Fletcher's depression, and in the end they complained to Gore that it was an intolerable situation for everyone. Gore: 'It was very difficult. Andy's been my closest friend since we were 12. But, for the others, he'd become unbearable. I justified it by thinking that it would be better for him if he went home and got some professional advice.' Fletcher wasn't pushed, he wanted to go but Gore recognized that it was the right thing for his friend and the band. Miller also recalls a conversation with Fletcher where the latter made it very clear that he wasn't going to play the added dates and needed a break. Miller: 'I remember speaking to Fletch about the U.S. tour and him saying, "Well, I'm not going on it." He just couldn't mentally do it, even if he wanted to. I think there was pressure from band members as well, saying he was impossible to be with. But I'm sure it was his decision to leave and not theirs. That's my memory of it. And it was never a question of him permanently leaving the band.'

So at the end of the Asian dates, Fletcher checked himself into a hospital where he told Daniel Miller that he was never going to do another tour with Wilder or Balmonte, who'd formed a party-hungry faction on the tour. Fletcher: 'Once I was back home I went into hospital for four weeks. I've recovered since. I took up yoga, relaxation. I think I'm a much stronger person now. Hopefully, there won't be a repeat.' Happily on 22 June 1994 Grainne gave birth to their son, Joseph.

Daryl Balmonte was drafted in as Fletcher's replacement for the rest of the tour, spending a week in Hawaii being coached by Wilder. 'Alan felt that a session player would be much more accomplished but they wouldn't know the songs, so it would be much harder,' says the friend-turned-roadie, tour manager and replacement band member. 'I wasn't asked, I was told. Dave phoned me up when we were in Australia. He said, "Fletch is going home, you're playing keyboards." I was like, Oh, OK. I think it was a natural thing. I would have been a bit offended if they hadn't asked me.'

The South America and Mexico tour opened on 4 April 1994 in Sao Paulo, Brazil. Over the next few weeks, the band performed in Buenos Aires, Argentina and Chile, where they heard the devastating news that Nirvana's Kurt Cobain had committed suicide. Gahan's instant response was confused, drug-addled anger: 'I had become a complete cliché of myself. I remember in Chile when I got the news that Kurt had blown his head off, my first reaction was that I was angry. I was pissed off. I felt like he'd stolen my idea, like he'd beaten me to it. That's how fucked up I was. I really was that gone.' On the same evening he shared an increasingly rare intimate moment with Gore, when they were able to communicate with each other – even if they were both off their faces at the time. 'It was in Chile, the same night as the Kurt Cobain thing happened. It was very late and we'd been drinking a lot. Whether Martin was drunk, I don't know if he can even remember it but it stuck in my mind anyway. He said to me that he feels like he gets his songs ... like something from God and he thought that he was losing it because he was drinking and stuff. For some reason, he thought he had to channel that work through me, and I was his voice, kind of thing, which I thought was the most beautiful thing he had ever said to me. I mean we were both in one of those I love you modes, but it really stuck in my mind like maybe I really am supposed to deliver some kind of message, you know.' This revealing comment highlights how insecure and vulnerable Gahan felt about his role as the band's singer and also seems to back up Wilder's description of Gore as an open character when he's drunk but often frustratingly forgetful and undemonstrative when he's not had a drink.

After completing dates in Costa Rica and Mexico, Depeche Mode were able to grab three weeks off before the final haul across America with the slightly altered, stripped-back production. Anton Corbijn, who had to re-edit some of his visual projections, notes, 'they are all quite keen on the money. They all expect to make a lot of profit.' This infamous 34-date trek across the States ran from 12

May to 8 July, taking the total number of people who saw Depeche Mode in 1993 and '94 to over two million. During this latest phase Gahan's 'antics' took on legendary status as he partied hard with the new support act, Primal Scream. 'I knew what I was doing,' says Gahan, 'it was all conscious stuff. I picked the Scream because I'd heard that they liked to party. And I really like their record and it sounded like it'd be a good time, like we'd be a good combination. And we did have a good time, it was a lot of fun. And I was able to function, whatever that was, and do whatever I had to do to get through the shows.'

Daniel Miller was exasperated by Gahan's enthusiastic push for the hard-living, drug-weathered Primal Scream. 'When I heard that Primal Scream were going to support them, I thought it was a complete joke,' he recalls. 'I'm just the record company at the end of the day and touring has always been a very separate thing from the records in terms of how it's planned, financially and everything else. I was very vocal when I heard about Primal Scream, I thought it was ridiculous but to be honest I don't think it made any difference who was the support band. The band were in their own bubble. The fact that they had some mates to do it with, well, they had plenty of other people they could party with. Dave wanted Primal Scream to party with him but I don't think he was that discriminating at that point. I don't think he would have been any different with or without Primal Scream. And legend has it, although I don't know whether it's true or not, that Primal Scream were shocked by the amount of stuff going on during that tour and they had to pull back.'

Gahan has described the new tour routine: 'There'd be a knock at the door before the show and it's Innes, or Throb or Bobby, from the Scream. "Have ye got a wee sniff, Mr G? I cannae make it tonight, I've been on the Jack all day. I just need a wee sniff." Really funny. And, of course, I'd supply them with what they needed. Bobby balanced it really well. He knew where to stop. I didn't. I didn't realize that nobody actually did play the game that hard. And the Scream proved that.'

'I'm not sure that Gahan suggested them but he jumped on it,' remembers Wilder, 'because he loved Primal Scream – their music and the fact that he thought it would be great to have someone in a similar condition to himself on the road. He literally spent more time with them than with us. He would go and stand on the side of the stage and watch them play every night. Sometimes he'd be there with his harmonica puffing away and later they'd all jam together in their hotel rooms. Martin would be there and Daryl but I wasn't interested in sitting in a hotel room all night and having serious head-to-heads with other musos, jamming!' Gahan: 'We had fantastic times, sitting up 'til seven, eight, eleven in the morning, in my room, with Mick Jones yabbering on at me, "You gotta eat! You gotta eat!"

Select magazine journalist Andrew Perry covered the tour: 'Gahan was obviously in awe of them but the Scream were in complete disarray from the minute they joined the tour in California. They'd just completed three weeks of gigs in Europe and another three weeks in Britain, and they were cream-crackered. When they landed in San Francisco, they were immediately given a hard time by customs who assumed they must be carrying drugs because they were a rock band. And that night they had to play in Sacramento.'

Primal Scream generated plenty of their own stories during their time on the road with Depeche Mode. On 31 May Joseph Flores, a Park Ranger, ' … received a call in my car from an officer who was having problems on the San Antonio river. She was calling for back-up because five young men had taken off everything except for their underclothes and jumped in the river near the 400 block of River Walk downtown. One of them had damaged the light on the front of her patrol boat when she approached them. When I got there, they were rowdy and very intoxicated. I had to arrest them and take them down to the jail in handcuffs. It was only then that we learned one of them was the guitarist for the group, Primal Scream.'

On 16 June at Jones Beach Amphitheatre, Wantaugh, New York, Perry was able to observe Gahan at close quarters. 'Gahan was in a right state by then, with ropey American rock chicks hanging around him, all ripped fishnets and stilettos, incapable even of putting their lipstick on straight. They had a roadie who would go out every night and pick out the 15 or 20 most beautiful girls in the crowd and take them backstage, evidently for the Mode's pleasure.

'Scream always took along boxes of records and had a couple of decks in the dressing room, so there were all these people dancing, and Dave Gahan sitting in the middle of the room in an armchair, apparently shovelling cocaine up his nose at a frightening rate.

Suddenly, he seemed to realize I was a journalist, and he pointed at me and one of his big flunkies came and got me. I had to kneel down beside the armchair to make it possible for him to talk to me. He started burbling on about how people didn't understand him, but then his mood changed suddenly and he said, "I'm gonna curse you!" and next thing I know he's bitten me on the neck. By now he was shouting and everybody was watching him until he stormed out of the room still yelling about putting a curse on me.

'I assumed he was completely out of it but then, on stage, he was totally together and professional. Mind you, the show was weird. Dave being a rock star for two hours, while the others were 20 feet up on podia tinkling away at synths.'

Despite these extreme stories, Bobby Gillespie has subsequently tried to shrug off the tour as ' … dead boring – I've never seen so few drugs in my life. That wee geezer, the singer, he had some but the rest of them didn't so we just got drunk the whole time. It was a waste of time.' Alan Wilder is also keen to make it clear that, ' … in spite of all these things it was the most successful tour with some of the best shows we'd ever played. I had a great time.' However, he does concede, 'What people have heard about that tour is all pretty much true. Everyone was indulging in their own thing, sometimes with destructive results but it's all part of the private way you deal with such a bizarre and unreal world.'

As the Devotional tour lurched into its final phase, Gahan often required cortisone shots for his voice and his performances continued to blow hot and cold. Depeche Mode fan Kevin C. Murphy recalls Gahan's troubling behaviour at the Great Woods Centre, Mansfield, Boston on 23 June: 'This was the worst of the three Depeche Mode shows I've been to, mainly because poor old Dave was staggering around on stage with a bottle for most of the time and generally looked like warmed-over ass. He screwed up the words to a few songs, which is embarrassing considering the crowd is singing along reverentially. Andy had gone back to England by this point and Alan Wilder looked irritated and ready to go. Martin seemed like the only one still stepping up to the plate. His solo set was probably the high spot of the show.'

At the band's concert in Detroit on 4 July there was a moment during 'Never Let Me Down Again' when the singer seemed

completely disconnected from the world around him. It was a vulnerable, rather desperate moment and I wrote in *Vox*: 'As Gahan claps
his hands and arches back with a wild grin, he sees an astronaut
beamed on to the screen behind him, one of the images created for
the tour by photographer/director Anton Corbijn. The figure looks a
little fragile and alone as he floats in space like a strung-out Major
Tom, projecting some of the dangerous frailties of the winged-man,
out on his own, below.' This was all the more alarming as there were
only three more shows to go before the world tour was finally over,
supposedly forcing everyone back into real life. It was hard to imagine the man up on the stage being able to adjust to normal, day-to-
day living.

St Andrews Hall, Detroit witnessed a big end-of-tour party
enhanced by erotic dancers and Martin Gore dressed up as a woman,
and less than a week later the last night of the tour took place at Deer
Creek Music Center, Indianapolis on 8 July. Marc Elfenbaum,
production manager at Deer Creek, remembers, 'That was quite
some night. During Depeche's set, the guys from Primal Scream
went out in the crowd and started firing off bottle rockets, which was
very dangerous and would have got them arrested, if our security
guys hadn't managed to defuse the situation. At the end of the show,
Dave Gahan decided to take a dive off the stage into the crowd, but
it was a 12-feet jump over the barrier, and he ended up going shoulder first into the seats which were fixed into a concrete floor. The
security guys waded in right away to stop him being mobbed, then
our first-aiders stretchered him off to St Vincent Hospital.'

Gahan: 'I came away from that tour with two broken ribs, haemorrhaging from the inside. I mean, it was 180 shows, I pushed myself
too far. My body was going on nothing, I landed on the crash barri-
ers and cracked two ribs. It took me 24 hours to feel anything I was
so drunk. Next day I was in incredible pain. They wanted me to stay
(in hospital) a while. I said, Look, I don't want to go into one of those
places, I'd rather do this on my own. So Teresa and I got a little cabin
up in Lake Tahoe, northern California and just kind of disappeared.
I was all strapped up for three weeks.'

Gahan didn't weigh more than 100 pounds at the end of the tour,
he was an addict and at eight o'clock every night he started to feel
twitchy as his body clock informed him it was approaching showtime.

'I was fried. Completely fried ... When the gigs were over and that was taken away from me and all the people around me had gone, all I was left with were the drugs.'

As soon as the tour was over, all the band members went their individual ways. This left Gahan cut off from the rest of the band who'd all gone home to England. No one picked up the phone. Gore later confessed, 'Because Dave went back to America, we didn't see him very often and we didn't speak on the phone very much, maybe not as much as we should have. Andy, I see all the time, because we have the same group of friends and so if I'm in London, I'm almost bound to bump into Andy at some point.'

While Andrew Fletcher continued to recuperate and spend time with his family through the remainder of 1994, Gore had to knock himself out with pills for the first few nights while he readjusted to life back at home. 'I got into some very bad habits on that tour. I was taking sleeping tablets every day and when I got home from the tour, I still had a couple left and so it gave me a few days of good sleep out of those tablets and I was totally back to normal.' On 27 August he married his partner Suzanne, and the outdoor party turned out to be the last time he saw Gahan for a long time – the singer arrived at four o'clock in the morning with various members of Primal Scream, after they'd jammed together earlier in the day on stage at the Reading Festival.

Alan Wilder broke up with his wife and took a holiday in the Scottish Highlands with his girlfriend, Hepzibah Sessa. During this peaceful time out, the pair shared an experience which was the final straw for the increasingly edgy survivor of several hazardous flights on the recent world tour. On 1 September 1994, an RAF Tornado on a routine training flight, crashed into a hillside near Lochearnhead, Perthshire in Scotland, killing two airmen on board. Wilder was showered with debris which scattered across the A85 road after the plane crashed some 200 yards away from his open-topped car.

'Hepzibah and I were on a peaceful drive north of Loch Earn and there were all these military jets, flying at low level,' says Wilder. 'We saw one coming straight at us. My girlfriend commented on how low it was flying, but I realized it was completely out of control. As I swerved off the road into a farm track, I heard the sound of the impact and witnessed an enormous explosion from which the smoke and debris almost engulfed me. Particles of carbon etc., began to rain down on to the open-top car. Beyond the bend, parts of the dead airmen's bodies were clearly visible in the road (i.e., parts of a seat-belt with guts attached, lumps of gore, etc), a parachute, burning shrapnel and a strong, sweet smell of fuel.

'Another few seconds and it would have hit us. I still have night-mares about it. It put me off flying for life. I didn't find religion or have any life-transforming experience but it left its mark. Both Hep and myself still have the odd nightmare. The thing that struck me was that such an instantaneous tragedy is immediately followed by the banality of continuing life. As two dead airmen were splattered across the road, the sun shone and the birds sang and no music played.'

This Twisted, Tortured Mess, 1994–7

Restless and still feeling lost in the post-tour comedown, Dave Gahan moved over to London for a short spell with Teresa. He's admitted he was filling up the vacuum left by the end of *Devotional* with more aggressive and greedy drug use. 'I spent a few months in London and that's when my habit got completely out of hand. In fact Teresa decided that she wanted to have a baby and I said to her, Teresa, we're junkies. Let's not kid ourselves, when you're a junkie, you can't shit, piss, come ... nothing. All those bodily functions go. You're in this soulless body, you're in a shell. But she didn't get it.'

They were together all the time in this short period following the Devotional tour, distanced from the real world in their own isolated bubble. 'That's something I have created for myself,' he confessed. 'You know, I chose to pull myself away from people and places, all due to trust and this guy only wants to be my friend because I'm in Depeche Mode, or whatever. I used that as an excuse and I found when I started using heroin, I didn't need anybody for a while. I'd be lying if I didn't say for a while it made me feel great. You know, but like anything if you over-use it, the novelty is gonna wear off and the feeling is gonna wear off. I almost got to the stage where I was picking and choosing people to be around me that I could just, boost the effect basically. That would make me feel like, yeah, you know this is the way it is man, so you know ...

'The bottom line is I didn't want to get clean. I thought I could control it. I thought I could do it maybe now and again, have a little party, little parties that lasted a month. And a month later, I'd be sitting there, shivering and wondering what happened.'

Gahan had fallen into a depressing pattern of using without feeling. 'Heroin stopped working for a long time,' he said of this stupefied period in his life. 'You're always chasing that first high and that goes away very quick. And then you've got to deal with just the constant depression and finding ways and means to get and use.'

Back in his Los Angeles apartment, the half-comatose singer withdrew in safety, surrounded by people who were constantly dropping by – a very mixed bunch of friends, dealers and sycophants. 'It was really bizarre,' recalls Gahan. 'We never lived alone. There was always somebody there. I didn't mind, I liked the company. At the time I was romanticizing about the idea of death and just slipping away. It wasn't part of the rock 'n' roll thing by then, it was just about me. I didn't like what I'd become and I didn't know how to end it. But, along with this, there was also something in me that wanted to live. I was always very afraid when I was on my own.'

However, when Gahan shot up heroin he wanted to be alone. 'I wasn't a social drug taker after the *Violator* tour, it was an isolated thing, in my house in Los Angeles. I had my own room, the Blue Room it was called, it was a blue closet and I'd shut myself in there.' Teresa and her best friend, Kippy, who lived with the couple, would occasionally knock on the door to see if he wanted anything. Gahan: 'I remember Kurt saying the same thing, he had a closet under the stairs. That was plenty enough room. I'd be in there with my candle and my spoon and that was it.'

Like Cobain, the singer was rich enough to indulge his habit as deeply as his body would allow it. 'In some ways it was much harder for me to hit rock bottom,' he explains, 'because I had an endless supply of fucking money. The dealers would come to me. It wasn't until the last year that most of my dealers began to cut me off. I'd been publicly getting into a lot of trouble with drugs so they didn't want to be around me any more.'

In this narcotic-driven environment it was impossible for Gahan to maintain an even keel, even when his son came to visit. 'Usually when he came out to visit me I'd been able to stop fixing for a while and keep it together. But it came to a point where I was so sick I rang my mother, and said, "Mum, Jack's due here in a couple of days and I've got a terrible flu. I can't cope on my own, can you come over?" I lied. There was a lot of lying going on.

'She came and I tried to do the whole thing – get up in the morning, make him his little egg, tried to be the dad. But I was kidding myself. I was cheating my son and I was cheating my mother. I knew it.

'One night after I'd put Jack to bed and my mum was asleep, I got my outfit together and banged up in the living room. Then I blacked out, overdosed. When I woke up I was sprawled across the bed. It was daylight and I heard voices from the kitchen. I thought, "Shit, I left all my shit out."

'I got up in a panic, ran down to the living room and it was all gone. So I ran into the kitchen and mum and Jack were sitting there, and I said, "What did you do with my stuff, mum?" She said, "I threw it in the rubbish outside." I ran out the door and brought in six black bags. If you can picture this insanity, I'm with my son and my mother – who, as far as I know, don't know anything about what's going on with me – and I brought in six bags, five of which were my neighbours', and emptied them out on the kitchen floor. I was on my hands and knees going through other people's garbage, until I found what I needed. Then I shut myself in the bathroom. Shortly after that, there's a knocking on the door. It bursts open and my son and my mother are there and I'm lying on the floor with the wounds open and everything. I say, "It's not what it looks like, Mum. I'm sick, I have to take steroids for my voice ..." All this fucking trash comes out of my mouth. Then I look up at my mum and she looks at me and I say, "Mum, I'm a junkie, I'm a heroin addict." And she says, "I know, love."

'Jack took my hand and led me into his bedroom and knelt me down on the floor and said to me, "Daddy, I don't want you to be sick any more." I said, "I don't wanna be sick any more either." He said, "You need to see a doctor." I said, "Yeah."

'Anyway I guess my mum must have rung Joanne. She came and picked Jack up and that was the last I saw of them for a long while. My mum stayed on for a bit to settle me down. She'd say, "We don't want you to die." And that didn't stop me, that didn't do it.'

Stung by guilt over the damage he was doing to his family relationships, Gahan resolved to kick his habit on his own over the Christmas holiday period at the end of 1994. ' I lay on the couch for a week like a zombie. Then one night, I turned to Teresa and I said, "I need help." So, I went into rehab for the first time.'

Over the next 12 months the singer would periodically check himself into a rehab clinic, opening up a whole contradictory mixture of self-deception and conscious lying to others. He's claimed that, 'Every time I tried to get sober, Teresa wouldn't stop her own using to help me. That's when you know it's over. Our marriage was pretty much non-existent anyway. We'd see each other occasionally, that was all. She didn't use like me, regularly. But in rehab they said that if one of us wasn't going to give up, it would be impossible for the other. I'd thought we loved each other. Now I think the love was pretty one-sided.'

However, Conway's apparent lack of support wasn't just selfishness; she had no reason to believe in Gahan's self-righteousness. After all, in Los Angeles, there was a long-established culture of pop stars, actors and celebrities checking themselves in and out of rehab – all lying to each other, themselves and in a bizarre, twisted way, actually self-aggrandizing their lives through this process. Gahan has admitted that he didn't take the rehab programmes at all seriously: 'I'd go to these meetings and be as fucking high as a kite among all these sober people. And you can't imagine a worse place to be when you're loaded. I used to go to the bathroom and shoot up, then come back and raise my hand and say, "I got 30 seconds clean!" I was taking the piss really, but I was doing it to myself.'

Daniel Miller was in touch with the situation via Jonathan Kessler, who lived in LA and stuck by the frontman through thick and thin. In fact, the accountant's close relationship with Gahan, coupled with his clear, sharp-witted business abilities, sealed Kessler's role as the band's full-time manager from 1994 onwards. Everyone felt they could trust him and if he could also help Dave Gahan overcome his drug problem, that would be a vital contribution to the future of the group. 'Jonathan was very good with Dave through all the ups and downs that you have with people in that condition,' remembers Miller. 'He was very solidly there.'

One time when the singer did manage to sober up after a six-week stay at a clinic in Arizona, he met his wife and passionately explained his desire to stay off heroin and remain clean. Conway didn't believe him and told her husband that she wasn't going to change. While that hardly helped his resolve, the cold, grim reality of straight, day-to-day living was the real reason he soon returned to his drugs: 'I was talking about the rest of my life here. So, of course, it wasn't long after that that I started using again but in secret. Gradually Teresa got sick and tired of picking me off the floor and she decided to split,' he confesses, in a more sympathetic portrayal of his marriage break-up.

Although they'd been partners in crime, and in many ways, brought out the worst in each other, Gahan did not break his habit when his wife left. 'Trust issues have been going on all my life, so when Teresa left I was then given the excuse to go out and get even more fucked up. I was hell-bent on going the whole hog. My wife had left me, my friends were disappearing and so I was surrounded by a bunch of junkies. And I knew exactly what was going on, y'know. I had money, I had me drugs and that's why they were around. I knew it and that fuelled my anger even more.'

He lived on his own, chasing his own '... shadows around the apartment. I imprisoned myself, became comfortable in my prison, or I thought I was comfortable. I was hiding from myself and what I was doing to myself. I could see it in people's faces.' Gahan was often reckless with his drugs, pushing himself further with a numb, fatalistic carelessness. Now that there were fewer friends around to keep an eye on him, he would sometimes overdose and get ripped off by his junkie friends. He remembers one time waking up on a dealer's lawn, wearing only his trousers, shoes and socks. His wallet, shirt, silver watch and jewellery were all stolen. As he slowly came round he worked out what had happened – he'd overdosed inside the house and had been thrown out. Gahan struggled to his feet and started hammering on the dealer's front door, slurrily taunting them with the fact they hadn't found the $400 that he'd hidden in his sock. The dealer was wearing his watch when she opened the door and let him in. The next week he went back to the same place to score again: 'I had to. They were my so called friends.'

While Gahan's life festered in Los Angeles, back in England there was no communication between Alan Wilder and the other members of Depeche Mode. In early summer 1995 he called a meeting in London with Andy Fletcher and Martin Gore to inform them he was leaving the band. This came as no surprise to Daniel Miller who was sure at least one band member would bail out after the Devotional tour. 'I knew something had to give,' says Miller. 'I knew that the four of them could never work together again. That was not going to happen. They had some kind of a discussion at some point, I can't remember when, and Alan said, "Look, the next album I don't really want you guys to be around in the studio." And that was it really. If somebody had to go it had to be Al. In the chemistry of the band, somehow, Fletch couldn't go because him and Mart were part of the same thing in a sense and Mart's the songwriter, so it had to be Alan. He was the one who was laying down the law a bit and saying this is how he wanted it to be for the next album. All the others were saying, "Well, that's not how we see things for the next record." '

Despite what he'd said to Miller from his sick bed, Fletcher had calmed down over the months following his breakdown and was telling friends he would work with Wilder again – as long as the west London man wasn't calling all the shots. Neither the unconfrontational Gore or the zonked-out Gahan had any intention of forcing the issue with Wilder, so it was very much the keyboard player's own initiative to make the break: 'I arranged a meeting at our offices to tell them I was leaving the band,' he explains. 'I sort of knew at the end of the tour that I wanted to go, but I thought, well, I'm going to give myself six months just to make sure that I haven't got clouded vision. And in six months I did feel exactly the same. I couldn't call Dave into a meeting so I phoned him but I couldn't get hold of him. I tried several times and he didn't return any of my calls so I sent him a fax saying, "Look, I've tried to call you, Dave. I can't get hold of you, I've just had a meeting with the others to say I've left the group. Good luck", and so on. In the meantime at this meeting, Martin was fine but Fletch seemed to take it quite personally which I couldn't really understand. I said to him, "Look, I've just had enough of being in a group. For whatever reason I'm not particularly enjoying it." He seemed to take it as a personal affront somehow. Martin didn't, he just said, "yeah, OK," and shook my hand. That kind of situation is never going to be comfortable.

'I don't think they knew what I was going to say. I think they were a bit surprised. I'm sure they knew I wasn't particularly happy because it must've been in my body language for the last couple of years and I know they've said Dave was in his own world and Alan was in his own world. But I don't think they expected me to say, "right I'm off", just like that.' Although this news was hardly a surprise, Fletcher's response in the meeting was probably a momentary flash of panic.

Wilder's resolve effectively meant there were now only two function-
ing members of Depeche Mode left – Gore and Fletcher. One insider
alleges, 'There's no doubt Alan thought he'd split the band when he
walked out of the meeting. He knew Dave was in a bad way, and he
didn't believe there was any realistic chance of another Depeche
Mode album – especially now he was gone. I think maybe he regrets
that decision now.' Wilder counters this, arguing that he's never
'doubted it or regretted doing it'. He adds, 'I think anyone has a right
to leave a group and do something different with their lives. For me
being in a gang, well, at a certain age it just doesn't feel right. I don't
feel bitter in any way but my personal feeling is that we'd peaked and
it was the right time to go.'

On 1 June 1995 Wilder issued a statement to the press: 'Due to
increasing dissatisfaction with the internal relations and working
practices of the group, it is with some sadness that I have decided to
part company from Depeche Mode. My decision to leave the group
was not an easy one, particularly as the last few albums were an indication of the full potential that Depeche Mode were realizing.

'Since joining in 1982, I have continually striven to give total
energy, enthusiasm and commitment to the furthering of the group's
success and in spite of a consistent imbalance in the distribution of
the workload, willingly offered this. Unfortunately, within the group,
this level of input never received the respect and acknowledgement
that it warrants.

'Whilst I believe that the calibre of our musical output has
improved, the quality of our association has deteriorated to the point
where I no longer feel that the end justifies the means. I have no wish
to cast aspersions on any individual; suffice to say that relations have
become seriously strained, increasingly frustrating and, ultimately, in
certain situations, intolerable.

'Given these circumstances, I have no option but to leave the
group. It seems preferable therefore, to leave on a relative high, and
as I still retain a great enthusiasm and passion for music, I am excited
by the prospect of pursuing new projects.

'The remaining band members have my support and best wishes
for anything they may pursue in the future, be it collectively or indi-
vidually.'

Part of Wilder's statement was clearly referring to his long-running frustration with Martin Gore, whom he believed didn't appreciate his workload or creative input into the music. There was also a certain degree of common sense in Wilder's thinking, given that the other band members were a non-musician and a singer who was a rock-star burn-out in LA. Emotionally, as well, the group's outsider shared Flood's unwillingness to put himself back into such a strained and drug-warped environment. Wilder wanted to make his own rules and he started afresh, releasing another Recoil LP, *Unsound Methods*, in 1997. He's also found personal happiness with Hepzibah Sessa and their daughter, Paris. 'There were a lot of different things I had to sort out at the end of the Devotional tour,' he says. 'I just wasn't enjoying being in Depeche Mode any more and I am now a lot happier in my work and in my home life.'

Bizarrely, despite the fact that for the second time in the band's history a key member had left, there was no immediate dialogue between Gore, Fletcher and Miller to suggest they thought this was the end of the band. As soon as the dust had settled, Martin Gore felt that Gahan was the real problem, not the absent Wilder. Fletcher's more combative nature meant that he was determined to prove to the departing musician that Depeche Mode could carry on without him. 'I think they undervalued Alan's input anyway and so perhaps that explains why they didn't worry about him too much,' notes Miller. 'I've always thought that he was underrated by the others and I know Alan thinks that. Or rather Dave valued what he did, Fletch played down what he did and Martin just was off in his world and didn't really think about it. And it wasn't just the musical element, Alan was the one who took the trouble to check things and listen to the cuts, he looked at the artwork, and so on. He took a lot of interest in all the aspects to it.

'I think there was also a background of financial tension because Fletch and Alan were earning the same amount of money. Al felt that he was putting in a lot of work and Fletch wasn't, and Fletch felt that he was being undervalued by Al. But I do want to stress that if there was financial tension, I always heard it second hand, nobody ever came to me about it. Obviously because Martin is the songwriter he earns a lot more money than the others but I think they all accepted it. Over the years there may have been a few discussions about that but I only heard about them from other people so I couldn't comment. No one in the band started claiming that they'd written part of such and such a song, none of that. Publishing often breaks up bands but in Martin's case they all had so much respect for him and understood his role, it was never a major issue.'

Gore's wealth has also been fattened by sound business investments. At one point in the early '90s he was the landlord of property in the Docklands area and was collecting £170,000 a year in rent from his former employer, National Westminster Bank. Andy Fletcher fared less well when his status as a Lloyds 'Name' resulted in a big financial loss, partly recuperated when he took legal action against the city institution.

In August 1995 Depeche Mode had a meeting to discuss their immediate future. Martin Gore had written five or six new songs, so the first question the band had to ask of themselves was whether they were in a strong enough mental and physical state to record a new album. Wisely they decided to adopt a cautious approach, encouraged by Daniel Miller who suggested they record one or two songs for a greatest hits compilation – the follow-up to *The Singles: 1981–85*. 'They'd been through all this shit and there really was a decision to be made – do they go back into the studio or not?' says Miller. 'We made it low pressure by agreeing we were going to do a "Best Of" album, so it was like, "let's just do a couple of songs and if that's as far as we get that'll be fine because at least we'll have a way of using them." '

Gahan: 'We had a meeting and decided whether we wanted to even make another record together. It was very unsure because everyone had a lot of time being involved in interests outside of the band.' Despite his vulnerable state, the singer's enthusiasm for Miller's tentative suggestion was fired up when he heard Gore's songs: 'I really wanted to record them. I really wanted to do the songs. A lot of the lyrical content and the feeling in the melodies really fitted with the way I was feeling and the stuff I was personally going through. It seemed like it would be a really good thing for me to do at that time because it was a way for me to work through my own personal problems. In retrospect, I wasn't ready and it was more important for me to take heroin than being in the band.'

Gahan had been in-and-out of rehab for a year but each time he would have a progressively more intense relapse into heroin when he

returned to his home or his room at the Sunset Marquis in Los
Angeles. To make matters worse, in August 1995 he came back from
a detox in the Sierra Tucson rehab, Arizona, and discovered he'd
been burgled. Everything had been taken – his Harley Davidson
bikes, the television sets, his stereo and recording equipment, even
small items such as cutlery. To add insult to injury the robbers had
reset his home's alarm code when they left, which convinced Gahan
that it had to be someone he'd trusted as only a few people knew the
combination. He believed his friends were taking revenge on him for
his attempts to get clean: 'My home was an empty shell. There was
nothing left. Just wires hanging out of the walls. It all seemed very
sinsister, like this fucked-up LA movie that I was actually in. And I
thought, "I'm not supposed to be fucking here. And perhaps if I'm
not around everyone else could get on with their lives." '

Gahan reacted by putting the place up for sale and renting a place
in Santa Monica. 'I thought everyone would be better off if I wasn't
around. I was hellbent on destruction.' He also went to the Sunset
Marquis for a few days and phoned his mother to tell her he'd just
come out of rehab again. He was shocked at her response. 'She said
Teresa had told her that I hadn't been to any rehab, and I wasn't even
trying to get clean like I'd promised. She didn't believe me.'

Gahan, who was in the hotel room with a girlfriend, shot up, drank
a bottle of wine, took some Valium pills and slashed his wrists. 'I was
in the middle of that phone call to my mum and I told her to hold on,
I'd be back in a minute, went to the bathroom and cut my wrists with
a razor, wrapped towels around them and came back to the phone
and said, "Mum, I've got to go, I love you very much." ' A friend
dropped by but initially Gahan '... acted like nothing was going on. I
put my arms down by my sides and I could feel them bleeding away.
I cut real deep, so I couldn't even feel my fingers any more. My friend
didn't have a clue what was happening until she noticed this pool of
blood gathering on the floor.' Gahan was almost unconscious by this
time and he was only brought round when the paramedics stitched
up his wrists without an anaesthetic. He was losing so much blood, it
would have taken too long to administer. 'The paramedic said to me,
"You silly sod, not you again." The same team of paramedics in West
Hollywood came and picked me up quite a few times. They were
starting to call me The Cat.

'When I woke up the next morning I was in a psychiatric ward, wrapped in a straitjacket, in this padded room. For a minute I thought I might be in heaven, whatever heaven is. This psychiatrist informed me I'd committed a crime under local law by trying to take my own life. Only in fucking LA, huh?' Gahan was then released into another room which was completely empty except for a bed. As a precaution there wasn't even a mirror in the room and he was denied both his matches and Zippo lighter. If he wanted to smoke he had to go outside and insert his cigarette into a wall-mounted lighter.

On 17 August 1995 the news broke of Gahan's attempted suicide when K-ROQ announced he'd been admitted to Cedars-Sinai Medical Center for treatment of 'lacerations'. An official statement was hastily released, declaring that Gahan was 'resting comfortably'. Detective Joel Brown of the West Hollywood Sheriff's Department summed up the injury as 'a two-inch (five-cm) laceration to his wrist'. The medicated rock-star confessed, 'It was definitely a suicide attempt. But it was also a cry for help. I made sure there were people who might find me.'

Gahan was released after a brief stay and went straight back to Sunset Marquis to shoot up some gear. He later recalled the period in his new Santa Monica flat as one of 'serious using' – 'as soon as I got out I was up to my old tricks. I'd clean up a bit, then use again. Every time I needed more, wanted it quicker – there was never enough. I just have to keep fucking going till I black out or whatever. That's my problem. Any addict's problem. They don't know when to stop. I didn't know when to stop. I went from worse to worse.

'I went through a phase for a little while, if I couldn't get dope, I'd be virtually shooting water, just squeezing out the cotton, getting whatever was left and banging off. I was definitely into the ritual side of things. In fact, now I think about it, the naughty excitement of going and getting it when the drugs weren't working any more, that was the big thing. Scoring without having me head blown off, that was it.'

By now the notoriety of his recent arrest meant that his connections no longer came to him. Using took him right into the heart of LA's darker side of life. He subsequently glorified the fucked-up machismo of LA's underworld with the warped excitement of an English junkie living abroad. 'I've had a few guns pointed at my head and shit like that,' he boasted to one journalist. 'But I mean, you walk into a crackhouse and what do you expect? Everybody's fucked out of their heads and they've all got .38s down the back of their pants.' The combination of drug-tilted paranoia and Gahan's macho ego also pushed him towards owning his own guns. He swaggered in 1997: 'I had a lot of guns, a 9mm, a .38 revolver and a 12-gauge shotgun too. I just thought they were out to get me. It was very much like the bit at the end of the movie, *Goodfellas* with the helicopters. I mean, if there were actually helicopters overhead or cars going by, I'd freak. I was so fucking paranoid, I carried a .38 at all times. Going downtown to cop, those guys you hang out with are heavy people, they have guns sitting on the table in front of them. I was scared of everything and everyone. I'd wait until four in the morning to check the mailbox and then walk down to the gate with the gun tucked in the back of my pants. I thought they were coming to get me. Whoever "they" were.'

He also continued to push his own limits with increasing dosages, claiming that he'd reached the point where he was shooting up heroin and cocaine speedballs because neither worked on their own. His emotions were often either dead or extreme, as he fantasized about '... shooting the big speedball to heaven – I just wanted to stop living in this body. Disappear. Stop. I wanted to stop myself. I wanted to stop living in this body. My skin was crawling, I hated myself that much, what I'd done to myself and everyone around me.'

Back in London, Depeche Mode had decided on a new producer for the tentative, toe-in-the-water sessions. Martin Gore recalls that after playing Daniel Miller his new demos, he remarked that the only concept for the tracks was that he liked the idea of them being 'quite hip-hop in a certain way'. That's why we started thinking about the dance angle and I think it was Daniel who first suggested Tim Simenon from Bomb The Bass. He said, "What about Tim, he's a nice bloke?" Gahan later remarked: 'There were loads of names being thrown at us but in the end we picked him because Martin and I really liked the Gavin Friday album that he did. *Shag Tobacco*'s an absolutely brilliant album, we really loved the sounds he produced with that. And also Tim's a big Depeche Mode fan.'

Brixton-born Simenon had followed the band's career right from their 'Photographic' debut on Stevo's Some Bizzare album. He also loved Daniel Miller's own projects, The Normal and Silicon Teens, as well as early Mute act Fad Gadget. Later Simenon got into hip-hop, electro, dub and house but he remained a Depeche Mode fan, particularly of their *Violator* LP. In 1988 when he was still only 20, the son of Scottish and Malaysian parents shot into the British charts with Bomb The Bass's dance single 'Beat Dis', released on Mute subsidiary Rhythm King Records. He went on to produce Neneh Cherry's hits 'Buffalo Stance' and 'Manchild' and co-produced Adamski's 'Killer'. He also worked with one of his early musical heroes, John Foxx, on a one-off project, Nation 12, releasing the 12" dance single 'Electrofear'. Foxx unfolds the young DJ/producer's working methods: 'I was into abstract, dance things and it was a good partnership, we did a lot of work together. Tim works in a very random way. He sniffs the air and doesn't speak about it much. He's a very tactile musician and has exquisite taste. Tim was choosing the beats, very instinctively, and cutting all these parts into his own patterns.' Gareth Jones has also worked with Simenon: 'When I hooked up with him, what really impressed me was his ability to strip away what's not right. He always reduces things to their essentials.'

Simenon's association with Mute via Rhythm King allowed him to drop by Daniel Miller's office and blag Depeche Mode records in the late '80s. He also worked on a few remixes for the band, re-tooling fresh versions of 'Strangelove', 'Everything Counts' and 'Enjoy The Silence'. Gore has declared that they'd met on quite a few occasions, and he'd always found the easy-going DJ to be a 'lovely person'.

The *Ultra* sessions, as they would eventually turn out to be, started in Eastcote, a cheap, tiny studio just across from the canal near Mute. 'Because there were so many changes this time around, we didn't set ourselves any great goals,' says Gore. 'We went into the studio with a very relaxed attitude: let's get back together, see how we're getting on, see how things go in the studio without Alan.' 'All of a sudden they started to remember what Alan Wilder did,' discloses Miller with a wry smile. The void left by the recently departed band member was filled on a practical, day-to-day level by the new producer and his studio team, which consisted of Q (an engineer), Kerry Hopwood (a programmer) and Dave Clayton (keyboard player). 'I'm not super technical,' says the self-confessed non-musician, Simenon. 'I understand what the computers do and I basically operate with people who enjoy reading manuals and are happy sitting in front of the computer for hour after hour. I make suggestions and they search for sounds. That's the way I've always made music. I have a box of records or sounds from CDs, which I'll be constantly feeding in as inspiration until a direction forms and we all focus on that.' Fletcher: 'I don't think the ideas have changed at all ... we just replaced Alan, as such, with a team of people.' Gore also remained dismissive of Wilder's contribution, insisting the new band set-up was preferable: 'Dave Clayton, the musician we are currently working with now, in a way fulfills Alan's role, but it's far easier to manipulate him. If Alan didn't like something, I am sure he would play it badly, but if we say to Dave, "can you try this out for us", he'll try it and he'll try his hardest to make it work for us. So I really enjoy the whole set up.'

During their first six-week period in Eastcote they worked on three songs, 'Useless', 'Sister Of Night' and 'Insight', creating backing tracks without finished vocals from the mostly absent Gahan. Simenon was given very little direction from Gore, who just informed him he wanted the songs to be quite beat-oriented. This gave the young producer freedom to experiment with his favourite band. 'That was a weird experience,' he confesses, 'but at the same time it was soothing because I knew their history, I knew their politics and I felt really comfortable. I just knew that it was going to work, it just had to, really.'

Simenon, who is a very low-key character, nursed them through these weeks with his thoughtful but easy-going approach. Daniel Miller would pop in to see how things were progressing but the significant change was Martin Gore's constant presence in the studio, although his new-found sense of responsibility didn't extend to sweating over a hot synthesizer. 'I hardly ever saw Dave Gahan in the studio and Fletch would drop by but Martin and I put a lot of hours in,' asserts Simenon. 'There were some fun times but generally it was fucking hard work. Martin and I spent a lot of time chin-scratching and then we got Dave Clayton to play a part, which is very different from Martin working with someone like Alan, who spends hours silently working on a keyboard sound.' However, Simenon's gentle, cognitive approach sometimes failed to coax out opinions about the musical direction from his quiet studio partner: 'Martin doesn't discuss the music a lot of the time,' he says, echoing Wilder's comments. 'I'd try to get him to talk about it, but generally if it's right he won't really say anything – if it isn't, he will, and then he'll suggest another idea. I'd be probing him a bit to get some feedback from him but because the session was so open there wasn't really a direction until it all came together at the end.'

Gahan has expressed some reservations about the new studio partnership, which was a step away from the organic, jamming approach favoured by Flood: 'Martin really enjoys working with Tim because Tim likes to work in the same sort of process as Martin, so they get on very well. I think Flood was a little more experimental and I don't mean that in a bad way to Tim, but Flood was willing to try a lot more stuff musically and dig deeper than sort of going with the same format of just programming everything, every song.'

The results of this initial period were encouraging enough for Gore to go away and write another three songs, including the unadorned, hard-sounding 'Barrel Of A Gun'. Simenon: 'At the end of the first period I suggested to Martin, "Forget the fucking chord changes, just get a relentless groove going" and he came up with "Barrel Of A Gun". There's still one chord change in it, of course!' By the end of this second Eastcote phase, they had six tracks ready for vocals. After a couple of phone conversations with Dave Gahan, it was agreed that Depeche Mode would relocate to New York to appease the singer who was fed up with flying over to England. Simenon recalls the band felt optmistic when they arrived in America: 'It seemed a positive thing that we were actually going to Dave's land and taking the next step with the record.' Initially Gahan lied to them that he was clean and the band tried to establish an upbeat mood in New York by clubbing most nights, in particular at the house club, The Tunnel, where Junior Vasquez was DJ-ing. However, within two weeks, the visiting musicians and producer were having crisis meetings in the back of taxis en route to the Electric Lady studio about the worsening state of Gahan's health. It wasn't that the frontman didn't turn up at the studio or wasn't trying, he just couldn't get it right – his vocals were shot to pieces and he found it hard to focus on his work. Gahan explains, 'When we started this album, 90 per cent of the time I was still strung out, and the rest of the time [rumoured to be their last two weeks in

Electric Lady] I was sick from kicking. It became very obvious that physically I wasn't able to stand up in front of a microphone for more than an hour without wanting to lay down and die.'

After spending ten days on a vocal for the song, 'Sister Of Night', Simenon confesses, 'We just didn't know what to do next. By that time everyone felt down and frustrated and there was obviously talk of, "Is it worth going on and what's the point?" At one stage, they were quite close to pulling the plug on the whole thing.' Gahan: 'They were nervous and scared. I was a chronic relapser. I was destroying everything, my life and theirs.' Gore admitted a year or so later: 'There were definite times during the recording of this record that I felt we wouldn't get it finished. I had to start thinking about finishing it as a solo artist, which I didn't really want to be.'

The band left the disastrous New York session in mid-May with some additional work on the backing tracks, a couple of new songs which Gore had written in a live room at the studio and one 'complete' vocal for 'Sister Of Night'. Despite Gahan's subsequent assertion that it's one of the best performances of his career, 'Sister Of Night' was actually pieced together from numerous different takes. Nevertheless, it's a haunting reminder for the singer of the tortured state of his mind at the time: 'I can hear how scared I was. I'm glad it's there to remind me. I could see the pain I was causing everybody.'

The band told Gahan to go home to Los Angeles and sort himself out. The singer had agreed to using a voice coach for the second time in his career, which was a significant step forward. Daniel Miller: 'After one of our crisis meetings, we all thought, Dave's got to have a singing teacher. He'd had a few singing lessons once and he'd hated it, so it had become a taboo subject. And we said, "this is the only way the album is going to work" and he agreed. He was actually quite open about it and not defensive at all. I think his decision to get a voice coach helped him. I saw it as a step forward, somehow, a way for him to say he wanted to get better as a singer and also make improvements in his own life.' As a concession to Gahan, it was agreed that Simenon and an engineer would fly to Los Angeles and work on the vocals with him, while Gore wrote some more new material. 'We got Evelyn in as a vocal coach and she was really good,' recalls Simenon. 'She came into the studio and said, "Well, Dave, hit this note" and he'd have a go. It was just another nice person to have in the studio and we did get one vocal from that session, for the song "It's No Good". Then the madness happened.'

According to Gahan, 'There was still the flame inside me that wanted to do this record but physically I just couldn't do it. I relapsed several times and after I knocked it on the head in New York I went back to LA and got back to my old tricks. Before I left I said to my girlfriend in New York – I met her in detox, she's been clean five years and she was instrumental in helping me admit I couldn't do what I was doing successfully any more – anyway, as I left she looked me in the eye and said, "You're gonna get high" and I said, "Yup." She says, "You don't have to" and I said, "I do." And I went to LA and had the worst binge I'd ever had.'

Gahan went 'fucking mental', a junkie with a self-confessed 'death-wish'. He checked back into the Sunset Marquis and shot himself up with coke and heroin speedballs. 'It was a particularly strong brand of heroin called Red Rum which has killed quite a number of people recently,' he detailed later. 'Of course, I just thought it referred to the racehorse, until someone pointed out that it spells "murder" backwards.'

At one o'clock in the morning of 28 May 1996 Gahan was preparing to shoot up. 'There was something weird about that night,' he's asserted. 'I remember saying to the guy I was with, "Don't fill the rig up. Don't put too much coke in it." I felt wrong.' He was sat inside his hotel bathroom with the dealer, while a girl he'd just met in the bar downstairs was waiting in his room. Only a few moments after injecting the speedball he passed out and the dealer tried to revive him. Gahan was dragged into his bedroom, panicking the girl who immediately phoned for an ambulance. The dealer, who was frightened of being arrested, slammed the receiver down and refused to let her make the emergency call. They struggled, the girl shoved him to the floor and the low-life ran off, only to return a few minutes later to collect his syringes and some of the dope. At 1.15 a.m. the emergency servives received a 911 call from an unnamed woman who claimed to be Gahan's room-mate. In the 15 minutes before they arrived, the girl tried to bring Gahan round by throwing water over him and rubbing his face with wet towels. After a few minutes Gahan had a cardiac arrest as a result of his partially cleansed system not being able to withstand the dosage. His hands started to turn blue and the colour slowly spread up his arms.

Afterwards he described the scene in the ambulance, as related to him by the paramedics: 'They gave me the full *Pulp Fiction* treatment and got a beat on the way to hospital. The first thing I remember was a paramedic in the background saying, "I think we lost him." All I remember about it was, it was really, really black and really scary, and I remember feeling that it was wrong. This was something really not supposed to be happening. I was thinking, I could control this, I could pick the date when Dave was gonna die. That's how fucked up my ego was. So I woke up and I was handcuffed to a cop and he was reading me my rights.'

Gahan was discharged at 8.30 a.m. the next morning and then immediately arrested and taken to the West Hollywood Sheriff's Station. LA County Sheriff's Lt. Steven Weisgarber announced that they'd found a large quantity of what apeared to be cocaine at the singer's home, as a result of which he was booked for possession of controlled substances and charged with being under the influence of a controlled substance. Gahan: 'Straight from hospital they threw me into the county jail for a couple of nights, in a cell with about seven other guys. A scary experience but not enough to scare me into quitting.'

He was released on $10,000 bail and made a rambling, disjointed statement outside the LA County Sheriff's office, all the time trying to keep quiet Jonathan Kessler, who wasn't convinced by the wisdom of Gahan's public confession: 'I'm a heroin addict, and, and I've been fighting to get off heroin – shut up Johnny – and, um, for a year. I've been in rehab twice and I don't wanna be like people like Kurt, that were ... and stuff like that. I wanna be a survivor.

'I mean I died again last night. So, I'm not ... I'm not ... my cat's lives are out. I ... I just wanna say sorry to all the fans and stuff, and, uh, I'm glad to be alive, and sorry to me mum as well.

'I just want them to know that it's not cool. It's not a cool thing to be an addict. It's not ... you know, you're a slave to it, and it took ... it's taken everything away from me that I loved, and so I'm going to rebuild my life.'

When Martin Gore heard the news he felt a mixture of sympathy, frustration, anger and resignation. He felt that Gahan hadn't taken either the band or his own problems seriously enough. 'That's when I thought Depeche Mode were over. We'd given him so many chances ...' As if to confirm Gore's worst fears the stupefied singer checked straight back into the Marquis and 'carried on' using for a couple of days. He argued with Kessler that it was all the fault of the 'dodgy dealer down town', insisting that if his regular Beverly Hills supplier had been available nothing bad would have happened. His friend, the youth TV presenter, Amanda de Cadanet, came around to visit at the Marquis and her face said it all. 'She could see I was fucked up again and tears were welling in her eyes. When she left it was like she was saying, Goodbye.' It was only after three or four days that it hit him, 'What the fuck was I doing? I'd died!' Gahan continues his account: 'I went back to the house I'd rented in Santa Monica and, um, sat on the couch and realized I was going nowhere ... I thought I was going to die. When I shot up, there was absolutely no feeling at all.'

He phoned his girlfriend in New York, a reformed heroin user herself, but she told him she couldn't help another junkie. 'I just couldn't do this to people any more. I didn't want my son to grow up and wonder why his dad died or killed himself. So I picked up the phone. For the first time in the couple of years I'd been in and out of detox, I picked up the phone and said, "I need help, I wanna get clean. What do I do?"

'Then Jonathan Kessler rang and told me there was a meeting with my lawyer about the bust. But when I showed up it turned out to be a full intervention. A Los Angeles specialist called Bob Timmons was there. He's worked with a lot of addicts in the entertainment business. They all said, "You're going into rehab right now." I said, "No fucking way." They said, "You are." I said, "All right, tomorrow" – thinking I could go home and cook up before I went, you know? But they said, "No, now." I was like, "What about this evening?" "No." I said, "A couple of hours. I need to call my mum." They let me go. Jonathan said he'd come and pick me up. I went home, did my last deal, had my last little party and checked into the rehab.'

Gahan went to the Exodus Recovery Center in Marina Del Rey, Los Angeles, the detox unit that both Kurt Cobain and Blind Melon's Shannon Hoon had checked out of prematurely with tragic consequences. It was a tough institution, more like a minimum security prison than a medical clinic. He was woken up at seven o'clock sharp every morning for a meeting with his counsellor and recovery group. These sessions would run throughout the day. Meals were eaten with plastic cutlery and he was not allowed to leave the center for the first five days while he was still doing cold turkey. At the lowest point of his withdrawal he was strapped down and watched around the clock while he had seizures almost every hour. He stuck with it and later asserted, 'For the first time I was listening. That was the difference. An addict thinks the world ends at them and that you're completely alone in this world. And you find there's a lot of people from different walks of life that are exactly the same as you. When I went to Exodus, I was making the admission that this shit had destroyed my life. It had taken away my son and left me fucking empty. It was fantastic for a couple of years. I'd be lying if I didn't say I thought I was fucking God! I felt brilliant – nothing mattered, man. I was high. And then it stopped. It stopped overnight and then I was always chasing that first high.

A year after their separation, Teresa Conway phoned him in Exodus to discuss their divorce. Shortly afterwards she served Gahan with the papers. It was a bitter break-up. 'She's suing me for a lot of money,' complained Gahan. 'I felt like I gave up a lot I already had – a wife and son – for something that seemed real at the time, but in retrospect was pretty painful. The first couple of years we were together were pretty good, but after that it started dwindling. A lot of it was based on lust – I could hang out with this girl, party and get laid.'

Gahan's resolve to get well was backed up by real fear. He faced two likely scenarios if he carried on using – he would probably die, or at best, spend time in prison. Even if he survived jail his criminal record would force him to leave America and it's almost certain that he wouldn't have Depeche Mode to fall back on by that time. In any case the band would find it extremely difficult to tour with a convicted drug addict.

When Gahan appeared in Los Angeles municipal court on 30 July 1996, the authorities were sympathetic because of his swift enrolment in a drug rehab programme. He was informed that as long as he remained off controlled substances for a year, all the charges would be dropped. As part of his probation, he was required to take two urine tests a week and any positive results would immediately result in jail. Gahan was also ordered into an outpatient programme which would allow him to work with Depeche Mode again. He moved into a 'sober living house' full of addicts like himself and then left Los Angeles altogether for a swish apartment in New York, overlooking Central Park. Effectively his decision to get clean meant a total abstinence from all drugs and alcohol, because he realized that as soon as his inhibitions were lowered he would be tempted to go out and score. He was starting a new life: 'I didn't have a choice,' he confesses. 'I was gonna be in jail for two years unless I did what the judge told me to do. Staying clean is all about time. It's not gonna happen overnight.'

Meawhile the band had continued to work at Abbey Road in London. Everyone, including Gahan, resolved to have one last go at finishing the record. Fletcher: 'We had to satisfy ourselves that Dave wanted to do it. There's a strong bond between us all. I think Alan thought that when he left the band it was going to be enough to split us up, but I think the bond is much stronger than he believed.' It was decided that Gahan would come over to London and record the rest of his vocals. He agreed, although subsequently admitted, 'It's emotionally and physically really hard to commute that all the time and it's something I'm looking forward to not having to do so much any more.'

This time around the atmosphere in the studio was surprisingly loose and relaxed, as the band members put their differences aside to, as Gahan put it, 'do something positive'. According to Gore, '... in some ways maybe it took a bit of pressure off us, because no one expected an album at all, let alone a good one'. Fletcher was candid about his feelings for Gahan at this juncture: 'If Dave had died in May, I wouldn't have felt guilty that I didn't do enough for him. He knew exactly what he was up to and I did as much as I could. But now, after what I've been through, if he's feeling depressed – he's waiting for news about his divorce from Teresa – he can talk to me, and I can help him. He realizes that I've suffered similar pains to him. Although I know Dave's volatile and he's got a lot on his plate, I hope he's going to be an inspiration, a success story.'

Gahan: 'It has taken a long while. But I'd say we've done our best work in the last few months. It progressively gets more and more difficult because when you know each other so well, little things become really big things. There is a lot of outside things now ... everyone's got families and they've got other interests outside of the band. A lot of time and energy is spent on these things and so less and less time really gets spent on making music together. When things go well, it's really good, but there's a lot of sitting around and waiting. The roles are very defined.'

Depeche Mode's old associate Gareth Jones was drafted in to engineer Gahan's vocals at RAK studios, where a vocal coach was installed, along with Gore and Fletcher. Compared to the previous agonies, the singer, who also attended AA meetings during the session, worked relatively quickly and completed his vocals in a month. He was very happy with his work, especially in the light of his deadened, dissipated performances in New York a few months earlier. He enthused, 'They really take you to a place, wherever that place may be, and they take you on a journey, tell you a story and you listen, you know, it draws you in.' Fletcher: 'Dave's vocals on this record are fantastic. When Dave was ill, some people were asking why we couldn't get rid of him, get another singer. But Dave would never come to me and say, Gore's being a pain, let's get another songwriter. His voice and Mart's songs are Depeche Mode.'

As soon as everyone was happy with a vocal take, Simenon would ferry the track over to Abbey Road to work on the music. The band spent an additional month in the studio after all the singing was completed, finishing *Ultra* in late 1996 – 15 months after it had started in Eastcote. Simenon and Gore had been in charge from start to finish. 'To be honest Dave had very little input into the whole direction until at the end in the mixing,' clarifies the Bomb The Bass leader. 'I'd be sending him tapes for his feedback but he wasn't in the studio, the same with Fletch, but generally Martin was the man.'

Simenon discloses that he was completely burnt out by the experience of working with Depeche Mode: 'I just felt fucked by the end of the recording, and I carried on working in January and February 1997, which was the worse thing I could've done. I nearly collapsed. I started to feel really ill. So I took a break and had a few months off. I was just mentally and physically exhausted.'

Gore and Fletcher also had a short holiday, with the songwriter abstaining from alcohol for seven months in 1997. Gahan continued the painful, sobering process of rebuilding his life: 'Having an addictive nature is something that I think you're born with, you know. From what I've learned so far, it's a day-to-day thing. Of course, in the early stages, you're more susceptible to relapsing. But as time goes on, for me personally I can't deny the fact that 75 per cent of the time now my life is a lot better. I'm a lot happier in my own skin. But at the same time, if I slack off, if I choose to get a bit complacent and kind of fall back into old habits, and I mean like withdrawing from people, isolating and choosing to hang out on my own and not making the effort to pick up the phone and talk to people about how I feel and go and meet people for coffee and get myself to meetings. If I don't do the legwork, I'm not going to stay sober for long. It might not be that I pick up, but I'm talking about a sickness in the head, or just being like stuck. That's a horrible feeling for anybody and I think a lot of people go through that just with being depressed and being in this kind of low-grade depression where everything and anyone that comes your way seems like such a big effort.

'I have to stay in touch with sober friends and people I got clean with or people that are there to help me. You know, I have a sponsor and I go to meetings and stuff like that. If you're in a room with a bunch of other people who have the same kind of problem, it's just a comfort in itself. I find that just sitting in a meeting for an hour and a half, I can just sit there and listen to other people and quite often somebody else who's sharing in that meeting about the way they feel or about being an addict, or about what they've been going through in the day will help me, you know.

'The only thing I don't have a choice about is my feelings ... they come and go, but they're really difficult to deal with when you've been using a long time. You've blocked them out for so long and they come on like a speeding fright train.

'There's little bits of David that come back every day and he ain't such a bad guy,' he explains, rather alarmingly disconnecting from himself by talking in the third person. 'I sit and watch Harry Enfield and I laugh my arse off. Or I cry at some soppy movie. I didn't have these normal feelings. I would sit and watch the weather channel for 12 hours of the day. It didn't matter, man ... days would go by, and years went by.

'A normal person is able to have a drink or two and say, "Whoa, I've had enough." That was not David. David was "More, more,

more, more" until I didn't have to think or feel any more. Being sraight has enabled me to stop and notice how all the chaos around me was created by me.

'If I thought I could go and have a drink I would, but to me it's an obsession. It doesn't matter if it's in a bottle of vodka or if you're banging a needle in your arm, at the end of the day, you're going to the same place – which is oblivion – and it's going to kill you. Twenty-four hours a day I used to be thinking of where I could go to be on my own and get up to my old tricks. I could be talking to my mother and be looking at her in the eye and be dying to get away.'

Gahan has also thrown light on the rigorous discipline of his drug rehab programme, which has created another extreme for the singer to embrace: 'It goes against the rules of the programme to be talking about this with people outside the rooms. When I share about how I feel in the rooms ... I can't wait to get back to my hotel now and phone my sponsor and tell him what's going on and he'll have some suggestions about how I could feel better. I just yearn to be comfortable in my own skin. It's happening but it's taking a while.'

Possibly encouraged by the importance of religion within the step-by-step structures of AA and rehab, Gahan has demonized his old addiction: 'I believe heroin is the devil because it takes your soul away. I think if there is a God there, he chooses to leave you and let you get on with it and that's what it feels like. You're this walking shell. I couldn't even look at myself in the mirror.

'I do a lot of praying. I don't pray for forgiveness but what I do is get on my knees and I thank God for keeping me sober another day. I pray to the ceiling in the hope that somebody's listening. But you know what? I feel a lot better doing it.'

Gahan's closer relationship with his son Jack has been the biggest and most immediate highlight of his new life. 'Just this weekend I got the opportunity to spend time with my son,' he told a writer in 1997. 'It was great, we went to see the movie, *101 Dalmatians*. One thing I notice about him now, which I didn't notice when I was using, is the way he looks at me. He looks at me with a lot of love and affection, and I never noticed that so much before as I did this weekend. I could look him right in the eyes. It wasn't like he'd be looking at me and I'd be feeling ashamed. It was almost like he was the adult and I was the child for a long time.

'It's been fantastic. I know from the way he acts around me that he knows if Dad says he's going to call or Dad says he's going to pick him up, I turn up. That wasn't the case for a lot of years.

'What's fantastic now is spending a couple of days with Jack. Being there. Being really there. Last night at the hotel I heard him kind of moaning and I went back into his bedroom and climbed into bed with him and just cuddled him and he went back to sleep ... six months ago I wouldn't have been able to do that. I wouldn't have wanted to, because of the guilt and the shame I felt about myself.'

I Find Myself, 1997–9

Depeche Mode confounded expectations in spring 1997 by releasing one of their most striking singles so far, the icy, electronic confessional 'Barrel Of A Gun'. For once Gore half-admitted that elements of Gahan's life had influenced the words, although he pointed out, 'It's only partly about the hell Dave's been through. It's written from my perspective … I have a problem with life, too.' Gahan: 'The lyrics and the intensity of the music both sum up the way I felt. Singing and recording it, I really got a chance to take a look at myself. It reflects the way I was feeling, the whole paranoia, the self-hatred.' The song became one of their biggest hits when it zoomed in at No. 4 in the UK, allowing the band to indulge in a rare appearance on *Top Of The Pops* with Tim Simenon on keyboards and Anton Corbijn taking over the drums. This display showed they were in good spirits after the traumas of the previous years. However, the single made an even bigger impression overseas, where it was No. 1 in four countries: Czech Republic, Sweden, Hungary, Spain.

British and American DJs loved Underworld's remix of the track but Martin Gore was exasperated: 'The original version of "Barrel Of A Gun" was about 83 beats per minute. When we received the "Hard Mix" back from them, we were sitting there thinking: what relevance does this speed bare to ours? Is it double the speed? And we timed it and it turned out to be about 148 bpm! When I rang them up and spoke to them, I asked: "Is there any chance you can fly some vocals in? Just so it has some relevance. Because there's not one sound of the original version on there?" And they said: "Well, we're not quite sure how that works, because the speed is different and I think it's in a different key." Different key, different speed, different song!'

On 14 April, 1997 Depeche Mode released *Ultra*, the album that no one, not even the band at various points, believed would be completed. It went straight in to the UK charts at No. 1, selling over 40,000 copies in its first week of release. It also topped the charts in Germany where it's out-sold *Songs of Faith and Devotion*, taking worldwide *Ultra* sales to three million. The LP has gone gold in America, UK, Germany, France, Canada, Spain, Sweden, Brazil, Belgium, Denmark, Czech Republic, Hong Kong and platinum in Italy. Opening with the stark, unyielding paranoia of 'Barrel Of A Gun', the album manages to sound electronic and sparse, yet also takes on fresh influences. Gore's love for twentieth-century music, including classical and Berlin cabaret, is expressed without clouding the final sound with too many elements. Right from the start the songwriter's demo for 'The Bottom Line' pushed the song in a Country direction through the rhythm and the roll of the words, and to enhance that element they introduced guitarist BJ Cole on pedal guitar. The album's most immediate track, 'It's No Good', has a bizarre lounge feel, while the Gore-sung 'Home' is a lovely, string-enhanced ballad. 'Sister Of Night' is a very soulful track, beautifully sung by Gahan. Refreshingly for Depeche Mode fans, the taut, textured electronics echoes late-'70s and early-'80s underground synthesizer pop – The Normal as opposed to Ultravox! Rhythmically there are slow breakbeats but it's a long way from being a trip-hop pastiche. 'Tim can make something that's 69 beats a minute quite groovy and that's quite important to us because we are in such slow territory,' notes Gore. 'In the past we have gone much faster than 100 bpm, but when I try writing anything faster now it just sounds silly to me, it just loses atmosphere. For me, this record is all about atmosphere.'

'I've always been convinced that dark atmosphere is most effectively conveyed through slow-paced tempos,' says Gary Numan, who explored sparse, acoustic percussion on 1981's *Dance* LP and loop-based atmospherics on his critically acclaimed *Sacrifice* ('94) and *Exile* ('97) albums. 'I think a sense of menace is almost impossible to create effectively if a song is racing along at a frantic speed.'

Ultra also features a tough industrial feel in the treatment of the rhythm sounds and the band's enthusiasm for the clipped, motorik beats of '70s German electronic music is underlined by a guest appearance from Can's Jaki Liebezeit. On-U-Sound's famous drummer, Keith Le Blanc, also makes an appearance on 'Useless', while Daniel Miller cameos with a System 700 on 'Uselink'.

Miller was very happy with the album's return to a 'stark type of recording. I think that's Tim's influence and Al not being there. Alan liked big arrangements, strings, choirs, dramatic piano things and I think Tim was trying to lay bare Martin's songs by making things more minimal and emotionally raw. It wasn't particularly discussed but that was how it developed. I think that was a very good thing because I'm the minimalist in the camp. That's not to criticize Al, because some of his arrangements on things like "Never Let Me Down Again" are absolutely fantastic, but arguably the emotions of the songs were flooded out a bit.' Gore echoed his comments in 1997: 'I think in some ways, it's very different to the last album and it would probably have made more sense as a follow-up to *Violator*. For me, the last album was a bit of a quirk, our pseudo-rock LP. This one's far more heavily electronic based, which is where our true roots are.'

Lyrically 'It's No Good' probes the frailties of human relationships, 'Barrel Of A Gun' expresses its conviction that life is set by pre-determined fate, and 'Sister Of Night' is self-absorbed alienation. As Dele Fadele wrote insightfully in *Vox*, ' "Sister Of Night" takes a more sinister route and deals with the power of addiction. Some might see it as a cryptic love song to a deadly drug, but it could just as well be sung to a person.' The sublime highlight of the album, 'Home' offers redemption. 'I think it's got quite a spiritual feel but religion is probably touched on less on this album than it has been in the past,' noted Gore at the time. 'I think I've overdone religion.' Prompted by the lyrics of 'Barrel Of A Gun', Gahan felt that *Ultra* '... definitely has a kind of destiny theme running through it. I think that destiny is pretty much plotted out for you anyway and during your life you might fall off the track a couple of times but generally you come back on board if you can. You know, sometimes it's just nicer to stay within the moment, within the day. Like, yesterday's gone and who knows about fucking tomorrow. I think one of the most difficult things about life is trying to just enjoy the moment that you have. All that kinda runs through the album, lyrically and stuff.'

In Britain, the press campaign was dominated by Gahan's revelations about his junkie past. Given the man's open nature and his all-

or-nothing approach to life there was an understandable need to confess and then move on, but in some ways it was an ill-advised tactic. Gahan realized with horror that he'd sealed his own fate: 'Even in ten years time, all I'll be to the press is Dave the junkie.' It also had the immediate side-effect of completely overshadowing the new album and encouraged a very bleak reading of *Ultra* in the critical reviews. For many people the album's subtly warm colours and understated beauty simply failed to register on first impression. *NME*'s James Oldham gave *Ultra* six out of ten: 'If these songs are about Gahan's decline as seen through Gore's eyes, then they're written in such blank and generalized terms as to be almost worthless as insights into his condition ... it's all too clinical. Issues are skirted, poetry is attempted and we're left clutching another instalment of stadium-orientated angst, at a time when we were expecting reflective intimacy. The needle rarely comes anywhere near this record. Against all odds, *Ultra* is just another Depeche Mode record.'

David Sinclair wrote in *The Times*: 'The biblical imagery of "The Love Thieves" is shackled to the sort of after-dinner chocolate soul tune that George Michael goes in for these days ... the tunes themselves recall nothing so much as the flatulent pop stylings of Tears For Fears, an impression exacerbated by Gahan's pompous delivery ... there is a weary feel to this album. It sounds as if, instead of providing inspiration, all the angst they have been through has simply worn them out.' *Mojo*'s Dave Rimmer: 'The results are dense, dark and unassailably mediocre. The more you listen to this album, the worse it seems to get.' *Select*'s Emma Morgan awarded the album a paltry two out of five but did at least enthuse, '... producer Tim Simenon's influence elsewhere has succeeded in eking out some genuinely touching moments rather than just the usual bombastic melodrama. The stunning "Home" takes its lead from Garbage's "Milk", melding an increasingly vulnerable rhythm to achingly vulnerable vocals from Martin Gore, while minor-key strings envelop the track like a comfort blanket.'

Ultra's standing seems to have been badly affected by the Gahan 'thingy' as Andy Fletcher once put it, with Gore bitterly concluding, 'the press we've received around this album isn't going to attract anyone'. However, that wasn't the only baggage the band were carrying with this album. It's clear from the reviews that the bombastic thrills of *Songs of Faith and Devotion* were still ringing in people's ears, disguising *Ultra*'s raw, stripped-back, elemental feel.

Vox's Dele Fadele gave the LP seven out of ten and recognized a transition: 'Depeche Mode's main achievement this time around is an intimacy, of sorts. The listener doesn't feel like they're stuck in a stadium hearing lofty pronouncements made at a great distance.' I wrote in a four out of five review for *Q*, 'an album of dry, dislocated, burnt-out and sometimes beautiful songwriting ... it sounds lived-in and dirty, rather than a bit pervy and self-consciously bleak'.

In America too, most of the reviews were lukewarm although at least *Rolling Stone* communicated the album's texture and atmosphere: 'moody, pulsating ballads such as "The Bottom Line" and "The Love Thieves" are ideal vehicles for Gahan's brooding baritone and for the band's ever-increasing sense of tender intuition'.

One of the band's commercial and critical problems in the U.S. (*Ultra* has not performed quite as well as their two previous LPs) was that although the 1997 kings of the American alternative scene, Marilyn Manson and Nine Inch Nails, do share artistic common ground (and the same troubled, white suburban audience) with the British synthesizer band, on *Ultra* Depeche Mode were pursuing a sparse, understated agenda rather than full-throttle, angsty anthems. Furthermore, the hype over electronica breaking big in the States that year also failed to include *Ultra*, as it crucially lacked the pulsey, disco-ey feel of *Violator*. The influential *LA Times* concluded, '*Ultra* won't woo any new fans grooving on electronica's latest wave.' Chris Carr is probably right when he says, 'They've always had an innate sense of timing and I think *Ultra* might have been slightly out. They're trying to earn the respect of their peers, because they were there before Massive Attack but the LP exists in a bit of a vacuum.' Gahan: 'I have no idea if Depeche Mode is still commercial. Before the radio stations played our songs in between The Eagles and Journey. Today we have to compete with bands like The Prodigy or The Chemical Brothers. I'm really surprised that "Barrel Of A Gun" had such a good chart position. The track is by far the most inaccessible that Depeche Mode have ever done.' Nevertheless, *Ultra* is likely to grow in stature over the next few years as it's a weathered, emotional record which reveals more with every listen.

The *LA Times* review must have been a disappointment to the

band who chose to launch the album in Los Angeles and London
with a three-song live performance. Wisely they decided against touring the album. 'We don't feel we can survive another tour,' admitted
Gore at the time. His colleague Gahan had instantly dismissed the
idea: 'It's taken this amount of time to find out what I really want to
do with myself and it's certainly not to go out on tour.' The British
event took place at Battersea's Adrenalin Village, with Nick Cave, the
Pet Shop Boys and an enthusiastic Gary Numan in attendance. The
NME's Simon Williams was not exactly invigorated by this first live
appearance since the Devotional tour: 'The pace is lethargic; the
synths are spooky; the vocals are half groaned, half moaned and
generally a bit, you know, deep. The vibe is vampish, Old Grave-ish
and bordering on the utterly relieved at having made it back from the
edge.' Chris Carr met the band backstage at the event: 'When I saw
Dave beforehand he was very nervous, but he's done it loads of
times, so he was up to it. It took a few minutes to settle in but once
he did, he was back.' The show was followed by a familiar scene back
at Martin Gore's flat as a big crowd of friends and acquaintances
gathered in Maida Vale. 'After Battersea I went back to his place and
there were too many people abusing his hospitality,' says Carr. 'He
must pay somewhere along the line. People were ransacking his
house, just because he's rich.'

Over the rest of 1997, a series of singles were lifted off the album.
'It's No Good' which is both bleak and humorous, shot into the
British Top 5. The accompanying video is one of Anton Corbijn's
most effective, featuring Gahan as a washed-out star playing the
cabaret circuit but still thinking he's Mr Big Shot. 'I thought Dave's
performance took it to another level,' says Corbijn, who gave the
visual mimic a chance to shine in public. 'Dave is the best actor in the
band, in fact I think he could be an actor if he wanted. Martin can't
act at all and Fletch over-acts. Dave's only problem is that he's somebody who starts over-enthusiastically on things and then he gives too
much of his energy and before the project is finished he's reached a
level where he can't do any more.' Outside the UK, it became one of
the band's biggest ever hits, reaching No. 1 in five countries: Czech
Republic, Sweden, Italy, Denmark and Spain.

Then came the album's best track, the redemptive 'Home', which
gave them their third successive chart-topper in Czech Republic in

June 1997 but stalled at 23 in Britain. In the wake of Brit-Pop's xenophobia, it's hardly suprising that the *Guardian*'s Ross Jones was dismissive about Depeche Mode's international standing. 'An arduously pompous opus drenched in swooping strings and severe synths. "Home" is the *English Patient* of techno-pop: stagey, arid, far too long, and likely to be an instant hit with pretentious Americans.' Home didn't come with an Anton Corbijn video. After nearly 20 promos together, the band and Daniel Miller felt it was time to try someone else and test whether the partnership had become too familiar and creatively lazy. Corbijn says he was frustrated by their decision: 'I don't think they saw the quality of the work I gave them. Maybe they realize it now because the videos they've made recently have no feeling for Depeche Mode. They look like they've been done by people who make adverts for life insurance. I think any visual feel and continuity they had has now gone.'

The follow-up was 'Useless', a more aggressive, bitchy track, which provoked *NME* to more critical venom: 'So they're back with another slice of Vorsprung durch techno doom rock which as ever is secretly half-decent, but will only ever be appreciated by slightly dysfunctional people who sit at the side of the class unnoticed. Plus all the Germans.' For once Martin Gore was actually enthusiastic about a remix for the single which only reached No. 28, describing Richie Hawtin's take on the album track 'Painkiller' as 'innovative'. He even preferred it to the original version, because '... the original idea for the song was for it to be quite soothing. That's why it was called "Painkiller". But our version ended up being quite hard. Richie Hawtin stripped it down and took it back to how it was intended, when it was a demo.' On the other hand, a DJ Shadow mix of 'Painkiller' wasn't released, reportedly because of problems clearing all the samples. However, the band weren't keen on it either. 'It's all over the place,' complained Fletcher, 'It's unusable.' Gore: 'He even used about half a verse from an old r'n'b song, happening over the top of it.'

Despite Ultra's success, in the UK it's already half-forgotten and is generally perceived as a failure. Gore rants, 'In this country we have always suffered, I think, mainly from a press campaign that went wrong. When we were doing OK in this country, but we were doing much better everywhere else, we started portraying ourselves as these enormous superstars everywhere else that didn't quite make it here. But the point that everbody missed was that we were doing quite well here too, we just weren't as successful as we were everywhere else. What the average person in the street seems to pick up from that is that we've never had any success at all here. I have so many people coming up to me, saying, Are you lot still going? You had a couple of hits in the early '80s, didn't you? And they remember "Just Can't Get Enough". We're considered as total has-beens in this country, by a large percentage of the population and I hate defending myself. Every now and then I get really angry when people say this to me and I say, "Our last album went to number one, how high do you have to get to be noticed?" '

It was also noticeable that a high-profile Depeche Mode tribute album, *For The Masses*, released in 1998, originated from America rather than the UK. British acts such as The Cure, Apollo 440 and Meat Beat Manifesto were very much in the minority on an album pieced together over the previous three years by the U.S. electronic act, Stabbing Westwood. There had been some bizarre LPs of Depeche Mode cover versions over the years, mostly from Sweden but *For The Masses* actually charted in America and reached the Top 20 in Germany, becoming the most successful tribute album of all time. Contributors included Smashing Pumpkins whose bare-bones version of 'Never Let Me Down Again' was originally released a few years previously, The Cure, who covered 'World In My Eyes' from *Violator*, plus The Deftones, Foo Fighters, Gus Gus and Monster Magnet. Rammstein's hilariously over-the-top take on 'Stripped' came out as a single, accompanied by a controversial Olympian video.

Meanwhile, the long-standing plan to release a 'Best of' LP finally hatched in 1998 with *The Singles: 1986-98*. It was heralded by the beautiful, melancholic 'Only When I Lose Myself', backed by two other new songs, 'Surrender' and 'Headstar'. All three tracks were recorded with Tim Simenon at Eastcote and Abbey Road. 'It was obviously nice to get another phone call from Daniel to say that they were doing a single,' recalls Simenon. 'It was a very different session to the whole *Ultra* experience. When Dave received Martin's demos he started work with the voice coach, Evelyn, a couple of weeks before coming to Britain. He got the melodies in his head and when he did come the session flew by. He was a changed man and it was a very comfortable session which only lasted a couple of months.' 'The stuff that we're doing now has a really heavy r 'n' b feel,' says Fletch of the new songs. 'A lot of that comes from Tim, who's really into Marvin Gaye and slow, sultry grooves. In our old age that appeals to us ... the zimmer frame stuff that doesn't go over 100 bpm.' Gahan: 'I think that the new single is a continuation of what we did with *Ultra*. We got a lot more soulful during the making of *Ultra*. I became a lot more confident about my singing. I don't mean I think I'm the greatest thing since sliced bread, it's just I have suddenly got in touch with myself again. I'm very grateful to have had the opportunity to be part of something that's really creative and makes me feel good.'

'Only When I Lose Myself' reached only No. 17 in the UK, despite its numerous remixes and different formats. 'I've always found love quite obsessional,' said Gore of the song's theme. 'People talk about co-dependency; to me I've always found there's something co-dependent about being in love – that's what love is all about.' For the video they went back to their old sleeve designer Brian Griffin, who had started making promos for Mute after a recent career in advertising. 'At a party about three years ago Dave Gahan was most forthcoming and interested in what I was doing,' explains Griffin from his Ladbroke Grove office. The promo, shot just north of Los Angeles, near Magic Mountain, in a disused research and development establishment, was full of images of wrecked cars and bizarre couples who've been brought back to life. While Gore liked the ethereal effect, he wasn't sure about the idea the director was trying to convey, and expressed his misgivings. MTV didn't like it as the band were hardly featured at all, except for some awkward looking shots of them in a glowing orange light.

In October 1998 Depeche Mode entered the UK charts at No. 5 with *The Singles 86-98* (along with an imaginative mix of promo items including a digital watch and a nylon bag with red digital logos), their 12th successive Top 10 album. The LP reached No. 1 in Germany, France, Denmark, Sweden and Czech Republic; Top 5 in Italy, Austria, Switzerland and Belgium; and Top 10 in Spain, Finland, Hungary and Ireland. In its wake a remastered version of *The Singles 81-85* re-entered the lower reaches of the British charts and missed the German Top 20 by one place. Q's Howard Johnson was enthusiastic about the '86–'98 compilation: '... a deep sense of melancholia which is naggingly addictive – this is a timely reminder that when it comes to being miserable bastards, Depeche Mode are state-of-the-art.' However, the band's currently unfashionable standing in the UK was reflected in the *NME*'s assertion, 'There's a black hole at the centre of these later songs, and it's not the thrilling moral vacuum they'd hope for, either. Compared with the inch-thick scuzz of the industrial crew, the articulate horrors of Nick Cave or Marc Almond's operatic sexuality, Depeche Mode sound like they dial up their redemption and absolution from room service.'

Oddly enough, Chris Carr's concern that the band had lost their innate sense of timing seemed to ring true again, as the compilation came out within weeks of 'Best of' LPs by numerous '80s acts, including Duran Duran, Culture Club and OMD. Obviously Depeche Mode are a cut above these bands but for those British fans who were beginning to question the band's relevance in 1998, it was an unfortunate coincidence.

More importantly for the group's future, they announced a four-month tour running up to the end of 1998. Gahan admitted he was 'scared' as he prepared for the shows by running on a treadmill in the gym every day for six weeks, and even Gore felt the need to impose a policy of only drinking twice a week on the tour. Tim Simenon, who DJ'd on the shows, admits that he didn't actually believe the Singles tour was going to happen until he was actually performing at the first show. 'I remember when we were making the *Ultra* album I thought, they're never ever going to tour again, it'll just be an album and that will be it. When the tour was mentioned I was like, "Mart, I'm there, I'll DJ for you." So that's what I did, I was the warm up act for 40 minutes before the band came on. It was great, hanging around and watching my favourite band for seven weeks. I watched the show every night.'

The Singles tour featured a very minimal stage presentation, as Anton Corbijn (who wasn't the band's automatic choice) finally granted Gahan's wish of cutting the effects down. This allowed Gahan to hold centre court, but within a more intimate band setting, emphasized by the presence of a drummer at the back and an additional session player on keyboards. The scaled-down set was intended to create a voyeuristic, peepshow effect, as if the crowd were in a booth looking at the band. 'I've always tried to make them very human visually rather than hi-tech,' opines 'visual director' Corbijn. 'They were very happy with the design, especially Dave because he likes the feeling of a band playing together. But it was a different experience for me because I felt more distanced from them.'

This bare, exposed stage also forced the audience to concentrate on the songs, which were all hit singles. In that way it was reminiscent of David Bowie's Sound and Vision tour, where he also cut down the visuals and concentrated on a hits-packed show. It also meant that the band could make serious money on this relatively short four-month jaunt. Anton Corbijn allows himself a smile, 'Now the accountant is the manager, of course he's very conscious of the costs of things.' Nick Duerden of Q Magazine, was certainly satisfied by the new, unadorned approach when he reviewed the band's gig at Hartwall Arena, Helsinki, 9 September 1998: 'Upon a very Zen stage, the minimal props Feng Shui'd to perfection, the band may lack the visual pyrotechnics that make U2 so consistently dazzling, but a menu of 19 formidable (mostly) hits can hardly fail.' Gore: 'If anything, playing the same songs every night makes life easier for us. Our motto is "we fear change".'

Backstage, drugs and liquor were conspicuous by their absence. 'No drugs were allowed,' confirms Simenon, 'that was completely stated to crew and band. I like vodka but I wasn't allowed that in the dressing room. It was just literally beer and wine. After the show Dave would come off stage absolutely pouring with sweat. In fact in the first couple of weeks he really ached, because of the non-stop physical exertion. When he walked off, Geoff, his AA and NA buddy, would be there and they'd hang out together. Geoff basically kept him company and they would very quickly get a car back to the hotel, so no one really saw him after the show. For the rest of us, there might be some aftershow parties but it wasn't an everyday thing. A lot of the drinking would happen at the hotel bar, so people could have a few beers, get in the lift and crash out – hardly wild rock 'n' roll stuff, really.

'The lack of substances was probably good for all of us. Everyone remained positive and there weren't any weird vibes at all. I think for Martin it was the first time he'd ever performed completely sober. I remember him saying, "all I had was a glass of wine before going on stage", and I'd say, "Well done Mart." I didn't see as much of Dave after the shows but he'd travel with us, he was at soundchecks, and he'd eat with us.' Daniel Miller observes, 'They were really able to appreciate the audiences and see what's going on a lot more than they ever did before. They don't feel that they're inside this cotton wool ball being pushed around the world. Martin hadn't gone on stage sober for years and obviously Dave is experiencing a similar thing. And they just came back saying it was great and that they were really feeding off each other on stage.' Anton Corbijn confirms this: 'I think they all looked happy on stage, maybe for the first time.'

Gahan admitted to the press that his recovery was still in a very early, tender phase and he'd have to leave the room if he saw someone chop out a line of coke. 'I'd want some. And I'd only want to test it, know what I mean? Mart and Fletch, they drink. Mart drinks a lot and they drink around me and sometimes that's a bit difficult, not because I want to get drunk, but just because I don't feel part of it.'

Disappointingly, the British arena shows drew a slightly more muted response to the other European dates, despite the fact the demand was enough for them to add a second Wembley Arena date. Cut off from the crutch of fanaticism or drugs, Gahan's performance was listless as he scurried around the stage trying to whip up a more full-blooded response. However, he burned on adrenalin at the shows in Milan, Paris and Berlin, where the audiences were so loud it was sometimes hard to hear the band. Simenon: 'In Germany it was like a religious mass, a real form of release.' As Sam Taylor concluded in his *Observer* review of their show at Waldstation, Berlin: 'Seeing them in Berlin, their spiritual hometown, is an upbraiding and slightly scary experience.' He counted '21,000 Euro-Goths' but still couldn't forget the band's Essex homeland. 'Dave Gahan is, truly, Basildon's own Michael Hutchence – with half the charisma and twice the self-destructive streak; yet somehow he is not only alive, but a bigger star than Hutch ever was.'

Anne Berning, label manager at Depeche Mode's German record company, Intercord, isn't surprised by the massive response in the country to the latest tour: 'Even when the band have been quiet for a while, their fans here have organized regular Depeche Mode nights, where as many as 1500 will turn up. There's also the hardcore who are almost like a secret organization. They group together and travel around the country when there's a tour and also organize their own events. I'd say the fans are not outgoing or macho – more timid, not socially active, more withdrawn sort of men. Three quarters of their fanbase is male and I think Depeche Mode's music probably helped them through their pre-pubescent years. There are younger fans too. The audience is constantly rejuvenating, it's not a stagnant thing. Depeche Mode also got a big kick when the country unified because a lot of their fans in East Germany had found it hard to get hold of their records, so when it all opened up there was suddenly this big influx of new fans from the east.'

After Europe, the first American dates in four years ran from 27 October and closed with two nights at Arrowhead Pond, Anaheim, California, three days before Christmas. No one in the band is prepared to confirm or deny that this will be their last tour. They've all admitted that they've thought of quitting in recent years. 'I think there's been a few times when the pressure's got to me and I think, is it all really worth it?' says Gore. 'But then, when you start weighing it up and you think, I do really enjoy this and I love the whole aspect of being in a band.' 'I think about it everyday,' acknowledged Gahan recently, when he was asked about whether he would leave Depeche Mode. He added, 'I think it's important to just focus as much as you can on what you're doing at the moment. It's impossible for me to predict what's going to happen in the future. It's not in my hands … thank God.'

On another occasion shortly before the tour he sounded very disillusioned with the band: 'I really believe that the more distractions and fixes I remove from my life, the better I'll feel about myself. The biggest of those is Depeche Mode. It's the one marriage that survived, but I'm not sure it works – for me, anyway. Jumping on a plane to go somewhere else and be told how wonderful I am doesn't feel good any more. It's not that I don't appreciate the attention to the work I do – I just don't appreciate the "importance" of it.'

Alan Wilder sympathizes with Gahan's difficulties, which he believes are down to a fundamental contradiction in his lifestyle: 'I find it sad that Dave needs to feel so humble now. You wouldn't wish him to be a heroin addict but there's something of him that's gone – and I'm only commenting as a pure observer now. I've had a little bit of contact with him, we're still friendly, but I'm looking from the outside. I think he looks a bit lost and not quite there any more. He's in constant treatment, in these AA and NA meetings every day and he says the whole basis of his treatment is that you have to come to terms with the fact you're not special in any way. So he's concentrating on humility all the time and that takes his edge away. He's at odds with his lifestyle and personality – the good side of his personality as well. It's difficult for him and I do feel sorry that he's found himself in this position because his natural instinct is to be very charming and open and he naturally becomes the centre of attention. But obviously this vulnerable charm is part of his problem as well.'

Gahan's 'new life' is still at a frail, immature stage, through recently given new strength by the singer's marriage to his New York girlfriend, Jennifer, who has been through similar experiences with addiction. He remains very open about the day-to-day struggles of staying sober. 'I've got a big problem thinking about tomorrow to be quite honest. The most important thing matters to me today is that I'm clean today – I have to do certain things during the day to make sure I don't forget what I am – and that's an addict.'

Meanwhile, Simenon feels the mood on tour was so charged and positive that it's 'very likely' there will be another album and tour. Fletcher has also told fans, pointedly: 'The atmosphere without Alan is great at the moment.' Martin Gore was planning to write new songs in the first half of 1999 and he's casually mentioned the idea of doing another album of cover versions to follow-up his solo debut, Counterfeit. It's also rumoured that for the first time in their career Depeche Mode have discussed the idea of signing a multi-million pound deal with another label after nearly 20 years on Mute. 'They're at an age where they might want a last big injection of funds,' observes a friend of the band. Chris Carr: 'It's no secret that they've become a cash cow for Mute. That's placed both of them in a difficult position. Daniel Miller has to work out whether the band are going to get bigger or face the fact they're on the decline.'

In reality Depeche Mode's current future is no more, or less certain than it has been since the mid-'80s. 'I think a lot of fans thought the Songs of Faith and Devotion tour was going to be their last,' notes Simenon. 'Now they think they won't see them again after the Singles tour. Who knows how long they can carry on? They might split up this year, or they'll still be going strong into the next century. I think a lot of the fans actually like that uncertainty.' This is a band who have survived every extreme and are still together. As Martin Gore said recently, 'Since *Black Celebration*, when I thought we were going to break up, there's been this impending doom scenario hanging over us, which never comes to fruition. We always seem to come through, somehow.'

Discography

Singles

20/2/81	Dreaming Of Me/Ice Machine (57)
13/6/81	New Life/Shout (11)
7/9/81	Just Can't Get Enough/Any Second Now (8)
29/1/82	See You/Now, This Is Fun (6)
26/4/82	The Meaning Of Love/Oberkorn (It's A Small Town) (12)
16/8/82	Leave In Silence/Excerpt From: My Secret Garden (18)
31/1/83	Get The Balance Right!/The Great Outdoors/Tora! Tora! Tora! *Live* (13)
11/7/83	Everything Counts/Work Hard/New Life *Live*/Boys Say Go! *Live*/Nothing To Fear *Live*/The Meaning Of Love *Live* (6)
19/9/83	Love, In Itself/Fools/Just Can't Get Enough Live/A Photograph Of You *Live*/Shout *Live*/Photographic *Live*
12/3/84	People Are People/In Your Memory (4)
20/8/84	Master And Servant/(Set Me Free) Remotivate Me (9)
29/10/84	Blasphemous Rumours/Somebody (16)
29/4/85	Shake The Disease/Flexible/Master And Servant *Live*/Something To Do (18)
16/9/85	It's Called A Heart/Fly On The Windscreen (18)
10/2/86	Stripped/But Not Tonight/Black Day/Breathing In Fumes (15)

14/4/86	A Question Of Lust/Christmas Island/People Are People *Live*/It Doesn't Matter Two (instrumental)/ Shame *Live*/Blasphemous Rumours *Live* (28)
11/8/86	A Question Of Time/Black Celebration *Live*/ Something To Do *Live*/Stripped *Live*/More Than A Party *Live* (17)
13/4/87	Strangelove/Pimpf/Agent Orange (16)
24/8/87	Never Let Me Down Again/Pleasure, Little Treasure/ To Have And To Hold (22)
28/12/87	Behind The Wheel/Route 66 (21)
13/2/89	Everything Counts *Live*/Nothing *Live*/Sacred *Live*/A Question Of Lust *Live* (22)
29/8/89	Personal Jesus/Dangerous (13)
5/2/90	Enjoy The Silence/Memphisto (6)
7/5/90	Policy Of Truth/Kaleid (16)
17/9/90	World In My Eyes/Happiest Girl (17)
15/2/90	I Feel You/One Caress (8)
26/4/93	Walking In My Shoes/My Slow Joy (14)
13/9/93	Condemnation/Rush/Personal Jesus *Live*/Enjoy The Silence *Live*/Halo *Live*/Death's Door/Rush (9)
10/1/94	In Your Room/Higher Love/Policy Of Truth *Live*/ World In My Eyes *Live*/Fly On The Windscreen *Live*/ Never Let Me Down Again *Live*/Death's Door *Live* (8)
3/2/97	Barrel Of A Gun/Painkiller (4)
31/3/97	It's No Good/Slowblow (5)
16/6/97	Home/Remixes (23)
20/10/97	Useless/Remixes (28)
7/9/98	Only When I Lose Myself/Surrender/Headstar (17)

Albums

5/10/81
Speak & Spell (10)
New Life/I Sometimes Wish I Was Dead/Puppets/Boys Say Go!/Nodisco/What's Your Name?/Photographic/Tora! Tora! Tora!/ Big Muff/Any Second Now Voices/Just Can't Get Enough

27/9/82
A Broken Frame (8)
Leave In Silence/My Secret Garden/Monument/Nothing To
Fear/See You/Satellite/The Meaning Of Love/A Photograph Of
You/Shouldn't Have Done That/The Sun & The Rainfall

22/8/83
Construction Time Again (6)
Love, In Itself/More Than A Party/Pipeline/Everything Counts/Two
Minute Warning/Shame/The Landscape Is Changing/Told You
So/And Then . . ./Everything Counts Reprise

24/9/84
Some Great Reward (5)
Something To Do/Lie To Me/People Are People/It Doesn't
Matter/Stories Of Old/Somebody/Master And Servant/If You
Want/Blasphemous Rumours

15/10/85
The Singles 81–85 (6)
Dreaming Of Me/New Life/Just Can't Get Enough/See You/The
Meaning Of Love/Leave In Silence/Get The Balance
Right!/Everything Counts/Love, In Itself/People Are People/Master
And Servant/Blasphemous Rumours/Somebody/Shake The
Disease/It's Called A Heart

17/3/86
Black Celebration (3)
Black Celebration/Fly On The Windscreen Final/A Question Of
Lust/Sometimes/It Doesn't Matter Two/A Question Of
Time/Stripped/Here Is The House/World Full Of Nothing/Dressed
In Black/New Dress

28/9/87
Music For The Masses (10)
Never Let Me Down Again/The Things You Said/Strangelove/
Sacred/Little 15/Behind The Wheel/I Want You Now/To Have And
To Hold/Nothing/Pimpf/Mission Impossible

13/3/89
101 (7)
Pimpf/Behind The Wheel/Strangelove/Something To Do/
Blasphemous Rumours/Stripped/Somebody/Things You Said/Black
Celebration/Shake The Disease/Pleasure Little Treasure/People Are
People/A Question Of Time/Never Let Me Down Again/Master
And Servant/Just Can't Get Enough/
Everything Counts

19/3/90
Violator (2)
World In My Eyes/Sweetest Perfection/Personal Jesus/Halo/
Waiting For The Night/Enjoy The Silence/Crucifix/Policy Of
Truth/Blue Dress/Interlude No.3/Clean

22/3/93
Songs Of Faith and Devotion (1)
I Feel You/Walking In My Shoes/Condemnation/Mercy In
You/Judas/In Your Room/Get Right With Me/Rush/One Caress/
Higher Love

14/4/97
Ultra (1)
Barrel Of A Gun/The Love Thieves/Home/It's No Good/Uselink/
Useless/Sister Of Night/Jazz Thieves/Freestate/The Bottom
Line/Insight

Bibliography

Take It Like A Man: The Autobiography Of Boy George by Boy George and Spencer Bright

Praying To The Aliens – An Autobiography by Gary Numan & Steve Malins, André Deutsch

Kraftwerk: Man Machine And Music by Pascal Bussy, Saf Publishing

Bowie: Loving The Alien by Christopher Sandford, Warner Books

Depeche Mode: Some Great Reward by Dave Thompson, Sidgwick & Jackson

Time Travel by Jon Savage, Chatto & Windus

Interview for The Singles 86–98 Video

In addition to the reviews and features mentioned in the book, research material was taken from my own articles in Q and Vox, plus others written by: Simon Williams, Phil Sutcliffe, Steve Sutherland, Jack Baron, Chris Heath, Carole Linfield, David Quantick, Peter Martin, Danny Kelly, Gavin Martin, Mark Jenkins, John Peel, Jenny Tucker, Carole Linfield, Spencer Bright, Craig Schmidt, Taylor Parkes, Johnny Cigarettes, Chris Roberts, Sean O'Hagan, Betty Page, Mark Cooper, Paul Moody, Clark Collis, Andrew Smith, Ian Fortnam, Helen Mead, Jeff Giles, Adrian Thrills, Paul Morley, Chris Bohn, Paul Du Noyer, Lynn Hanna, Brenda Kelly, Ray Rogers, Keith Cameron, Robert L. Doerschuk, Adam Sweeting, Steve Taylor, Mark Ellen, Eric Watson, Karen Swayne, Chris Burkham, Mat Snow, Bill Prince, Eleanor Levy, Jane Solanas, Damon Wise, Paul Mathur, Ian Cranna, Max Bell, Chris Jagger, Andy Darling, Nancy Culp, Sam King, David Sinclair, Bill Bruce, Melinda Gebbie, Andrew Vaughan, Francesco Adinolfi, Robert Sandall, Jan Gradvall, Andy Gill, Sam

King, Alex Kadis, John McCready, Marisa Fox, Lee Davies, Jon Wilde, Andy Strickland, Stuart Maconie, James Brown, Bruce Dessau, Jasper Rees, Pete Clark, Paul Lester, William Shaw, Jennifer Nine, Katherine Yeske, Andrew Harrison, Ben Willmott, Andrew Mast, Edwin Pouncey, Dele Fadele, James Oldham, Sara Scriber, Mike Gee, Rene Passet, Robin Bresnark, Robert Johnson, Tony Fletcher, Andrew Smith, Steven Daly, Jon Matsumoto, John Gill, Gary Bushell, Neil Tennant, Martin Townshend, Peter Martin, John Norris, Mark Scheerer, Stefan De Batselier, Victoria Harper, Glyn Brown, Caroline Sullivan, Olaf Tyaransen, Michaela Olexova, Gareth Grundy, Emma Morgan, Randee Dawn, Ray Rogers, Ross Jones, Dave Rimmer, Ian Masterson, Paul Colbert, X-Moore.

Their features were published in:
Sounds, Record Mirror, NME, Q, Melody Maker, Vox, Smash Hits, No1, The Guardian, Observer, The Times, Spin, Rock CD, Rolling Stone, Alternative Press, Time Out, The Sunday Times, Daily Telegraph, E&MM, Underground, Press Magazine, Zig Zag, The Face, Arena, Ultra, Insight, The Wire, Blitz, Daily Mail, City Limits, Select, Daily Mirror, TV Guide, MTV News, Details, Keyboard, Out, Daily Mail, Winnipeg Free Press, Globe, Uncut, Future Music, Los Angeles Times, The Guardian Guide, Mojo, Sound On Sound, Reuters, The Independent, The Mail On Sunday, Ray Gun, Modern Rock Live, For Him Magazine, I-D, Video Pulse Magazine, Music, Mixmag, DJ Magazine, BAM, CNN, Shunt, Hot Press, Daily Express, Evening Standard, Bong, Gay Times.

OTHER COOPER SQUARE PRESS TITLES OF INTEREST

LENNON IN AMERICA
1971–1980, Based in Part on the
Lost Lennon Diaries
Geoffrey Giuliano
300 pp., 70 b/w photos
0-8154-1073-5
$27.95 cloth

DESPERADOS
The Roots of Country Rock
John Einarson
304 pp., 31 b/w photos
0-8154-1065-4
$19.95

MADONNA
Blonde Ambition
Updated Edition
Mark Bego
288 pp., 195 b/w photos
0-8154-1017-4
$18.95

ANY OLD WAY YOU
CHOOSE IT
Rock and Other Pop Music,
1967–1973
Expanded Edition
Robert Christgau
360 pp.
0-8154-1041-7
$16.95

DREAMGIRL AND SUPREME
FAITH
My Life as a Supreme
Updated Edition
Mary Wilson
732 pp., 150 b/w photos, 15 color
photos
0-8154-1000-X
$19.95

FAITHFULL
An Autobiography
Marianne Faithfull with David
Dalton
320 pp., 32 b/w photos
0-8154-1046-8
$16.95

Colonel Tom Parker
The Curious Life of Elvis
Presley's Eccentric Manager
James L. Dickerson
300 pp., 35 b/w photos
0-8154-1088-3
$28.95 cloth

ROCK SHE WROTE
Women Write about Rock, Pop,
and Rap
Edited by Evelyn McDonnell &
Ann Powers
496 pp.
0-8154-1018-2
$16.95

GOIN' BACK TO MEMPHIS
A Century of Blues, Rock 'n'
Roll, and Glorious Soul
James Dickerson
284 pp., 58 b/w photos
0-8154-1049-2
$16.95

MICK JAGGER
Primitive Cool
Updated Edition
Chris Sandford
352 pp., 56 b/w photos
0-8154-1002-6
$16.95